The Economics of Gender in Mexico: Work, Family, State, and Market

Cover Art

Family, 1996. Silkscreen by Roberto Fantozzi, Peru
World Bank Collection

Roberto Fantozzi was born in Peru in 1953. In 1976 he won a first prize for photography in a competition sponsored by the University of Lima, after which his activity in the photography field increased significantly. In 1981 he obtained an M.A. from the Rhode Island School of Design on a Fulbright Fellowship. He has participated in important contemporary photography exhibitions in Mexico, Cuba, Ecuador and Brazil. In 1986 he was included in the II Biennial of Havana, and since then has participated in numerous international exhibitions in Latin America and in the United States. Fantozzi lives and works in Lima, Peru.

This work is included in the collection of the World Bank Art Program, which makes particular efforts to identify artists from developing nations and to make their work available to a wider audience.

The Economics of Gender in Mexico: Work, Family, State, and Market

Elizabeth G. Katz
Maria C. Correia
Editors

The World Bank
Washington, D.C.

ISBN 0-8213-4886-8

Library of Congress Cataloging-in-Publication Data

The economics of gender in Mexico : work, family, state, and market / edited by
Elizabeth G. Katz, Maria C. Correia.
        p. cm.
    Includes bibliographical references.
    ISBN 0-8213-4886-8
        1. Sexual divisions of labor--Mexico. 2. Labor market--Mexico. 3. Mexico--
    Economic conditions--194– I. Katz, Elizabeth G., 1964– II. Correia, Maria Cecilia.

HD6060.65.M6 E27 2001
306.3'615'0972--dc21

00-066781

Contents

Tables

Figures

Boxes

Foreword

As Mexico enters the 21st century, the distinct roles and responsibilities of men and women are changing profoundly, particularly with respect to schooling patterns and labor market participation. Yet while men's and women's roles overlap more today than they ever have, gender continues to limit the expectations and opportunities of Mexicans. This book presents an economic analysis of the effect of gender on the well-being of individuals and households in Mexico. The analysis includes the impact of gender on educational attainment and returns to education in the labor market, child labor and its downstream effects on labor market opportunities, men's and women's participation in urban and rural labor markets (including the microenterprise and *maquila* sectors), the determinants of off-farm employment for *ejido* residents, and the well-being of women and men in old age. While each of the chapters was originally written as a separate study, together they represent a life-cycle perspective on the importance of gender in determining the well-being of Mexicans. The book concludes with a short discussion of the current status of gender policy in Mexico and policy recommendations

The studies compiled in this volume are a direct result of the interest of the Government of Mexico in better understanding and empirically explaining current gender roles and relations in Mexico, as well as their policy implications. In the World Bank's Latin America and Caribbean Region, gender became an explicit area of attention in 1997 when the Region created a Gender group within the Poverty Reduction and Economic Management Unit. Since that time, the World Bank has worked closely with the Government of Mexico on the analytical front—as this volume demonstrates—and in translating the results of this research into policies and operational programs.

We hope that the work presented in this book will stimulate discussion and debate among policymakers, academics, and the general public, and ultimately help expand opportunities for both women and men in Mexico. We also hope that it can serve as a foundation for developing and strengthening programs and services dedicated to dealing with gender and development issues. The World Bank is eager to participate in these ongoing discussions and to work together with our Mexican counterparts—both governmental and nongovernmental—on activities and projects that address the important gender issues raised in this volume.

Olivier Lafourcade
Country Director, Colombia,
  Mexico, Venezuela
Latin America and the
  Caribbean Region

Guillermo Perry
Chief Economist
Latin America and the
  Caribbean Region

Acknowledgments

We have benefited from the comments and enthusiasm of many people who read earlier versions of this book. We are particularly grateful to the late Dr. José Gomez de León Cruces, National Coordinator of the National Program for Education, Health and Nutrition (PROGRESA), who generously took the time to review the manuscript and make extensive comments. We would like to thank Javier Alatorre, Marina Ariza, Mercedes Barquet, Antonieta Barrón, Rosa María Camarena, Francisco Cos-Montiel, Maria Guadalupe Escoriza, Gabriel Medina, Patricia Muñiz Martelón, Maria de Lourdes Murguial, Mercedes Pedrero Nieto, Elia Ramírez, Clementina Sastre López, and Gina Zabludovsky, all of whom generously gave their time to review the manuscript and participate in a workshop in April 2000 to discuss the contents of the book. Dulce María Sauri, who at the time was Executive Director of the National Council for Women, was instrumental in promoting this research in Mexico and facilitating its publication. Erwin Roeniger, at the Ministry of Finance and Public Credit, was our primary liaison among key stakeholders, and Alfonso Ramírez Lavín, World Bank consultant, provided strategic advice throughout the process.

We would like to thank many people at the World Bank. In the Mexico Department, Olivier Lafourcade and Marcelo Giugale provided invaluable support and advice. Adolfo Brizzi, Michael Geller, Selpha Nyairo, Dora Posada, and Guillermo Perry provided guidance and assistance at different points in the production process. Finally, we are very grateful to Elizabeth Waters, who orchestrated the publication.

Acronyms and Abbreviations

CONMUJER	*Coordinación General de la Comisión Nacional de la Mujer*
Conteo	National Survey of the Population and Housing Count
EAP	Economically active population
ENAMIN	*Encuesta Nacional de Micronegocios*
ENE	*Encuesta Nacional de Empleo* (National Employment Survey)
ENECE	*Encuesta Nacional de Educación, Capacitación y Empleo* (National Survey of Education, Training and Employment)
ENEU	*Encuesta Nacional de Empleo Urbano* (Urban Employment Survey)
ENIGH	Mexican National Household Survey of Income and Expenditures
FGT	Foster, Greer, Thorbecke Index
GDP	Gross domestic product
ILF	In the labor force
IMSS	Instituto Mexicano del Seguro Social

INEGI   *Instituto Nacional de Estadística, Geografía e Informática*

ISSSTE   *Instituto de Seguridad Social al Servicio de los Trabajadores del Estado*

LAC   Latin America and the Caribbean

LFP   Labor force participation

MFA   Multifiber arrangement

NAFTA   North America Free Trade Agreement

NRE   National Rainfed Equivalent

OLF   Out of the labor force

PROCAMPO   *Programa de Apoyos Directos al Campo* (income support program)

PROGRESA   *Programa de Educación, Salud y Alimentación* (Education, Health and Nutrition Program)

SECOFI   *Secretaría de Comercio y Fomento Industrial*

SREFS   *Encuesta Regional de Servicios Financieros a Unidades de Producción Rural*

SSA   *Secretaría de Salud* (Ministry of Health)

Introduction

Elizabeth Katz and Maria Correia

Mexico is undergoing significant demographic, social, and economic changes, and the distinct roles of women and men in the Mexican economy are rapidly changing. In both urban and rural areas, large numbers of young Mexican women are entering the labor force, and as girls' education reaches parity with boys', we can expect this trend to intensify. However, women continue to face unique constraints on their economic activities—constraints which are largely related to their household roles and responsibilities. Macroeconomic change also affects Mexican men, who must respond to shifting labor market opportunities and government policies.

This volume examines gender differences in the Mexican economy, with a focus on the labor market. We examine gender issues over the course of the life cycle, beginning with education and child labor, continuing with adult urban and rural labor force participation, and concluding with the situation of elderly Mexican men and women. While each chapter uses different data sources and analytical methodologies, the volume as a whole is guided by a gender perspective that examines the situations of both women and men as distinct groups and in relationship to one another.[1] Drawing on national labor market statistics, specialized regional household surveys, and firm-level data, the chapters that comprise the volume are rich in detailed quantitative analysis, which is presented in relatively nontechnical language geared toward a wide audience including citizens, advocates, practitioners, and policymakers.

This book has its origins in the commissioning of a series of technical papers by the World Bank, in collaboration with several Mexican government agencies, including the *Comisión Nacional de la Mujer* and the *Secretaría de Hacienda y Crédito Público*. A number of additional studies resulted from the first national Workshop on Gender Analysis and Public Policies in April 1997. As the high quality and comprehensive scope of the individual papers became recognized, Mexican policymakers and World Bank staff agreed that combining them into a single, nontechnical volume would increase access and help inform gender analysis and policy formation in Mexico. To this end, several rounds of peer review, revision, and editing were undertaken, resulting in the present volume.[2] A workshop held in Mexico City in April 2000 elicited comments from prominent Mexican and international scholars, which were also incorporated into the chapters.

Gender-Related Trends

What are some of the major gender-related trends in the Mexican economy, and in the labor force in particular? Table I.1 summarizes some of the relevant national-level statistics related to gender differences in Mexico. In terms of basic demographics, women outlive men by an average of six years, and both women and men enter their first marriage in their early 20s. Mexico's total fertility rate of just under three children per woman is about average for the Latin America region, and approximately 65 percent of childbearing-age married women (and/or their husbands) are estimated to be using some form of contraception. Female labor force participation is estimated to be about half that of male participation—37 percent of Mexican women are either employed or looking for work, compared to 79 percent of men. In terms of sectoral distribution, men are more heavily concentrated in agriculture and industry, while almost 70 percent of the female workforce are employed in the service sector. Finally, the Duncan Index of segregation, which measures the percentage of workers that would have to change jobs in order to achieve perfectly balanced gender representation across sectors or occupations, stands at approximately 40 percent.[3]

Several major themes emerge from the individual chapters. They can be summarized as follows:

Gender and Life Cycle. The role of gender in influencing economic activities and outcomes varies across the life cycle. Beginning with school-age children, girls (almost 15 percent of whom report domestic labor as their primary activity) are forced to leave school or combine domestic work with their education, while boys (over 50 percent of whom have entered the labor force by age 15) exhibit higher repetition rates due to their income-generating responsibilities. These patterns are especially strong among poor households and in rural areas. As adults, women are subject to a higher earnings penalty for having combined work and study as children, which may be due to the nature of the occupational concentration of girls and women in domestic services, the skills of which are not valued in other sectors of the economy.

Despite their often low earnings, young, single women in sectors as different as the rural *ejidos* and border *maquiladora* factories are entering the workforce in record numbers. Married women generally exhibit low

Table I.1. Mexico: Selected Demographic and Economic Indicators

	Women	Men
Life expectancy	75	69
Average age at first marriage	21	24
Total fertility rate	2.8	
Contraceptive prevalence rate	65	
Labor force participation rate	36.9	78.7
% labor force in agriculture	13	30
% labor force in industry	19	24
% labor force in service sector	68	46
Duncan Segregation Index[1]		
By sector	41.4	
By occupation	39.5	

1. The Duncan Index of segregation is the percentage of female or male workers who would have to change jobs in order for the occupational or sectoral distribution of the two groups to be the same—in other words, for men and women to be equally represented across occupations or sectors. It is calculated as $D = \frac{1}{2} \Sigma_i \mid M_i - F_i \mid$ where M_i = the percentage of males in the labor force employed in occupation or sector i, and F_i = the percentage of females in the labor force employed in occupation or sector i.
Sources: GENDERSTATS; *World Development Indicators 2000*; INEGI; CONAPO.

labor force participation rates and formal sector work experience; the evidence presented in several of the chapters suggests that gender-specific responsibilities for housework and childcare constrain their economic activity. Married men, meanwhile, are more likely to work when they have young children, and to use older children and other household members as sources of unpaid labor for income-generating activities. Finally, gender differences among elderly Mexicans are largely manifest in the greater reliance of women on family support in old age.

Marriage Market and Labor Market. Key to gender analysis of the Mexican economy is understanding the complex interaction between household formation, age- and gender-specific household roles, and labor force participation. By taking a life cycle perspective, the volume suggests that women, more so than men, are "tracked" at different stages toward specialization in either domestic or market labor. For example, girls who drop out of school in order to help cook, clean, and look after their younger siblings are often ill-prepared as adults for anything but domestic work. Girls who manage to stay in school have a better chance of entering the paid labor market, which must then be balanced against marriage and childbearing, as long as Mexican women continue to have major responsibility for household work. The choice between building up labor market "assets" and family "assets" is keenly felt by elderly Mexicans—most of whom are women—who rely either on formal employment-linked pensions and medical care, or on their children for support in old age.

.Region, Generation, and Gender. Significant differences in gender roles and gender disparities exist across urban and rural Mexico, and across the younger and older generations of Mexican women and men. For example, gender disparities in secondary school attendance are significantly larger, and the domestic labor responsibilities of girls are significantly greater, in rural compared to urban areas. Likewise, while national data indicate higher earnings profiles for women than for men, decomposition analysis of a rural sample suggests that women's labor force participation would increase from 28.5 percent to 85.1 percent if they faced same returns to endowments as men, and gender differences in productive characteristics are more important in explaining microenterprise-based gender earnings differentials in rural than in urban settings. Generational differences, meanwhile, are especially apparent in the rural *ejido* sector, where young men and women are more highly educated than their parents and therefore more able to pursue diversified income-generation strategies, including significant participation in off-farm employment and migration.

Organization of the Book

In keeping with the life cycle theme, the book is organized roughly in chronological order, beginning with the experience of Mexican girls and boys in the educational system and child labor market, continuing through analysis of the adult labor market (which is divided between urban and rural, with separate chapters on the *maquiladora* and microenterprise sectors), and ending with a chapter on gender differences among the elderly. Here, we briefly summarize the main findings of each chapter.

In Chapter 1 on gender and education, Susan Parker and Carla Pederzini argue that Mexico has made significant progress in narrowing the gender gap, especially among primary school students. There remains a small male bias in school attendance during high school and university, but this is not reflected in the number of years of completed schooling, because boys are more likely to fall behind and repeat grades. Several interesting findings regarding gender differences in the determinants of school attendance among 12 to 15 year olds (the age group where the gender gap in attendance is largest) are the negative impact of a disabled family member on boys' attendance, the significant positive response of girls' attendance to school breakfast programs, and the strong negative role of rural residence on girls' attendance. Interestingly, the presence of young children and a parent's absence from the household decreases both boys' and girls' school attendance probabilities by similar magnitudes, suggesting that gender roles may be more flexible for youth in households with high dependency ratios or absent parents.

Chapter 2, by Felicia Knaul, examines child labor in Mexico. Knaul finds that, if unpaid domestic work is excluded from the analysis, men enter the labor force earlier than women and accumulate significantly more years of work experience. For both men and women, the returns to education are higher than the returns to experience, and earnings profiles (returns to education and experience) are generally higher for women than for men. However, the earnings penalty for combining work and school is higher for women than for men; a possible explanation for this lies in the gender bias of the occupational distribution of young workers, in which girls, who are disproportionately represented in domestic services, accumulate skills and experience that are not rewarded in other sectors of the economy.

The Appendix to Chapter 2 focuses on the need to include unpaid domestic work in the measurement of child and youth economic activity rates. An inclusive definition implies a more than doubling of rates of work activity among female children and youth compared to conventional estimates (from 7.6 percent to 16.7 percent), and reverses the gender bias of child labor statistics (14 percent of boys are working). Counting home-based domestic work, which significantly reduces school attendance for those children performing a minimum of 20 hours per week of unpaid labor, also increases the overall incidence rate of child and youth labor in Mexico by 25 percent, compared to figures using standard definitions (15.5 percent versus 12.3 percent). Market-based child labor, in which 11 percent of urban boys and 37 percent of rural boys participate, is even more incompatible with school than home-based work: of those boys working at least 20 hours per week, only 40 percent of urban and 46 percent of rural child laborers are able to combine their work with school.

Chapter 3, by Wendy Cunningham, finds that household roles are more important than sex in determining the labor market activity of Mexican men and women. For example, labor force participation rates for women range from 25 percent for married women to 51 percent for single mothers to 69 percent for single, childless women, and the latter group is better represented in the formal sector than either married or single men. In addition, unlike single mothers and husbands, wives—13.2 percent of whom enter the labor force during recessionary periods—demonstrate an insurance-motivated added worker effect and a propensity for informal sector self-employment when the economy is deteriorating. The chapter argues that real economic necessity of the type faced permanently by single mothers and temporarily by wives whose households suffer significant income losses is generally met by women delegating or combining their domestic responsibilities with market work, preferably in the formal sector.

Chapter 4, by Susan Fleck, reviews recent trends in the *maquiladora* sector. The gender recomposition of the *maquiladora* labor force—in which women's share of employment fell from 78 percent to 57 percent between 1975 and 1998—is traced to changes in the types of industries that make up the sector, and the increasing attractiveness of *maquiladora* employment to men. Not only do women make up a smaller and smaller percentage of the *maquiladora* workforce, but they are also disproportionately concentrated in those industries with the lowest wages and benefits (such as textiles and apparel). Even within particular *maquiladora* industries, women consistently earn less than men, on average.

Another special sector of the Mexican economy—microenterprises—is explored in Chapter 5, by José Pagán and Susana Sanchez. They find that female-to-male earnings ratios in this sector are 36 percent in rural areas and 50 percent in urban areas. Differences in the types of men's and women's businesses explain a relatively small proportion (less than 5 percent) of this gender earnings gap, while gender differences in productive and personal characteristics, such as enterprise size and owner's level of education, explain 35 percent of the gap in urban areas and 42 percent in rural areas.

Chapter 6, the first of two chapters on rural labor markets, by José Pagán and Susana Sanchez, uses Oaxaca decomposition analysis with data from three rural states to examine gender differences in labor force participation and distribution between wage and self-employment. It finds that human capital, household demographic composition, and local labor market conditions explain only a small percentage of the low labor force participation rate of rural women, and their relatively high self-employment rate, suggesting that structural features of the rural labor market—such as gender-based employer preferences—act in such a way as to dissuade women from entering wage and salaried employment.

Chapter 7, the second rural labor market chapter, by Elizabeth Katz, uses a national survey of Mexican *ejidos* (agrarian reform farms), to examine gender and generational differences in off-farm labor market participation. In addition to marked regional and sectoral disparities, the results suggest that young, educated women are entering the rural labor market to a much greater extent than the older generation of women. Moreover, unlike their male counterparts, the labor force participation of women is not significantly affected by larger landholdings or the receipt of government support payments. This suggests that the labor supply behavior of young rural women is somewhat autonomous with respect to income derived from the family farm.

Chapter 8, by Susan Parker and Rebeca Wong, looks at the welfare of the Mexican elderly from a gender perspective. The broad finding is that elderly Mexican women are extremely dependent on their status as wives, widows, or mothers in order to receive income and healthcare. Since most women outlive their spouses, they are more likely to live in extended family arrangements in old age, where their adult children provide them with food and shelter. If they have a pension or healthcare coverage, it is almost always as a widow or a dependent. In this sense, the marriage market, combined with the profamily orientation of the Mexican institutions that provide formal employment-based pensions and health insurance, has been a particularly important avenue for elderly Mexican women to achieve a decent standard of living.

The book concludes with Chapter 9, by Elizabeth Katz and Maria Correia, which reviews the current status of gender policy in Mexico and outlines specific policy recommendations from the individual chapters.

Notes

1. The gender analysis is confined mostly to human capital and labor market issues; the book does not address other important topics such as reproductive health and violence.

2. From the World Bank's perspective, this book also represents a continuation and enrichment of the frequently referenced *Women's Employment and Pay in Latin America* (Psacharopoulos and Tzannatos 1992). This previous publication was largely limited to the analysis of gender differences in labor force participation and earnings, using Oaxaca decomposition analysis.

3. By way of comparison, the Duncan Index of occupational segregation for the United States is estimated to be 33.8, and for sectoral/industrial segregation, 26.6 (Blau, Ferber, and Winkler 1998).

References

Blau, Francine D., Marianne A. Ferber, and Anne E. Winkler. 1998. *The Economics of Men, Women and Work*. Upper Saddle River, N.J.: Prentice Hall.

CONAPO. 2000. "Evolución Reciente de la Población Económicamente Activa en México, 1991–1996." www.conapo.gob.mx/sit98/pea.htm

GENDERSTATS. genderstats.worldbank.org.

Psacharopoulos, George, and Zafiris Tzannatos. 1992. *Women's Employment and Pay in Latin America: Overview and Methodology.* Washington, D.C.: World Bank.

World Bank. 2000. *World Development Report 2000.* New York: Oxford University Press.

1

Gender Differences in Education in Mexico

Susan W. Parker and Carla Pederzini

A highly educated labor force is one of the key factors in promoting economic growth, and low levels of education are highly correlated with poverty. Lack of adequate education levels has been one of the most important factors contributing to the persistence of high levels of poverty in Latin America (Londoño 1996).

Perhaps just as important as the overall level of education in a country is its distribution. In most countries, the level of schooling for females is lower than for males, in spite of the fact that women's education has been demonstrated to have substantial positive external effects, whereas returns to men's education are mostly private (Schultz 1993). Besides generating private returns from labor market participation, women's education has a strong impact on numerous other variables as well, such as their children's health and mortality, and their own fertility and reproductive health. A large literature exists which has demonstrated that social returns to investing in women's education outweigh the social returns to investing in men's education (Schultz 1993; King and Hill 1993).

In Latin America, gender differences are generally lower than in other developing countries, although the growth rate in overall education levels has been less than in other regions (Inter-American Development Bank 1996). Furthermore, since 1960 there has been a large general expansion in education within the region and a sharp decline in gender differences between men and women. Primary school enrollment and completion statistics show no differences by gender in most countries, and to a large extent these trends carry over to secondary education. Those countries most likely to still have gender gaps favoring males in education among youth are poorer countries, such as Bolivia, whereas in wealthier countries there are no significant differences between males and females in educational attainment, except in very poor and indigenous areas (Bustillo 1993).

This chapter concentrates on the determinants of education in Mexico, an area in which there has been little empirical investigation. Mexico is an interesting case study because, like much of Latin America, it has experienced strong recent growth in educational attainment. Nevertheless, given its level of GDP, the current level of educational attainment in Mexico continues to be deficient. A 1996 study by the Inter-American Development Bank argues that the Mexican population has on average two and a half years less of education than it "should" have, given its level of GDP compared to other Latin American countries. Possible explanatory factors include the high level of income and social inequality in Mexico, which implies unequal access to basic services such as health and education.

This chapter has two central goals: (a) to analyze the determinants of the level of education of boys and girls in Mexico by concentrating on the effects of family background, economic and poverty status of the family, supply of schooling, and demographic variables; and (b) to shed light on the factors which may affect gender differences in education.

Our results find that the overall gender gap in education in Mexico has diminished to the extent that there are no apparent gender differences in years of completed schooling for individuals under age 25. This is suggestive of a new equality in educational achievement—one that appears to be repeating itself in a number of other Latin American countries. Nevertheless, rural children have far lower educational achievement than urban children, and gender gaps, while not large, appear to be higher there as well. In terms of the factors that have contributed to the reduction of the gender gap, one of the most important is that of the mother's education, so that the increased educational achievement of women tends to have a greater impact on their daughters than on their sons.

This chapter describes the educational system in Mexico and trends in educational attainment over several decades, provides a brief description of the existing theoretical and empirical literature on the determinants of educational investment in children and evidence on differential investments between girls and boys, and provides a detailed descriptive analysis of current trends in schooling attainment of individuals aged 6 to 30. We then turn to the empirical models, where we estimate the determinants of school attendance[1] and of falling behind in school. The regressions focus on child, family, and community characteristics. We conclude with interpretations and policy implications. For all of the empirical analysis, we use the 1995 National Survey of the Population and Housing Count.

Data

The National Survey of the Population and Housing Count (Conteo) was carried out in 1995 as a census of the population. The Conteo has two parts, including the short census questionnaire applied to the entire population, and a more detailed household questionnaire that was applied to a subsample of the population at the same time, which we use as the principal database for this paper. This data set includes information on all individuals in the household, including their labor market behavior, educational level and whether they are currently studying, all forms of monetary income including program transfers, and demographic and health information.

For three reasons the Conteo is the best available information for the purposes of our study. First, it has a very large sample (over 50,000 households), which implies that it is sufficiently large to carry out disaggregations by population group. Second, it includes all monetary income sources at the individual level, whereas many other data sets in Mexico include only labor or employment income. Third, it has by far the most complete information on educational attainment, compared with other available data, including number of years studied, number of years dedicated to technical careers, and whether individuals are currently attending school, and if not, whether they have ever attended.

The Educational System in Mexico

With the creation of the Secretary of Education in Mexico in 1921, the provision of education officially became a federal responsibility. The Mexican education system consists of mandatory free primary education, and as of 1992, secondary education. As might be expected, primary coverage is almost universal in Mexico, but secondary coverage lags substantially behind.[2] At the high-school level (*preparatoria*), students may choose between a curriculum oriented toward preparation for higher education, a curriculum oriented toward technical school, or a curriculum which prepares them for entering the workforce. Nevertheless, by the high-school level, as we will see, the majority of youth are no longer attending school.

Technical school is an option which is quite common, particularly among women. Technical school is normally 1 to 3 years, which can be done after primary, secondary, or high school. Generally, technical school involves training for a particular skill or occupation, such as computing, nursing, secretarial, and electronic technicians. About 16.5 percent of all women (compared to 8.6 percent of men) report that they have attended technical school, and the percentage of female workers with a technical school education is approximately 23.5 percent (compared to 9.6 percent of male workers). Of individuals between ages 12 and 30 who attend technical school, 65.6 percent are women.

University-level education is attained by only a small fraction of the population. Approximately 18 percent of men aged 25 to 40 and 12 percent of women aged 25 to 40 report having completed at least one year of university-level education.

Overall levels of education have been increasing steadily over the last 50 years, as measured by average years of schooling attained. The level of education has increased dramatically between the older and younger generations for individuals living in both urban and rural areas (Figure 1.1). For example, whereas the average years of completed schooling for individuals between the ages of 25 and 29 in urban areas is approximately 10 years of schooling, for the population aged 65 and older, this figure is only about 4 years of schooling for women and 5 for men.[3]

Figure 1.1 also shows that both currently and historically, education levels are much lower in rural areas than urban areas, although there has been some closing of this gap.[4] For the population above age 40, years of completed schooling in rural areas are less than half those in urban areas. The level of education in rural areas is particularly low for individuals above age 65, where the average level of educational attainment is only 1.5 years for men, and 1.2 years for women.[5]

Figure 1.1 demonstrates that the education gender gap is generally larger for the older generations than for youth and younger generations. This implies that differences in educational attainment between men and

Figure 1.1 Average Years of Schooling by Age Group, Rural/Urban Residence, and Gender

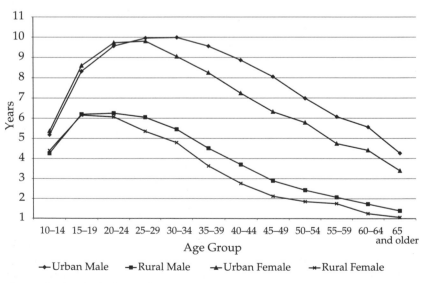

Source: Authors' calculations from *Encuesta del Conteo,* 1995.

women are becoming smaller over time. With respect to number of years of schooling, higher education levels of men than of women begin to appear only in the age group 20 to 24, and are increasing thereafter. Nevertheless, it is important to mention that the gender gap appears to be decreasing after age 50. We believe that this tendency can be at least partially explained by a selection mechanism. Women tend to have a longer life span than men, and given that it is probable that individuals who live longer also have higher education levels, a decreasing educational gap by gender could be explained.

It is important to emphasize the role of technical school in gender differences in education. The Conteo is the first data set in Mexico that allows the accurate measurement of number of years spent in technical school. Because girls and young women are much more likely to attend technical school than boys and young men, the Conteo allows a more accurate measurement of the educational gap by gender. Without correct accounting for technical school, there would appear to be a larger gap in years of completed schooling than is actually the case. Although this also raises the issue of whether technical schooling should be "counted" in the same manner as other types of schooling, here we consider one year of technical schooling to be equivalent to one year of schooling.[6]

The descriptive evidence presented here shows large increases in education levels of the population over time, and evidence that gender gaps in education between men and women have decreased. The considerably large declines in the gender gap are noteworthy and similar to trends in other Latin American countries. While we know of no obvious large-scale, gender-specific policies in education in Mexico over the last 30 years that would have contributed to the reduction of the gender gap (with the exception of PROGRESA; see Box 1.1), we mention two factors here that may be related. The first relates to the general expansion in education, which implies additional schools and easier access to these schools. Parents may be more reluctant to send their daughters than their sons to schools that are not located close by or that require substantial travel. A general expansion in education facilities could through this mechanism have a larger impact on girls' school attendance than on boys'.

A second factor that might be related to the reduction of the gender gap is the increase in women's labor force participation, which has coincided with the period of reduction of the gender gap. The rise in labor force participation of women in Mexico has been the fastest of all countries in Latin America, with increases in the participation rate of 256 percent between 1970 and 1990 (Valdés and Gomáriz 1995). While Mexican female labor force participation was well below the average of the region in 1970, this increase has allowed Mexico to "catch up" with the rest of the region. Male labor force participation, on the other hand, has fallen over this period. The implications of increases in labor force participation for education investment are numerous; probably the most important is that overall increased participation of women implies larger returns to investing in education for girls. That is, if parents expect that their daughters are likely to spend more years working in the labor market, they might invest more heavily in their daughters' education.

Theoretical and Empirical Literature on Educational Investments in Children

Economic theories on the determinants of investment in education usually begin with the theory of human capital, whereby individuals choose to invest in education depending on the costs and benefits of this investment (Becker 1964). Costs include both direct expenditures associated with schooling and indirect costs representing opportunity costs (usually forgone earnings during the time of studies), whereas benefits refer to the increase in the present value of lifetime earnings associated with education investments. Investments in education are therefore expected to increase with expected returns and decrease with increased costs.

This general theory of human capital includes a focus on gender, related to the organization of work in households. According to Becker, either because of biological differences or discrimination, both of which may affect women's expected returns to educational investments, women's investment in human capital may be lower than men's. Mincer and Polacheck (1982) demonstrate that one's perspectives on time use and labor market participation in the future help to determine investments in human capital. Because of their larger responsibilities for household tasks, women anticipate shorter periods and interrupted periods of

---

Box 1.1 The PROGRESA Program

The *Programa de Educación, Salud y Alimentación* (Education, Health and Nutrition Program, PROGRESA) was implemented in 1997, after the Conteo was carried out. Its goal is to combat poverty and reduce the education gap between boys and girls in poor rural areas of Mexico by providing monetary supports tied to investment in human capital. Families receive grants for sending their children to school, and the grants at the secondary level are slightly higher for girls. Thus, the program is designed to compensate for the greater tendency of girls in isolated rural areas to drop out after primary school. Currently the program serves approximately 2.6 million families in marginalized rural areas.

employment, which may motivate them to invest in human capital differently from men, both in quantitative and qualitative terms.[7]

Another reason why gender differences in education may exist can be found in the large percentage of returns to education for women which are social, implying that women receive less of the benefit of their investment. Men, on the other hand, capture a larger fraction of the total returns to education in the labor market (Schultz 1993; King and Hill 1993). In the case of the human capital decisions of children, these are often viewed as decisions made for children by their parents (see Box 1.2).

Intrahousehold allocation models provide an alternative focus on viewing family resource allocation decisions (Thomas 1990). Under these models, heterogeneity of preferences between family members is permitted, such that the outcomes may reflect the level of bargaining power of the different members. These models allow the income, assets, and educational level of different people in the household to have different impacts on outcomes. Numerous studies have found evidence of differential impacts of resources controlled by women versus resources controlled by men. (See Haddad, Hoddinott, and Alderman 1997 for a summary of recent literature.) In this chapter, we allow men's and women's education levels to have different impacts on boys' and girls' education, and in this way test to some extent the implications of intrahousehold models.

Box 1.2 Why Parents May Invest More in the Education of Boys than of Girls

Decisions by parents to invest differently in their sons' and daughters' education may be due to differences in the expected net (of costs) returns to boys' and girls' education. Girls may be viewed as having a lower expected return to educational investments, so that it may be more "efficient" and not necessarily openly "discriminatory" to invest more in a son's schooling.

King and Hill (1993) focus on various reasons for why the costs and returns to male and female education may differ from the perspective of parents. For example, if schools are located far away, parents may be more reluctant to allow daughters to travel long distances than sons. With respect to benefits, girls may face lower returns to human capital investments because of labor market discrimination or because of less time spent in the labor market, thereby reducing the benefits to investing in the education of girls. Parents may also be motivated to invest in children who will be more likely to support them economically in their old age. If parents' expectations are that their sons will be more likely to provide economic support in their old age, they may be more likely to invest in sons' education.[8]

Empirical Studies on Schooling

There are a number of empirical studies relevant to our analysis, and here we briefly mention some of the most recent and relevant studies in the context of Mexico.

There have been very few studies which empirically analyze the determinants of education in Mexico. One exception is Post, Garcia, and Flores (1998) who analyze rates of continuation from primary to secondary school in the different states of Mexico, with particular focus on mandatory secondary education, which was implemented in 1992. The authors argue that community characteristics are important for analyzing gender differentials in education; that is, the more marginated the state, as measured by lacking basic services such as water, and high illiteracy rates, the greater the inequality in girls' education. They also analyze the determinants of being a full-time student for the age group 13 to 15 in Mexico in 1984 and 1992, finding that family resources had a larger impact on children studying in 1992 than in 1984.

Palafox, Prawda, and Velez (1994) analyze the determinants of schooling achievement in Mexico using an interesting database on cognitive achievement scores in math and Spanish of children in primary schools. They find that male students tend to do better in both mathematics and Spanish than female students, even after controlling for socioeconomic characteristics. Parental education levels are positively associated with student achievement, as is living in a two-parent family.

Knaul and Parker (1998) consider the relationship between schooling and work participation of urban youth in Mexico, looking at the determinants of beginning a work spell or leaving school in the context of the economic crisis of 1995. They find that schooling tends to be more related to market work for boys and domestic work for girls.[9]

Current Trends in Educational Achievement in Mexico

This section presents trends in school attendance and educational attainment of the population of individuals between ages 6 and 30, taking into account differences at the urban–rural level and differences by income level. We chose this age group in order to provide a full picture of educational attainment, given that even at age 25, over 5 percent of the population still report that they are attending school.

Figure 1.2 presents the percentage of the male and female population attending school. The figure shows that by age 8, the percentage of children attending school is over 95 percent. It is interesting to note that school attendance increases from age 6 to age 9, which is evidence of a certain degree of late enrollment, although this late enrollment does not appear to differ by gender. School attendance begins to fall by age 11, with important declines in attendance beginning at age 12, an age which (usually) coincides with the end of primary school. At this age, it is also important to note that a gender gap begins in attendance. For example, at age 13, 87.0 percent of boys are attending school compared to 82.4 percent of girls. These trends suggest that more girls than boys tend to end their education at the primary level. Nevertheless, by ages 16 and 17, which normally correspond to the end of secondary-level education, boys begin to drop out at the same rate as girls. At age 19, a gap begins once again, presumably resulting from young men entering college at a higher rate than young women. For example, 27 percent of males aged 19 are attending school, whereas 24 percent of females of this age are attending school.

Figure 1.3 considers these trends by rural–urban residence. In Mexico, rural areas are generally defined as localities with less than 2,500 residents. Rural areas tend to have a higher percentage of population in poverty, lower access to health and educational services, and less social infrastructure of roads, water systems, telephone services, and other services.

Figure 1.2 Percentage of Population Attending School, by Age and Gender

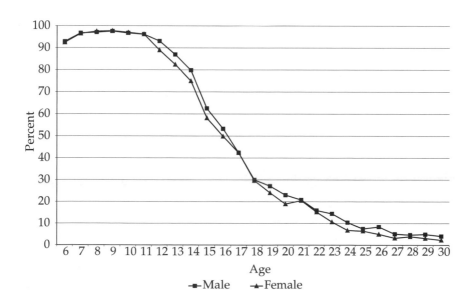

Source: Authors' calculations from *Encuesta del Conteo*, 1995.

Figure 1.3 Percentage of Population Attending School, by Urban/Rural Residence, Age, and Gender

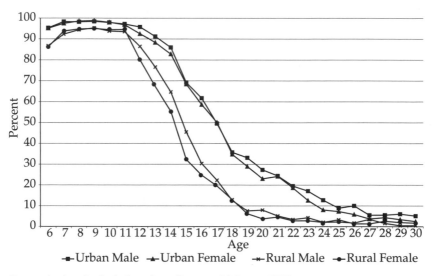

-■-Urban Male   -▲-Urban Female   -✕-Rural Male   -●-Rural Female

Source: Authors' calculations from *Encuesta del Conteo*, 1995.

The percentage of the population attending school is uniformly lower for rural areas than for urban areas. Figure 1.3 also shows that the gender gap in school attendance is larger in rural areas than in urban areas. In the case of urban areas, attendance appears to be about the same for boys and girls until age 17, at which boys begin to have a higher school attendance than girls. This presumably corresponds to the age at which individuals begin to enter college. In rural communities, a gender gap in attendance begins at age 11 and is larger. For example, by age 13, 76.6 percent of boys are attending school in rural communities compared to only 67.2 percent of girls. By age 17, there appears to be little difference in school attendance between boys and girls; more noticeable are the very low overall attendance rates of both boys and girls.

Figure 1.4 presents the relationship between school attendance and per capita household income level, divided into 5 groups (constructed by quintiles based on per capita income). It is clear that lower levels of per capita household income are associated with lower school attendance. It is particularly noteworthy that the lower-income groups show evidence of very late entry to school, as enrollment increases sharply from ages 6 to 9. This is an important tendency, because late entry implies that even before they begin school, children are in some sense "behind" in school, and this is likely associated with an increased risk of

Figure 1.4 Percentage of Population Attending School, by Per Capita Income Quintile and Age

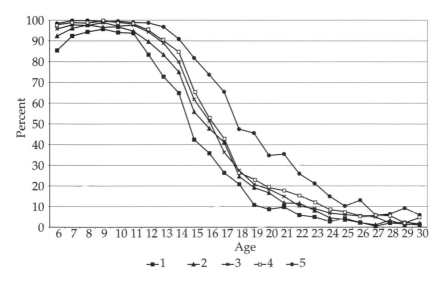

Source: Authors' calculations from *Encuesta del Conteo*, 1995.

school dropout at earlier ages. This raises the question of why lower-income households send their children to school later, and presumably is also related to gaps in educational attainment between urban and rural areas.

Figure 1.5 shows the number of years of completed schooling for individuals aged 6 to 30 by urban and rural areas. The gender gaps evident in school attendance are not obvious in years of completed schooling. Actually, for urban communities, there is a "reverse" gender gap which seems to favor girls—as girls appear to have a higher number of completed years of schooling than boys until their mid-20s. For the rural communities, the number of years of completed schooling is more or less equal until age 24, where a gap begins, with men having a higher number of years of completed schooling than women.

Figure 1.6 shows number of years of completed schooling by income group. Again, there are very clear tendencies that families with higher levels of income tend to have children with higher levels of schooling, even at very young ages. A noticeable gap in the number of years of schooling between the lower-income groups and the upper-income groups is already evident in children by age 8, and the gaps only increase with age.

Figure 1.5 Average Completed Years of Schooling, by Urban/Rural Residence, Gender, and Age

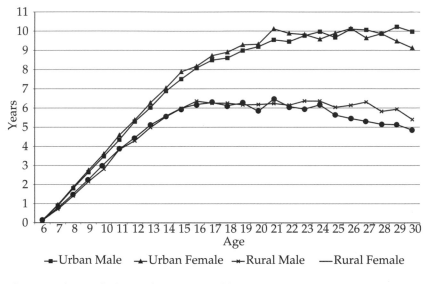

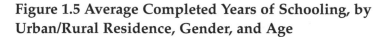

Source: Authors' calculations from *Encuesta del Conteo,* 1995.

Figure 1.6 Average Completed Years of Schooling, by Per Capita Income Quintile and Age

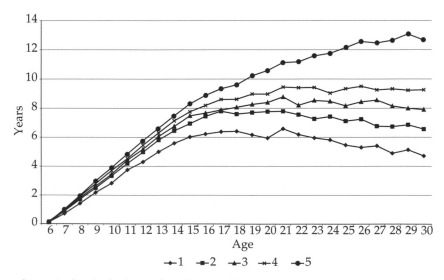

Source: Authors' calculations from *Encuesta del Conteo,* 1995.

The conflicting patterns of school attendance and years of completed schooling are quite striking. Why does a significant and important gender gap in attendance beginning at the secondary level of schooling not coincide with a reduced number of years of schooling at these ages, even in rural areas where attendance gaps are quite large?

One possible explanation is that while fewer girls attend school, those that do attend do better in school than boys. That is, they are more likely to complete school levels on time, are less likely to fall behind in school, and are less likely to repeat grades. While we do not have explicit information on repeated grades, we can look at the extent to which children fall behind in school, where we define falling behind by the schooling gap (Behrman, Birdsall, and Szekeley 1999). This schooling gap is defined as the number of years behind where a child should be in school, assuming the child entered school on time and progressed normally through school—that is, never repeating a grade.[10] Note that the schooling gap reflects a number of different educational outcomes, including late entry, intermittent school attendance, grade repetition, and dropout. While a schooling gap due to late entry for a child who progresses normally through school may be the same as for a child who started "on time" but has repeated grades, this analysis cannot, unfortunately, distinguish between the different causes.

Table 1.1 clearly shows that by age 9 the schooling gap begins to become larger for boys than for girls, both in urban and rural areas.[11] There are also large differences between urban and rural residence, with children living in rural areas being farther behind in school at all ages. By age 12, for example, boys in rural areas, on average, are 1.7 years behind where they should be in school, whereas the corresponding figure in urban areas is 0.71. Rather than late entry, it seems likely that these higher levels of schooling gap are reflective of a higher degree of grade repetition or intermittent attendance for boys than for girls. While we do not have direct information on age at entry to school, the descriptive analysis above did not seem to suggest differences in late entry by gender.

We have found, however, that with respect to attendance, girls begin to drop out of school at a higher rate than boys beginning at age 12, particularly in small communities and in low-income households. Nevertheless, we have found that these differences in attendance do not necessarily translate into immediately overall higher levels of education for young men, but rather these differences show up in terms of educational attainment after age 20. The reasons for this are that even though boys have higher rates of attendance than girls, particularly in rural areas, they tend to be more likely to fall behind in school.

The degree to which both boys and girls (particularly boys) fall behind in school is an important correlate in schooling achievement. The phe-

Table 1.1. Average Schooling Gap: Years Behind in School by Age, Gender, and Residence

	Rural			Urban		
Age	Boys	Girls	All	Boys	Girls	All
8	0.59	0.49	0.54	0.20	0.13	0.16
9	0.85	0.73	0.79	0.36	0.25	0.30
10	1.19	0.93	1.06	0.53	0.39	0.46
11	1.16	1.15	1.16	0.66	0.41	0.54
12	1.71	1.55	1.63	0.71	0.62	0.67
13	2.01	1.88	1.95	0.97	0.73	0.85
14	2.45	2.41	2.43	1.12	0.95	1.04
15	3.02	3.00	3.01	1.49	1.11	1.30
16	3.64	3.81	3.73	1.92	1.83	1.88
17	4.75	4.72	4.73	2.51	2.28	2.40
18	5.75	5.88	5.81	3.40	3.10	3.25

Note: Years behind in school = age minus completed years of schooling (includes technical school) minus 6.
Sources: Encuesta del Conteo, 1995; author's calculations.

nomena of late entry and grade repetition, which these trends presumably reflect, are important issues in Mexico and are likely related to labor market participation and domestic work at early ages, which although they may not immediately result in school dropout, are likely to promote grade repetition and subsequent dropout.

This complex picture of educational attainment in the younger generations suggests that both attendance and school performance (that is, whether a student successfully completes the year of study) while in school are important indicators of long-run school attainment.

Empirical Models and Sample

We now turn to our estimation models of the determinants of educational investments in boys and girls. The estimation methods are based on reduced form models of the demand for education.[12,13]

Consistent with the descriptive data presented above, we estimate two separate dependent variables in our empirical model: school attendance and the schooling gap. Behrman and Knowles (1999) argue for the necessity of using various indicators of education rather than simply using the usual completed years of schooling. It should be noted that the second model, that of schooling gaps, clearly represents a more long-term measure of schooling attainment than that of current school attendance because in some sense it represents the accumulated result of educational achievement since the child started school. While it might then not seem appropriate to include variables indicating a family's current economic situation, it should be noted that nearly all of our variables are variables which have some degree of permanence[14] (see "Independent Variables" section below).

Samples Used in the Analysis

In our analysis we focus on youth aged 12 to 15. We chose this age group for several reasons. First, the descriptive evidence above suggested that a gender gap in attendance begins to appear at age 12 between boys and girls, and is particularly high between ages 12 and 15, which is precisely the age at which children should be attending secondary school. Second, the analysis showed that the largest gaps between boys and girls in terms of falling behind in school begin after age 11.

Finally, we are concerned about sample selection issues which occur after age 15, particularly for girls. In our sample, we use only children who are children of the household head and/or spouse of the household head because these are the only children for whom we can identify their parents, and henceforth we analyze the impact of parent characteristics on child schooling. Nevertheless, this raises sample selection questions as to whether these children and youngsters are representative of the sample of all children. In particular, there may be biases arising from excluding youngsters who marry at an early age and leave the household to form their own household, an effect which is particularly important for girls.[15]

Independent Variables

We consider several sets of independent variables, including characteristics of the child; characteristics of the parents, including level of education; household and demographic characteristics; and community-level characteristics, including the supply of secondary schools.

Characteristics of the Child and Siblings. Characteristics of the child included in the model are the age and sex of the child. We also experimented with variables measuring birth order, including dummy variables measuring whether the child was the oldest or youngest.[16] Some recent evidence has found that middle children do worse in terms of household schooling investments (Parish and Willis 1993). Nevertheless, these variables were found to be insignificant in all cases and were left out of the final models.

We also include measures of children aged 0 to 5, children aged 6 to 11, and other siblings aged 12 to 20 in the household. We expect that the presence of younger children may have a negative impact on schooling, due to either additional domestic responsibilities or economic necessity. Other siblings of school age may have a negative impact on education through tradeoffs between quantity and quality, or through the "dilution" of family resources. Nevertheless, we recognize that these measures of other children in the household can be considered to be endogenous. The estimated coefficients on these variables should be treated as correlations, with no implication of causality.

Characteristics of the Parents. We are particularly interested in the potential effects of the education levels of the father and mother. Parental education should have a positive influence on child education through such factors as parental influence, a home environment more oriented toward study, and the greater ability of parents to help children with homework. It is also likely to pick up the economic status of the household, although we include a number of other measures of economic status.[17] Some previous literature in other countries has demonstrated that the educational levels of the father and mother have different impacts on the level of education of sons and daughters. In particular, it has been found that the mother's level of education generally has a greater impact on child education outcomes, particularly those of girls.

We also include a dummy variable measuring whether the father of the child is present in the household. This variable may pick up both economic and work effects and motivational or psychological aspects associated with schooling. Parents absent from the household may place additional work burdens on children, for example, if children enter the labor force to replace adult labor or if children at home engage in more domestic work to make up for parents. Previous studies in both Mexico and other countries have found that children of single parents often perform worse in school, even when controls for income status are in place (Gómez de León and Parker 1999; Garasky 1995). These worse outcomes are often attributed to motivational and psychological factors associated with a parent's separation or divorce. In our case, there are very few mothers of children not living in the household, whereas approximately 15 percent of fathers are absent from the household. Almost all of the households where fathers are absent are female headed.

Characteristics of the Household. The economic status of the household, as demonstrated in the descriptive statistics, should be a fundamental determinant of educational determinants and differences in education between boys and girls. Economic status affects educational investments in children through the ability of the household to pay direct and indirect costs of their child's schooling. Poorer households have fewer resources with which to finance such aspects as transportation and school supplies. Additionally, the opportunity cost of children attending school may be higher for poor households in terms of forfeited income and help with domestic chores.[18]

We include a measure of the household's unearned income levels to capture the effects of income on educational investments. We exclude labor income from the measure of income levels for two reasons. First, given that work decisions of children are clearly endogenous, we consider child and youth income to be endogenous to their educational decisions. Second, in a family labor supply model the labor force decisions of all household members are jointly determined, so that it would also be inappropriate to consider adult labor income as exogenous to children's educational investments.

As additional indicators of economic status and wealth, we also include whether the floor of the household dwelling is an earth floor and whether the household has running water inside the house. Finally, we include a measure of whether there are any disabled individuals in the household. This variable may be important to the extent to which children may substitute for the labor of disabled individuals.

Characteristics of the Community. The availability, distance, and accessibility of schools are key variables for measuring the costs of attending school. We use measures of the number of per capita secondary schools, where per capita refers to the secondary-school-age population (ages 12 to 15) as indicators of the supply of schools in the municipality.[19] We do not have direct measures of the distances to schools for the children in each community. Rather, we use an (admittedly crude) indicator of altitude in the municipality as a measure of difficulty of access to schools in rural areas only.

Table 1.2 provides the means and standard deviations of the variables used in the analysis. The table shows the differences in the education variables by gender. It is important to note that the differences between boys and girls, both in attendance and in the schooling gap, are significant both in urban and rural areas. The table also makes evident the lower economic status of children in rural areas compared to urban areas. For example, in urban areas over 60 percent of households report having running water in their dwelling, compared to only 20 percent of households in rural areas. Table 1.2 also shows the much higher levels of education of parents in urban compared to rural areas. In general, parental education levels are more than twice the level in urban as in rural areas. As expected, the number of children in the family is much larger as well in rural areas.

Table 1.2. Means and Standard Deviations of Variables Used in the Analysis: Youth Aged 12 to 15

| | Urban (Localities >2,500) | | Rural (Localities <2,500) | |
	Girls	Boys	Girls	Boys
Child Characteristics				
% of children attending school	83.9 (32.2)	85.7 (35.0)	63.0 (48.3)	71.9 (44.9)
Schooling gap	0.87 (1.66)	1.15 (1.76)	1.97 (2.10)	2.09 (2.08)
Age	13.5 (1.12)	13.5 (1.12)	13.5 (1.10)	13.4 (1.10)
Number of kids 0 to 5	.511 (.784)	.499 (.791)	.842 (1.02)	.816 (1.01)
Number of kids 6 to 11	.992 (.949)	.952 (.953)	1.37 (1.10)	1.38 (1.10)
Siblings in household aged 12 and older	2.83 (1.69)	2.78 (1.69)	3.68 (2.08)	3.73 (2.16)
Parent Characteristics				
Years of schooling of mother	5.74 (4.07)	5.79 (4.19)	3.02 (2.83)	2.95 (2.74)
Years of schooling of father	6.50 (5.42)	6.66 (4.65)	3.40 (3.01)	3.33 (2.97)
Father absent from household	.139 (.328)	.123 (.328)	.084 (.277)	.086 (.280)
Household Characteristics				
Unearned household income (per capita)	33 (196)	29 (198)	23 (82)	25 (107)
Presence of disabled persons in household	.097 (.289)	.104 (.306)	.132 (.338)	.129 (.335)
Dwelling has running water inside	.631 (.483)	.636 (.481)	.201 (.401)	.175 (.378)

Table 1.2 *(continued)*

	Urban (Localities >2,500)		Rural (Localities <2,500)	
	Girls	Boys	Girls	Boys
Dwelling has	.121	.123	.387	.392
earth floor	(.326)	(.329)	(.487)	(.488)
Community Characteristics				
Secondary	.0001	.0001	.0004	.0004
schools	(.00005)	(.00005)	(.0003)	(.0003)
per capita				
Altitude			1,139	1,142
			(864)	(855)

Note: Standard deviations in parentheses.
Source: Encuesta del Conteo, 1995.

Regression Results

Our principal focus in the discussion of the regression results is on differences in the determinants of education by gender, although we also compare the results between urban and rural areas. [20,21]

School Attendance. Beginning with school attendance in urban areas (Table 1.3), the results show large impacts of parental education on attendance of girls and boys. The education level of both parents is highly significant, and for girls the education level of the mother has a larger positive impact than the level of education of the father. The reverse is true for boys; the education level of the father has a larger impact on their school attendance than the level of education of the mother.

Family Income Level. With respect to the impact of family income on school attendance in urban areas, for both boys and girls the results show that family income has an important positive impact on children's schooling. The size of the impact is larger for boys than for girls by about 30 percent. A larger impact of family income on boys' education is consistent with an interpretation that boys' education is more responsive than girls'; that is, it is subject to larger changes with income fluctuations. In other words, increases in family income are more likely to be spent on boys' education, whereas decreases in family income are more likely to hurt boys' education than girls.

Family income has a positive impact on school attendance for both boys and girls in rural areas and, as in urban areas, the impact is larger for boys' school attendance than girls' school attendance. Compared with

Table 1.3. Determinants of the Probability of School Attendance by Urban and Rural Residence: Youth Aged 12 to 15 (marginal effects; Z statistics)

	Urban (localities >2,500)		Rural (localities <2,500)	
	Girls	Boys	Girls	Boys
Child characteristics				
Age	−.060*	−.066*	−.155*	−.135*
	(−17.9)	(−21.6)	(−21.2)	(−21.5)
Number of kids 0 to 5	−.028*	−.021*	−.019*	−.008
	(−6.06)	(−5.14)	(−2.04)	(−0.99)
Number of kids 6 to 11	−.002	−.005*	−.015*	−.010
	(−0.55)	(−1.26)	(−1.62)	(−1.23)
Siblings in household aged 12 and older	−.011*	−.003	−.008	−.004
	(−3.93)	(−1.08)	(−1.43)	(−0.87)
Parental characteristics				
Years of schooling of mother	.013*	.008*	.021*	.017*
	(10.3)	(7.02)	(6.12)	(5.44)
Years of schooling of father	.011*	.011*	.019*	.020*
	(8.93)	(10.5)	(5.61)	(6.61)
Father absent from household	−.036*	−.031*	−.058*	−.122*
	(−3.33)	(−3.11)	(−1.90)	(−4.41)
Household characteristics				
Log of household per capita unearned income (*100)	.070*	.095*	.137*	.239*
	(1.98)	(2.81)	(2.22)	(4.49)
Presence of disabled persons in household	−.006	−.034*	.014	−.036*
	(−0.57)	(−3.23)	(0.60)	(−1.80)
Dwelling has running water inside	.036*	.024*	.063*	.035
	(4.45)	(3.27)	(2.99)	(1.77)

Table 1.3 *(continued)*

	Urban (localities >2,500)		Rural (localities <2,500)	
	Girls	Boys	Girls	Boys
Dwelling has	–.034*	–.043*	–.044*	–.049*
earth floor	(–3.11)	(–4.29)	(–2.59)	(–3.34)
Community characteristics				
Secondary	–0.014	–0.084	1.03*	0.65*
schools	(–0.18)	(–1.25)	(2.71)	(2.06)
(1,000*)				
Altitude			–.047*	–.031*
(1,000*)			(–4.81)	(–3.55)
N	7086	7292	4197	4504
Model				
statistic	Chi2(12)=1,203	Chi2(12)=1,212	Chi2(13)=756	Chi2(13)=760

* Significant at the 10 percent level or less.
Note: Standard deviations in parentheses.
Source: Encuesta del Conteo, 1995.

urban areas, the magnitude of the impact is much larger, indicating that income has an even larger impact on educational investments in rural areas than in urban areas. This can be interpreted as evidence that income "matters" more for schooling attainment in rural areas, or that differences in educational outcomes by income levels are greater in rural areas than in urban areas.

Absence of the Father and Presence of Disabled Household Members. Absent fathers have a negative effect on school attendance. In urban areas the father's absence from the household has an important negative impact on the probability of both their male and female children attending school. The magnitude of the impact is similar for boys and girls and suggests that the father's absence reduces the probability of attending school by over 3 percentage points.

Nevertheless, this negative impact is much larger in rural areas than in urban areas, and in rural areas, the father's absence from the household has a negative effect twice as large for boys as for girls. The results suggest that for boys living in rural areas, the father not living in the household reduces the probability that they attend school by over 12 percentage points. This again suggests that boys tend to leave school and work in the labor market when their father is not living in the household.

The presence of disabled individuals is negatively and significantly related to the probability of school attendance only in the case of boys, reducing attendance by 3.4 percentage points. This negative effect of disabled members likely suggests that boys may substitute for family disabled workers in the labor force, thereby reducing the probability that they attend school.

Presence of Small Children in the Family. On the other hand, small children in the family have a larger negative effect on school attendance for girls than for boys, although it is significant for both. This may reflect the possibility that older daughters have additional domestic responsibilities associated with younger brothers and sisters that are incompatible with school attendance, whereas more younger brothers and sisters may increase the probability of entering the labor force for older brothers. In the case of siblings one's age or older, the evidence indicates that this negatively affects the attendance of girls only, which may indicate that in large urban families, girls are the ones most likely to be excluded from educational investments, at least in terms of school attendance.

School Attendance in Rural Areas. Turning now to school attendance in rural areas, the educational level of the mother and father continues to be a significant determinant of school attendance in all of the samples. Again, the impact of the mother's education has a larger positive impact for girls, whereas the impact of the father's education is greater for boys. The estimated impact is quite large and demonstrates that in rural areas, the education of the mother and the father has an impact twice as great as in urban areas. For example, for girls, each additional year of the mother's education increases the probability of attending school by 2.1 percentage points, compared to 1.9 percentage points for each additional year of the father's education.

Supply of Secondary Schools. Finally, at the community level, the supply of secondary schools is positively and significantly related to the probability of school attendance for both boys and girls only in rural areas, with a larger impact for girls. This is consistent with evidence that the supply of secondary schools is a bigger problem in rural areas, and suggests that increases in the supply of schools in rural areas will have a greater impact on the school attendance of girls.

Regressions of the Schooling Gap

We now turn to the regressions of the schooling gap, beginning with urban areas. (Note that a *higher* schooling gap indicates greater years behind in school, and thus implies a more negative outcome, the reverse of our indicator of school attendance.) Table 1.4 shows that, as in school attendance, parental education levels are a key determinant of educational attainment. Nevertheless, unlike school attendance, the impact of the mother's education level is greater than the impact of father's education level for both girls and boys. This differential finding from school attendance may suggest that over the longer run, the mother's education level plays a greater role in the educational attainment of both boys and girls, although it should be emphasized that the father's education level is also significant in both groups and its impact is not small.

Absent fathers tend to increase the schooling gap in urban areas only for boys, again supporting the idea that absent fathers result in a higher probability of working, thus causing boys to fall behind in school. As with the results for school attendance, the presence of disabled individuals affects the probability of only boys falling behind in school, whereas the number of younger children in the family has a positive effect of falling behind in school only for girls.

With respect to the determinants of the schooling gap in rural areas, parental education again has a strong impact and, as was the case in school attendance, the impact is much greater in rural than in urban areas (Table 1.4). The mother's education level has a greater positive impact on schooling outcomes than the father's education level for both boys and girls. The size of the impact is again much greater in rural than in urban areas, indicating that parental education levels make a greater difference to children's education in rural areas. The income measures show the important impact of income on increasing children's achievement. As has been seen throughout the empirical analysis, the impact of household income is greater for boys than for girls.

Table 1.4. Determinants of the Schooling Gap by Urban and Rural Residence: Youth Aged 12 to 15 (coefficient estimates [t-statistics])

| | Urban (localities >2,500) | | Rural (localities <2,500) | |
	Girls	Boys	Girls	Boys
Child characteristics				
Age	.159*	.238*	.448*	.384*
	(9.92)	(14.6)	(17.4)	(15.6)
Number of kids 0 to 5	.116*	0.068	.149*	.089
	(4.56)	(2.60)	(4.40)	(2.67)
Number of kids 6 to 11	.024	.040*	.036	−0.22
	(1.04)	(1.68)	(1.04)	(−0.65)
Siblings in household aged 12 and older	.067*	.075*	.037*	.092*
	(4.55)	(5.03)	(1.79)	(4.60)

(Table continues on the following page.)

Table 1.4 *(continued)*

	Urban (localities >2,500)		Rural (localities <2,500)	
	Girls	Boys	Girls	Boys
Parent characteristics				
Years of schooling of mother	−.077* (−13.5)	−.056* (−9.47)	−.147* (−12.4)	−.136* (−11.5)
Years of schooling of father	−.034* (−6.80)	−.045* (−8.80)	−.081* (−7.14)	−.100* (−9.08)
Father absent from household	.038 (0.74)	.182* (3.23)	.299* (2.82)	.333 (3.26)
Household characteristics				
Log of household per capita unearned income (*100)	.290 (1.50)	−.334* (−1.78)	−.499* (−2.22)	−.572* (−2.65)
Presence of disabled persons in household	.344* (5.73)	.583* (9.65)	.115 (1.38)	.325* (4.01)
Dwelling has running water inside	−.324* (−7.81)	−.397* (−9.20)	−.272* (−3.60)	−.182* (−2.36)
Dwelling has earth floor	.647* (10.9)	.650* (10.6)	.805* (12.8)	.718* (11.9)
Community characteristics				
Secondary schools (1,000*)	0.339 (0.936)	0.275 (0.739)	−3.55 (−2.62)	−.851* (−0.68)
Altitude			−.032* (−0.89)	.078* (2.23)
N	7,074	7,292	4,197	4,505
Model statistic	F(12,7074) = 139	F(12,7279) = 157	F(13,4197) = 101	F(15,4491) = 100

* = Significant at the 10 percent level or less.
Note: Standard deviations in parentheses.
Source: Encuesta del Conteo, 1995.

Absent fathers tend to increase the schooling gap for both girls and boys in rural areas, with a greater impact on boys than on girls. Small children in the household are likely to increase the extent to which children fall behind in school, and once again, the effects are greater on girls. In both samples, older siblings have a positive and strong impact on the probability of falling behind in school, providing support for the "dilution" of the family resources argument. Finally, the supply of secondary schools in rural areas appears to increase attainment for only girls.

These results demonstrate the unquestionably large effects of family background—the educational level of mothers and fathers, and variables measuring the economic status of the family—on the schooling attainment of children. These impacts are, in general, much greater in rural than in urban areas, showing that family background is even more important in rural settings.

Family income has a very important significant impact on increasing educational investments, and the magnitude is consistently higher on boys' education than on girls' education in both urban and rural areas. Our interpretation of this finding is that boys' education is more responsive than girls' education; that is, there are larger changes in response to changes in family income. This implies that families are more likely to spend additionally on boys' education in good economic times, and remove them from school in poor economic times, thereby reducing their educational attainment.[22]

Variables which in some degree measure the capacity of (or lack of) households to supply labor to the market tend to have much greater negative impacts on boys, whereas variables indicating the necessity of domestic work have greater negative impacts on girls. This is consistent with the argument that labor market participation interferes more with the schooling of boys and domestic work interferes more with the schooling of girls. It is also clearly related to the higher participation in the labor market of boys at a young age (Knaul and Parker 1998). Knaul and Parker suggest that a more inclusive definition of work should be used in analyses of child work and school attendance.

The Gender Gap Revisited

To what extent do gender gaps continue to exist in our schooling indicators, even after controlling for certain individual, family, and community variables? Table 1.5 provides predicted probabilities of school attendance derived from the probit regression[23] for boys and girls. The difference in the values between boys and girls can be interpreted as the impact of gender evaluated at the mean value of all other independent variables. We also present the ratio of the predicted value of girls' school attendance to boys' school attendance as a measure of gender differences. Values below 100 percent measure the extent to which girls' school attendance is lower than boys', controlling for other factors.

For the group of boys and girls aged 12 to 15, Table 1.5 shows that there continues to be a very large gender gap in attendance in rural areas, and a smaller gender gap in urban areas favoring boys. Nevertheless, the size of this gender gap varies depending on household characteristics. Both in urban and rural areas, the gender gap is generally larger with lower educational levels of parents, particularly that of the mother, indicating that family background is not just an important determinant of overall schooling levels, but of the difference in schooling levels between boys and girls as well.

We turn now to the predicted schooling gap by gender, derived from the regression equations for boys and girls (Table 1.6). (Recall that a larg-

Table 1.5. Predicted Probabilities of School Attendance

| | Urban Areas | | | Rural Areas | | |
	Girls	Boys	% Ratio (G/B)	Girls	Boys	% Ratio (G/B)
All	.841	.859	97.8*	.632	.723	87.4%*
Age 12	.932	.958	97.3*	.826	.890	92.8*
Age 13	.884	.915	96.6*	.711	.794	89.6*
Age 14	.811	.838	96.8	.558	.663	84.2*
Age 15	.730	.727	100.4	.411	.501	82.0*
Mother: no schooling	.654	.719	91.0*	.532	.634	83.9*
Mother: completed primary	.873	.884	98.8	.729	.822	88.7*
Father: no schooling	.671	.693	96.8*	.527	.629	83.8*
Father: completed primary	.860	.876	98.2	.731	.813	89.8*
Father absent from household	.814	.832	97.8	.629	.690	91.6*

* Significantly different from 1 (100 percent).

er schooling gap is a negative outcome, so that values of our indicator below 100 percent indicate a more favorable outcome for girls). Table 1.6 confirms that this gap is fairly large in urban areas, showing that overall, boys are a significant number of years behind where they should be in school than girls. In rural areas, however, the schooling gap is comparable for both sexes, although slightly larger for boys. In contrast to urban areas, the gap does not seem to be particularly variable with family background. In urban areas, the difference between girls and boys is greatest (that is, boys do worse relative to girls) in families where the father is not present, perhaps indicating that boys bear a greater burden of this absence in terms of their ability to attend and complete school on time.[24]

These results confirm the earlier descriptive evidence which suggested that girls are at a greater risk for dropout and boys are at a greater risk

Table 1.6. Predicted Schooling Gap: Average Number of Years Behind in School

| | Urban Areas | | | Rural Areas | | |
	Girls	Boys	% Ratio (G/B)	Girls	Boys	% Ratio (G/B)
All	.863	1.14	75.7*	1.96	2.05	95.6*
Age 12	.600	.781	76.8*	1.34	1.53	87.6*
Age 13	.792	1.00	79.2*	1.74	1.86	93.6
Age 14	.976	1.24	78.7*	2.21	2.27	97.4
Age 15	1.10	1.54	71.4*	2.62	2.62	100
Mother: no schooling	1.69	1.94	87.1*	2.73	2.78	98.2
Mother: completed primary	.823	1.09	75.5*	1.24	1.36	91.2
Father: no schooling	1.60	1.93	82.9*	2.62	2.73	96.0
Father: completed primary	.904	1.19	76.0	1.35	1.44	93.8
Father absent from household	.934	1.35	69.2	2.02	2.07	97.6

* Significantly different from 1.

for falling behind in school. The school attendance of girls is particularly problematic in rural areas, whereas the problem of boys falling behind in school is, relative to girls, significantly greater in urban areas.

Conclusion

Over the last four decades important progress has been made in improving educational attainment in Mexico. The average number of years of schooling attained has doubled, and gender differences in education have been substantially reduced. Nevertheless, given its level of GDP, Mexico still lags behind other Latin American countries in terms of education. Furthermore, large differences in educational attainment between rural and urban areas remain—differences which are clearly related to economic status.

The gender gap in education has fallen substantially over the last 30 years; overall, girls and boys below age 20 do not display significant differences in educational attainment, as measured by years of schooling completed. Nevertheless, the existing educational difficulties of children appear to differ substantially by gender. By age 12 girls are less likely to enroll in school than boys. This is consistent with fewer girls going on to secondary school after finishing primary school.

In spite of these trends, a gender gap in years of completed schooling by age does not show up between boys and girls until after age 20. The reason for this is that while boys enroll more in school, they are more likely to repeat grades and fall behind in school. The policy implication which emerges as a result of this analysis is that policies should be aimed at stopping the dropout of girls after primary school and at trying to understand why boys who are enrolled in school are more likely than girls to fall behind in school.

Men are still more likely to enroll in college than women. An important issue for the future with respect to gender and education, particularly in urban areas, will be attendance at the university level and the types of majors women choose to study and the careers they choose to enter. In many Latin American countries, it has been shown that women tend to be concentrated in traditionally female areas, such as education and health (Bustillo 1993).

While perhaps not specifically oriented to increasing girls' education, the general expansion in education levels in Mexico might have had a greater impact on girls' attendance if schools were more easily accessible; girls are more likely to drop out of school if schools are located outside of the community. Although important for both genders, the supply of secondary schools is a larger determinant of girls' schooling than of boys' in rural areas. Thus, an obvious policy implication for continuing the reduction of the gender gap and increasing overall education levels in rural areas is to continue the construction of secondary schools.[25]

PROGRESA, *Programa de Educación, Salud y Alimentación*, the Education, Health, and Nutrition Program, is an example of a new program targeted at promoting the educational level of boys and girls in poor, rural contexts. The results in this chapter may suggest that it is unnecessary to give higher grants to girls than to boys, if girls' achievement is now, overall, compatible with boys', (although the analysis in this paper has not specifically focused on the highly marginated areas where PROGRESA operates). Initial results of the program show that school enrollment has increased significantly for boys and girls, with evidence of a higher impact on the school enrollment of girls (PROGRESA 1999; Schultz 2000). It remains to be seen whether the higher level of grants for girls will go "too far" and lead to a reverse gender gap, if parents become more likely to send girls to school than boys.

Another clearly important factor behind the reduction of the gender gap in education is the effect of parental education levels. Of the impacts of parental education on boys and girls, the one that is always of largest magnitude is the impact of the mother's education on the schooling of girls. We have found evidence that the education of parents is highly important in explaining educational outcomes, even after controlling for a number of other income status variables. We have also shown that the largest gender gaps favoring boys are in households where the parents, particularly the mother, have lower education levels, so that increasing parental education levels will continue to help reduce this gender gap. Gender gaps favoring boys are clearly related to economic background, and households with more unfavorable indicators (low parental education and income) are much more likely to show gender gaps in education which favor boys.

Research in other countries has shown that resources controlled by women tend to have more favorable impacts on children's welfare outcomes than resources controlled by men. The evidence that the mother's education level generally has a greater impact than the father's with respect to more long-term measures of educational attainment of children points toward the confirmation of these findings within Mexico. This is consistent with intrahousehold research, which has shown that greater bargaining power of women tends to have a greater positive impact on children's well-being. This should not be interpreted to mean that the impact of fathers is unimportant. In general, they are also very significant determinants of their children's educational attainment.

Finally, our analysis has pointed to a relationship between the necessity of child labor within households and their schooling attainment, in ways which differ by gender. Absent fathers and the presence of disabled household members have strong negative effects on schooling attainment above all for boys. It is likely that these variables have negative effects on schooling for boys because they show the necessity for child labor to substitute for adult labor supply.

In the case of girls, however, small children in the household have a negative and significant impact on schooling outcomes in all cases, whereas the same is not true for boys. This would seem to indicate that girls are likely to do worse in school when domestic needs are greater at home, as is presumably the case with small children in the household. This suggests that different types of work appear to interfere with the schooling achievement of boys and girls. For boys, educational attainment appears to be worse the greater the need for additional household labor supply to supplement family income. For girls, on the other hand, domestic work appears to play a greater deterring influence to school. The issue of which type of work (if any) may be more "compatible" with school is an important issue, and one which should continue to be explored in future research.[26]

Notes

1. In this paper, we use interchangeably the terms *school attendance* and *enrolled in school*. The indicator is derived from the question "Is _____ currently attending school?" We have no information on absentee rates of children enrolled in school.

2. Approximately 10 percent of children attend private primary and secondary schools.

3. See Bracho and Padua (1995) for an analysis of education levels over time using the various census data.

4. These tables may overstate the differences between rural and urban areas, because presumably an important proportion of the individuals who currently live in urban areas migrated at some point in their lives from rural areas, and individuals who migrate may be likely to have a higher educational level than those who stay.

5. Whereas education levels have increased over time in all areas of Mexico, there exist vast differences in educational achievement by state. In general, the southern poor states have the worst indicators of education, and Mexico City has the most favorable. See Martínez Rizzo (1992) and Palafox, Prawda, and Velez (1994) for a description of educational differences among states.

6. One way to measure equivalency in this sense would be to compare the returns to education from different types of schooling. Parker (1995) finds that returns for salaried workers to technical school are actually higher than returns to other levels of schooling for women and comparable to high-school and college returns for men.

7. An alternative perspective is provided by Frances Vella (1993) who maintains that the attitudes toward female work, which may be constructed independently of the education system, are those which determine investment in human capital. Her results demonstrate that the attitudes of women toward women's work are developed in youth and can lead to substantial reductions in human capital investment, labor supply, and returns to education.

8. Parish and Willis (1992) provide an interesting set of alternative hypotheses to viewing educational investments in daughters and sons. First, the authors focus on altruism, which implies that aside from their own consumption, parents care about the well-being of their children. If there is more altruism toward sons than daughters, sons will receive larger transfers than daughters. Under the hypothesis of "resource dilution," large families result in lower levels of education for all children. Middle children are those who are most affected. The number of children and the order of birth can affect the education opportunities even in the absence of manipulation in favor of the own interest of the parents. The authors also focus on the potential role of credit restrictions or conditional altruism. The lack of capacity of the individuals to obtain credit against their future income as collateral implies that the current conditions of the family will determine whether investments in education are made. Parents are willing to finance only those children who, according to their perception, are in a condition to return the resources. This can explain gender discrimination, according to the authors, because sons may have greater possibilities to pay back investments.

9. In the context of Latin America, King and Bellew (1991) analyze the gender inequality in Peru between 1940 and 1980, arguing that gender inequality in education has decreased substantially. Important determining factors of school enrollment include the education level and wealth of parents. Their findings suggest that wealthier parents are more likely to send daughters to school. Barros, Fox, and Mendoça (1997) demonstrate the lower probability of school attendance among children living in female-headed families in Brazil. Also with respect to Brazil, Levison (1991) and Psacharopoulos and Arriagada (1989) show the importance of similar factors as well as education of parents and family income on both labor force participation and school attendance. The importance of parental education levels as determinants of both child work and school attainment are also shown in Lam and Schoeni (1992) and Parish and Willis (1992).

10. The schooling gap is defined as G = age minus years of completed schooling minus 6.

11. Note that we do not know whether boys and girls who are currently not attending have permanently dropped out or will return to school at some point.

12. The (parental) demand for education of children is expected to depend on factors affecting the expected returns from the educational investments, and factors affecting direct and indirect costs of schooling. This framework implies the following model of demand for schooling:

$$E_{ij} = B_0 + B_1 X_i + B_2 X_{ij} + \delta_i + \varepsilon_{ij}$$

where E_{ij} represents the educational investments in child j in household i, X_i represents the vector of explanatory variables common to all members of the household (within these are community characteristics which are obviously identical for all household members), and X_{ij} represents the characteristics specific to the child (Parish and Willis 1993). The error term is specified in two parts, one term which is specific to each child, and another which is common to all siblings. Because of the common part of the error term to each child in the same family (δ_i), we estimate robust (Huber-White) standard errors.

13. Note that our sample may contain different children from the same family (who all then obviously have the same household characteristics), suggesting it may be appropriate to estimate a household fixed effects model where all characteristics (observed and unobserved) at the level of the household are "differenced out." This model has the advantage of assuring that unobserved heterogeneity at the household level is not biasing the estimated coefficients, with the corresponding disadvantage that the impact of individual household variables cannot be analyzed. This model, however, requires variation in outcomes within each group (in this case the household) and so results, in our case, in the loss of the majority of the sample.

14. Behrman and Knowles (1999) have shown that a long-term indicator of income (for example, permanent income) leads to much larger estimates of the impact of family income on schooling than indicators of current income.

15. Comparing the marital status of girls between ages 16 and 20 demonstrates that girls who are not children of the household head are much more likely to be married (about 10 percent compared to 1 percent of those living with parents). That is, they have most likely left the household they grew up in to form another household with their husband. This implies a selection in that the girls who remain living in their original household with their parents are much more like-

ly to continue studying than girls who leave their household to marry. This further justifies our restriction of sample to individuals below age 16.

16. Unfortunately, we have no information on children who are no longer living in the household, so that the oldest child in the household is not necessarily the oldest child of the parents. Additionally, we do not know if a mother's fertility has been completed, so that the youngest child may not be the last child.

17. Where education is missing for parents, we impute the mean value.

18. In this paper we do not attempt to analyze the complicated relationship between child work and school attendance. See Knaul and Parker (1998) for an analysis of the interrelationships between work and school in the context of longitudinal data for Mexico.

19. While we have access to information on the supply of schools at the level of the locality, unfortunately the database of the Conteo does not contain information on the locality, so we are unable to match this school information to the locality level. Instead, we use the next level of geographic aggregation, the municipality.

20. Note that estimating separate models is equivalent to estimating aggregate models where boys and girls are estimated together, with a dummy variable distinguishing whether the child is a boy or a girl with interaction terms between gender and the other independent variables.

21. We carried out a likelihood ratio test to evaluate whether the coefficients in the model for girls differ from that of boys. With a chi-squared statistic (16) equivalent to 49, we clearly reject that boys and girls can be pooled together.

22. Note that this may partially reflect the fact that the data used come from 1995, a year of severe economic downturn. It would be important to repeat this analysis for years of different economic circumstances to see if these findings hold up.

23. A probit regression is used when the dependent variable of interest, in this case school attendance/enrollment, can take on only two values, 0 or 1 (representing that the child attends school or does not attend school). The probit regression permits us to analyze how variables such as parental educational levels affect a child's probability of attending school.

24. Note that in a number of Latin American countries, a "reverse" gender gap in boys' and girls' schooling has begun to appear at the secondary level (Duryea

and Areunds-Keunning 1999). Given this evidence it would seem important to be watchful of continued tendencies in urban areas in Mexico.

25. In urban areas, we found no overall significant impact of the supply of secondary schools. This is not to suggest that educational services are unimportant in affecting educational attainment in urban areas. It may be that quality is a greater issue in urban areas, although unfortunately we have no indicators in this paper of school quality.

26. See Gómez de León and Parker (2000) for evidence that in poor rural areas of Mexico, domestic work tends to interfere with school for girls, whereas market work and farm work are more incompatible with school for boys.

References

Barros, Ricardo, L. Fox, and Rosane Mendonça. 1997. "Female-headed Households, Poverty and the Welfare of Children in Urban Brazil." *Economic Development and Cultural Change* 45(2):231–57.

Batista Gomes-Neto, Joao, and Erik Hanushek. 1994. "Causes and Consequences of Grade Repetition: Evidence from Brazil." *Economic Development and Cultural Change* 43(1):121–48. The University of Chicago.

Becker, Gary. 1964. *Human Capital, A Theoretical and Empirical Analysis, with Special Reference to Education.* New York: Columbia University Press.

Behrman, J., N. Birdsall, and M. Szekeley. 1999. "Intergenerational Schooling Mobility and Macro Conditions and Schooling Policies in Latin America." Inter American Development Bank, Office of the Chief Economist, Working Paper No. 386. Washington, D.C.

Behrman, J., and J. Knowles. 1999. "Household Income and Child Schooling in Vietnam." *World Bank Economic Review,* forthcoming. Washington, D.C.

Bracho, T., and J. Padua. 1995. "Características y valor económico de la educación y la formación especializada en el empleo en México." *Revista Latinoamericana de Estudios Educativos (México)* 25(1):9–42.

Bustillo, Ines. 1993. "Latin American and the Carribean." In E. M. King and M. A. Hill, eds., *Women's Education in Developing Countries.* Baltimore: The Johns Hopkins University Press.

Duryea, Suzanne, and Mary Arends-Keunning. 1999. "New Gender Gaps in Schooling: Adolescent Boys at Risk in Latin America." Presented at the 1999 Population Association Meetings of America. New York.

Garasky, Steven. 1995. "The Effects of Family Structure on Educational Attainment: Do the Effects Vary by the Age of the Child?" *American Journal of Economics and Sociology* 54(1):89–105.

Gómez de León, J., and S. Parker. 1999. "The Well-Being of Female-Headed Households." Paper presented at the 1999 Annual Meeting of the Population Association of America. New York.

_____. 2000. "The Impact of Anti-Poverty Programs on Children's Time Use: The Case of PROGRESA in Mexico." Paper presented at the 1999 Annual Meeting of the Population Association of America. Los Angeles.

Haddad, L., J. Hoddinott, and H. Alderman, eds. 1997. *Intrahousehold Resource Allocation in Developing Countries: Methods, Models and Policy.* Baltimore: The Johns Hopkins University Press for the International Food Policy Research Institute.

Inter-American Development Bank. 1996. "Como organizar con éxito los servicios sociales." In *Progreso Economico y Social en América Latina. 1996.* Washington, D.C.

King, Elizabeth, and Rosemary Bellew. 1991. "Gains in the Education of Peruvian Women." In *Women's Work, Education and Family Welfare in Peru.* World Bank Discussion Papers. Washington, D.C.

King, Elizabeth, and Anne Hill, eds. 1993. *Women's Education in Developing Countries: Barriers, Benefits and Policies.* Baltimore: The Johns Hopkins University Press.

Knaul, Felicia, and Susan Parker. 1998. "Patterns over Time and Determinants of Early Labor Force Participation and School Dropout: Evidence from Longitudinal and Retrospective Data on Mexican Children and Youth." Paper presented at the 1998 Annual Meeting of the Population Association of America. Chicago.

Levison, Deborah. 1991. "Children's Labor Force Activity and Schooling in Brazil." Unpublished doctoral thesis. University of Michigan.

Londoño, José Luis. 1996. "Pobreza, desigualdad y formación de capital humano en América Latina, 1950–2025." Washington, D.C.: World Bank.

Martínez Rizzo, Felipe. 1992. "La desigualdad educativa en México. *Revista Latinoamericana de Estudios Educativos (México)* 22(2):59–120.

Mincer, Jacob, and Solomon Polachek. 1982. "La inversión de la familia en capital humano: Las ganancias de la mujer." *Estudios sobre la mujer.* Secretaría de Programación y Presupuesto, México.

Palafox, Juan Carlos, Juan Prawda, and Eduardo Velez. 1994. "Primary School Quality in Mexico." *Comparative Education Review* 38(2).

Parish, W. L., and Robert Willis. 1993. "Daughters, Education and Family Budgets. Taiwan Experiences." *Journal of Human Resources* 28:863–98.

Parker, S. 1995. "Niveles salariales de los hombres y mujeres asalariados y trabajadores auto-empleados en el México urbano 1986–1992: Un enfoque microeconómico." In *Capital Humano, Crecimiento, Pobreza: Problematica Mexicana.* Universidad Autonoma de Nuevo León, Mexico.

Post, David, Rosario Garcia, and Rocio Flores. 1998. "Public Policy and the Equality of Access to Secondary School in Mexico." Mimeo. Pennsylvania State University.

PROGRESA. 1999. "Más oportunidades para las familias pobres: Evaluación de resultados del Programa de Educación, Salud y Alimentación, Primeros Avances." Secretaría de Desarrollo Social, Mexico.

Psacharopoulos, George, and Ana Maria Arriagada. 1989. "The Determinants of Early Age Human Capital Formation: Evidence from Brazil." *Economic Development and Cultural Change* 37(4):683–708.

Schultz, Paul. 1993. "Returns to Women's Education." In Elizabeth King and Anne Hill, eds., *Women's Education in Developing Countries: Barriers, Benefits and Policies.* Baltimore: The Johns Hopkins University Press.

_____. 2000. "School Subsidies for the Poor: Evaluating a Mexican Strategy for Reducing Poverty." Processed.

Thomas, Duncan. 1990. "Intra-Household Resource Allocation: An Inferential Approach." *Journal of Human Resources* 25(4).

Thomas, Duncan. 1994. "Like Father, Like Son: Like Mother, Like Daughter: Parental Resources and Child Height." *Journal of Human Resources* 29(4):950–88.

Valdés, Teresa, and E. Gomáriz. 1995. "Mujeres Latinoamericanas en Cifras: Tomo comparativo." Ministerio de Asuntos Sociales y FLAC-SO, Santiago, Chile.

Vella, Frances. 1993. "Gender Roles and Human Capital Investment: The Relationship between Traditional Attitudes and Female Labour Market Performance." *Economica* 61:191–211.

2

The Impact of Child Labor and School Dropout on Human Capital: Gender Differences in Mexico

Felicia Marie Knaul

Child and youth labor force participation has both long- and short-term consequences for individual, family, and social welfare. It can hinder school attendance and be harmful to the health and psychological well-being of children. In the long term, child labor may affect educational attainment and physical and mental development, with resulting consequences throughout the life cycle.

One measurable link between the short- and the long-term effects is that beginning to work at a young age lowers educational attainment and can lower productivity and adult earning capacity. The effect on productivity will be reflected in the returns to education and to experience. It is an empirical question as to whether the gains from early experience (but lower education) are outweighed by the gains from staying in school (and not working). This question has an important gender dimension. Since the nature of employment both early in life and as adults differs among males and females, it is likely that the returns to education and to experience would also vary by gender. This would be particularly true if one group gains more "marketable" experience than the other, or if their work is more compatible with school attendance. In this case the long-term penalties of dropping out of school and/or working early in life would differ by gender.

This chapter assesses the long-term impacts of school dropout and of working early in life, in terms of labor market returns later in life. The analysis is based on retrospective household survey data from Mexico. Through these data it is possible to observe the wages and other characteristics of adults later in life, and to link these data to information on the age at which these individuals started working and when they quit school. By linking these data the research assesses the effects of age at entry into the labor force and school dropout on adult labor market outcomes.

The empirical approach of the chapter is to modify the standard neo-classical model of returns to human capital by using alternative ways of measuring "early experience." The analysis explicitly acknowledges the fact that early work may not necessarily be coincident with school dropout. Through this modified approach it is possible to disentangle the effects of various combinations of work and schooling on returns to labor later in life and to develop a taxonomy of effects of early employment and/or school dropout. The models also allow for differences in the nature of early employment for boys and girls, and thus test whether gender differences do exist.

The findings of this chapter show that there is indeed a penalty for dropping out of school and working early in life. They suggest that there are positive returns to early labor market experience, but that these depend on continued progression through the school system. The earlier children drop out of school and enter the labor force the greater the penalty they pay in terms of adult earning capacity. Those who never go to school and only work accumulate the least education and marketable experience. Those who complete high school tend to have higher accumulated human capital and greater earning capacity.

The results also indicate strong gender disparities. At every level of schooling and early employment, girls pay a greater penalty than boys for not continuing in school or for working while in school. One of the hypotheses put forward as to why this is so relates to the "nature" of the work boys and girls do. The types of early employment that boys engage in (industrial, services, etc.) may be more complementary to the occupations they choose later in life. Thus, early work experience counts as real experience. Further, their work may be more complementary to remaining in school for longer periods. Girls, however, tend to be concentrated in activities in which there is little accumulated experience and low complementarity with education (domestic work). Thus, the returns to their "experience" are low because the "experience" they gain early in life does not count in the labor market, or it is in the type of occupations where education is not rewarded.

The findings have important policy implications. In Mexico and in the rest of Latin America, school enrollment of girls is on a par with or sometimes greater than that of school enrollment of boys. Still, despite a reduction in differences in educational attainment among boys and girls, gender disparities in labor market outcomes are persistent. Our results suggest one piece of information relevant to explaining gender differences in adult labor market outcomes. The male–female wage differences later in life may be partly explained by differences in the types of employment that men and women undertake when they are young. For the same number of years of early work and school dropout, girls suffer more in terms of labor market returns later in life than do boys. Policymakers who are interested in the "efficiency" of educational investments may gain from taking a closer look at the gender-differentiated effects of early employment and dropout on labor market returns in Mexico.

This chapter provides a brief overview of the literature and of the data, summarizes the theoretical framework and the models used in the chapter, examines the results of earnings equations that model early entry into the labor force and school dropout, and summarizes the major points of relevance to policy decisions and highlights directions for future research. The Appendix considers the implications of excluding home-based household work in the definition of child labor.

Literature Review

Studies on developing countries tend to focus on the relationship between school and work during the school-going age, with the objective of testing whether work hinders schooling.[1] However, there has been relatively little empirical work evaluating the effects of work during school-going age on labor market returns in later years.

Several studies from developing countries on the relationship between school and work during the school-age period provide important insights for this chapter. A common finding is that a large proportion of working children attend school (Post and Pong 2000; Patrinos and Psacharopoulos 1993; Levison 1991; Knaul 1993, 1995). A volume of studies (Grootaert and Patrinos 1999) considering the determinants of child labor, home care work, and schooling suggests that among poor families, interventions to allow for the combination of school and work may provide interim solutions to prevent school dropout associated with child labor. Alessie, Baker, and Blundell (1992) show that in Côte d'Ivoire there are important differences in the impact of various socioeconomic and labor market variables on the probability that children work, depending on whether the child worked and attended school in the initial period. Knaul (1995) develops models similar to those used in this chapter and finds that in Colombia there is a payoff to delayed entry into the labor force, and a tradeoff between work and schooling. The return to a year of education or experience is reduced when schooling is combined with work, and only partially offset by the return to experience.

The empirical literature evaluating the impact of early labor market experience among adolescents in developed countries is of particular relevance to this study. This research is mixed in its findings on the tradeoffs between school and work, and the long-run impact on adult earning capacity (Rich 1993). On one hand, there are a number of studies that suggest that teenage workers have lower grade point averages and weaker career and educational attainment. Post and Pong (1999, 2000) present evidence from a range of both developed and developing countries demonstrating a negative relationship between employment and educational achievement among 13 and 14 year olds. On the other hand, not all the evidence on the effects of youth work on long-term returns to education and experience is negative. Several studies from the United States have shown that individuals who were employed during high school tend to have more stable employment records and higher earnings as adults. Others have found that working during high school is associated with punctuality, dependability, and personal responsibility (Steinberg, Laurence, Greenberger, Garduque, Ruggiero, and Vaux 1982; Steinberg, Laurence, Greenberger, Garduque, and McAuliffe 1982). Job switching during high school and short periods of unemployment are associated with higher average wages for adults up to 10 years later (Becker and Hills 1983). The impact of early labor force participation may be related to factors such as the intensity of the work and age of the child (Post and Pong 1999).

There has been some quantitative research on child and youth labor force participation in Mexico. Several researchers have documented that families have responded to economic crises and to unemployment of the family head by sending children and women to the labor market (González de la Rocha 1988, 1995; Beneria 1992; Chant 1994). There are also several studies that have considered child labor in particular occupations, industries, and sectors, including the street or informal sector (Cos Montiel 2000; Brizzio 1996). Christenson and Juarez (1987) find that the education level of parents, family income, family size, and female headship increase the likelihood of child labor.

A few studies have considered the impact of child labor on schooling. Using the National Household Income and Expenditure Survey of 1992, Abler, Rodríguez, and Robles (1998) show that female youth who work in their home have lower school attendance rates than other groups of young workers. Binder and Scrogin (1999) use data collected through direct interviews with children in Guadalajara, Arandas, and Tijuana to consider the determinants of labor force and household work. They find that the occupation of the household head is an important determinant of hours worked. Labor force hours tend to reduce leisure time, although the effect on academic performance and desired schooling is negligible. Knaul and Parker (1998) use retrospective data to analyze the long-term relationship between school dropout and labor market entry. Workers are more likely to be behind in school, and hours spent studying are lower among children who work longer hours. Their analysis suggests that both labor market entry and school dropout are associated with negative shocks to household income and to the reorganization of families, such as divorce. Levison, Moe, and Knaul (2000) estimate the determinants of studying and working for youths aged 12 to 17 in urban Mexico using the national employment survey. This research contrasts a definition of work that includes household domestic work, with the traditional definition of market-based employment, which excludes household domestic work. Results based on the traditional definition indicate that girls are more likely than boys to specialize in school, while those based on the more inclusive measure of work indicate that girls are less likely than boys to specialize in school.

Very few studies have been undertaken on particular policy interventions or programs on behalf of child workers or to increase school attendance. Almost no studies have considered the demand side or the role and responsibilities of employers, both of which are important areas for future investigation. Gómez de León et al. (2000) cite evidence of an important impact of monetary educational grants provided through the *Programa de Educación, Salud y Alimentación* (Education, Health and Nutrition Program, PROGRESA) on promoting school attendance and decreasing child work. The reduction in labor force participation is more evident among boys than girls, which is likely to be associated with the low rates of paid work among females. This finding suggests the importance of analyzing the role of unpaid labor among females.

Other literature of direct relevance to this chapter considers the measurement of education and experience in the analysis of returns to human capital. Lam and Levison (1992) find that the definition of the experience variable may have important effects on the variance in earnings for groups with low levels of experience. A series of studies evaluates the returns to the quality and quantity of schooling in Brazil, and finds that the results are highly sensitive to accounting for early entry into the labor force in the experience measure (Behrman and Birdsall 1983, 1985; Eaton 1985). Behrman and Birdsall (1985) note, "...the standard definition of experience should not go unquestioned in settings where many children leave school well before the age of 15, but may or may not immediately begin full time work."

Data

The data used here come from the *Encuesta Nacional de Empleo* (National Employment Survey—ENE), and in particular from the associated module called the *Encuesta Nacional de Educación, Capacitación y Empleo* (National Survey of Education, Training and Employment—ENECE). The data were collected in the second trimester of 1995 by the *Instituto Nacional de Estadística, Geografía e Informática* (INEGI) and the *Secretaría del Trabajo y Previsión Social*.

The ENE and ENECE cover both the urban and rural areas of Mexico and include approximately 110,000 individuals. The samples are divided into urbanized and less urbanized areas. Urbanized areas include the major urban centers with 100,000 or more inhabitants and state capitals. The less urbanized areas are comprised of low-density urban centers of 2,500 to 99,999 inhabitants and rural areas. The unfortunate consequence of these groupings is that the results presented in this chapter are not easily divided into rural and urban areas, given that the low-density urban centers are quite large. For this reason, the majority of the results are given only at the national level, with a dummy variable to indicate differences between the urbanized and less urbanized areas.

The ENE includes information on educational attainment, demographic characteristics, and family structure for all household residents. The survey also contains a household module with information on physical characteristics and ownership of the dwelling. The main body of the questionnaire is devoted to a standardized battery of questions on employment, unemployment, and labor market withdrawal applied to all household residents aged 12 and over. This part of the survey also includes information on time spent on household work, market work, and studying.

The ENECE includes detailed information on education and labor market histories based on retrospective questions on the age at which individuals took their first job and the age at which they left school. The information on age at first entry unfortunately does not specify what is considered as "entry" or a "first job" either in terms of hours worked or duration of the work. There are no specific instructions in the interviewer's manual. The data also include a variety of questions related to labor market experience. In addition to the standard variables (age and years of schooling) used to construct potential or traditional experience measures, there is information on the total number of months worked during the individual's lifetime.

The Empirical Framework: Modeling the Effects of Early Labor Force Entry and School Dropout

The human capital model provides a framework for examining the effect of early entry into the labor force, and the tradeoff between working and attending school. Individuals invest in themselves through education and training that lead to increases in future earnings and nonmonetary benefits. This investment is associated with both direct costs and time costs that arise due to the deferral of earnings and the possible reduction of a person's working life (Mincer 1974; Becker 1993).

The human capital earnings function described in Mincer (1974) differentiates between schooling and "post"-schooling investments that

may be referred to as training or on-the-job experience. The basic earnings function includes the amount of completed schooling and work
experience.

This equation is estimated empirically as a log linear function, a
basic formulation commonly used in the literature. A quadratic term
for years of experience incorporates diminishing returns in terms of the
training that is received through labor market experience. The basic
equation is:

$$Log\ Y_i = \beta_0 + \beta_1 s_i + \beta_2 e_i + \beta_3 e_i^2 + X'\beta + \mu_i \tag{1}$$

where, for each individual i, log Y is the natural logarithm of earnings or
wages at time t, e represents years of work experience, s is years of schooling, and X is a matrix of control variables that may include personal, family background, and labor market characteristics. The error term is represented by μ.

In the absence of more detailed information on training and time actually spent in the labor force, potential time spent in the labor market is
used as a proxy. In most of the literature, potential experience is defined
as "age minus years of completed schooling minus the age at beginning
to attend school" (often age minus highest completed grade 6). This traditionally used measure of potential experience presents several limitations for the study of child labor and schooling, while modifications of
the experience and education measures make it possible to incorporate
early work experience and the interactions with schooling.

The limitations of the traditional measures are related to the timing
and interactions between work and school. First, years of schooling is
typically not available and number of grades successfully completed is
used as a proxy. This leads to an overestimation of the number of years of
out-of-school experience when grade repetition is frequent. Second, children start school at different ages and the age is often not reported. Third,
labor market attachment is not necessarily continuous. Part-time work,
temporary employment, and unemployment are prevalent. Finally, and
key to the analysis presented in this chapter, in-school work is common
in both developing and developed economies. These phenomena are likely to differ significantly by gender.

In this chapter, the earnings equation is specified in such a way as to
allow for differences between early and late labor market experience,
between in-school and out-of-school work, and the interaction of school
and work at different stages of schooling. The summary statistics (means
and standard deviations) of the dependent and independent variables are
given in Table 2.1 and a discussion of these variables follows.

(Text continues on page 58.)

Table 2.1 Means and Standard Deviations of Dependent and Independent Variables

	All						Positive Wage Earners					
	Male		Female		All		Male		Female		All	
	Mean	SD	Mean	SD	Mean	SD	Mean	SD	Mean	SD	Mean	SD
Dependent variable												
Hourly wages and earnings							9.71	25.46	8.41	11.00	9.26	21.59
Nat. logarithm of hourly wages and earnings							1.83	0.86	1.76	0.82	1.80	0.85
Independent variables												
Human capital variables												
Education:												
Years of education	9.01	4.95	8.19	4.65	8.58	4.81	8.95	4.97	9.36	4.82	9.09	4.92
Education categories:[1]												
Some or completed primary school	0.35	0.48	0.38	0.48	0.36	0.48	0.37	0.48	0.30	0.46	0.34	0.47
Some or completed jr. high school	0.23	0.42	0.20	0.40	0.22	0.41	0.24	0.43	0.20	0.40	0.23	0.42
Some or completed high school	0.18	0.38	0.22	0.42	0.20	0.40	0.17	0.37	0.27	0.44	0.20	0.40

(Table continues on the following page.)

Table 2.1 (*continued*)

| | All | | | | | | Positive Wage Earners | | | | | |
| | Male | | Female | | All | | Male | | Female | | All | |
	Mean	SD	Mean	SD	Mean	SD	Mean	SD	Mean	SD	Mean	SD
Some or completed college-level degree	0.21	0.40	0.14	0.34	0.17	0.37	0.20	0.40	0.19	0.39	0.19	0.40
Experience:												
Potential (traditional): (age − years of education − 5)												
Linear	19.57	13.24	20.70	13.57	20.16	13.43	20.43	12.55	18.60	12.44	19.79	12.54
Squared	558.29	645.46	612.51	671.67	586.76	659.91	574.57	623.93	500.75	585.26	549.04	611.84
Total years worked during life:												
Linear	17.68	12.72	8.42	9.99	12.82	12.28	18.89	11.96	12.75	10.48	16.76	11.84
Squared	474.46	553.21	170.68	337.42	314.90	477.61	499.82	542.70	272.24	396.41	421.13	508.66
Years that combined studies and work	1.79	3.01	0.80	2.01	1.27	2.58	1.84	3.05	1.08	2.39	1.58	2.86
Combinations of work and study by categories												
Combined work and primary school, then dropped out	0.13	0.33	0.05	0.23	0.09	0.29	0.13	0.34	0.06	0.23	0.11	0.31
Combined work with primary school, then passed to jr. high school	0.03	0.18	0.01	0.10	0.02	0.14	0.04	0.19	0.01	0.10	0.03	0.16
Combined work												

and jr. high school, then dropped out	0.06	0.23	0.03	0.17	0.04	0.20	0.06	0.24	0.03	0.17	0.05	0.22
Combined work with jr. high school, then passed to high school	0.02	0.15	0.01	0.12	0.02	0.13	0.02	0.15	0.02	0.13	0.02	0.15
Combined work and high school	0.06	0.23	0.07	0.25	0.06	0.24	0.06	0.24	0.09	0.28	0.07	0.26
Labor force participation variables												
Dummy rural–urban (rural = 1)	0.17	0.38	0.17	0.37	0.17	0.38	0.16	0.37	0.11	0.32	0.15	0.35
Home ownership:[2] Owns home or has it	0.78	0.41	0.78	0.41	0.78	0.41	0.76	0.43	0.78	0.42	0.77	0.42
Mortgaged	0.15	0.35	0.14	0.35	0.14	0.35	0.16	0.37	0.15	0.36	0.16	0.36
Lent without paying rent or other arrangement												
Overcrowding Number of rooms per resident	1.19	0.73	1.20	0.72	1.20	0.73	1.18	0.73	1.28	0.78	1.22	0.75
Number of bedrooms per resident	0.48	0.31	0.48	0.31	0.48	0.31	0.46	0.31	0.52	0.34	0.48	0.32

(Table continues on the following page.)

Table 2.1 (*continued*)

| | All | | | | | | Positive Wage Earners | | | | | |
| | Male | | Female | | All | | Male | | Female | | All | |
	Mean	SD	Mean	SD	Mean	SD	Mean	SD	Mean	SD	Mean	SD
Home charateristics												
Predominant building material: [3]												
Wood	0.07	0.25	0.06	0.24	0.07	0.25	0.07	0.26	0.06	0.24	0.07	0.25
Adobe (mud brick)	0.07	0.25	0.07	0.25	0.07	0.25	0.06	0.25	0.05	0.22	0.06	0.24
Asbestos or metallic sheathing	0.00	0.06	0.00	0.06	0.00	0.06	0.00	0.06	0.00	0.05	0.00	0.06
Paper board sheathing	0.00	0.06	0.00	0.06	0.00	0.06	0.00	0.07	0.00	0.06	0.00	0.06
Other building material	0.01	0.07	0.00	0.07	0.00	0.07	0.01	0.07	0.00	0.06	0.00	0.07
Roofing material: [4]												
Palm fronds or wood	0.10	0.29	0.09	0.28	0.09	0.29	0.10	0.30	0.08	0.28	0.10	0.29
Asbestos or metallic sheathing	0.12	0.32	0.12	0.32	0.12	0.32	0.12	0.33	0.10	0.30	0.11	0.32
Paper board sheathing	0.04	0.19	0.04	0.19	0.04	0.19	0.04	0.19	0.03	0.17	0.04	0.19
Other building												

material	0.01	0.12	0.01	0.12	0.01	0.12	0.01	0.12	0.01	0.10	0.11
Flooring material:[5]											
Wood, tiles or other covering material	0.50	0.50	0.53	0.50	0.52	0.50	0.49	0.50	0.57	0.50	0.50
Earthen floors	0.06	0.24	0.06	0.23	0.06	0.23	0.06	0.24	0.04	0.19	0.22
Does not have											
Interior bathroom	0.06	0.23	0.05	0.22	0.05	0.22	0.05	0.23	0.03	0.17	0.21
Electricity	0.02	0.15	0.02	0.14	0.02	0.15	0.02	0.15	0.01	0.11	0.14
Interior sewage connection	0.14	0.35	0.14	0.34	0.14	0.35	0.14	0.35	0.09	0.29	0.33
Telephone service	0.60	0.49	0.58	0.49	0.59	0.49	0.63	0.48	0.53	0.50	0.49
Sample size	37,288		41,250		78,538		26,921		14,229		41,150

1. The excluded category was zero years of education.
2. The excluded category was renting home.
3. The excluded category was built of brick, concrete, Stone.
4. The excluded category was concrete or brick roofing material.
5. The excluded category was plain concrete flooring (no covering material).

Discussion of Variables

The wage functions are estimated using a direct measure of time spent working during the individual's life. The information on "total years worked during lifetime" is from the survey question that explicitly asks about the total number of months that the respondent has worked during his or her lifetime. This variable is likely to suffer from recall error, yet have important advantages over the potential measure of experience.[2] The direct formulation of the experience measure includes part-time and in-school work undertaken at any time of the life cycle, and excludes labor market absences, be they of short or long duration. Finally, it also accounts for late entry into the labor force, which is particularly common among women. The data show that the differences in the experience measures are large for females. For both males and females, the measure of "potential" experience (age minus highest school grade completed minus age at entering schooling) is higher than the measure from total time spent working during the lifetime. The traditional measure gives a mean of 21 years of work experience on average, compared to 8 years using the direct measure of total years worked during lifetime.

In-school work experience is modeled in two ways. First, a linear term is added for potential in-school experience below age 18. This is defined as the difference between the age at entry into the labor force and the age at school dropout. The coefficient on this term is expected to be negative because the young person is unlikely to spend as much time in school or at work as on either activity if undertaken individually. This negative coefficient must be deducted from the returns to education and experience in order to develop a measure of the net returns to a year of time in which school and work are combined. Thus, the negative coefficient cannot be interpreted as a negative return to in-school work, but rather compared to the other returns.

For the second model, education is given as a step function with a dummy variable for primary, junior high school, high school, and university education. Five interaction terms are also added to indicate individuals who (a) combined work and primary school, and then dropped out of school during or after primary; (b) combined work and primary school, and continued on to junior high school; (c) worked during junior high school and went on to high school; (d) worked during junior high and then dropped out of school; and (e) combined work with time spent studying in high school. The inclusion of these five interaction dummy variables provides a complete way of differentiating between combinations of work and school at different levels of the educational cycle, and dropping out of school at different points in the cycle. The underlying assumption of this approach is that once a child enters the labor force he or she continues to work at all later phases of the educational cycle.

The dependent variable in all of the regression analysis is the logarithm of total hourly earnings. Earnings include wages and income of all workers, be they salaried or independent. The variable exclusively reflects monetary earnings from the primary job, because in-kind and secondary salaries are not reported.[3] Hours are based on the week prior to the survey. In order to estimate gender differences, each regression is estimated separately for males and females. The regressions all include a dummy variable to indicate whether the person is living in one of the large urban areas or in the less-urbanized parts of the country. The sample is restricted to adults between ages 18 and 59.

Caveats Regarding Econometric Analysis

A series of caveats regarding the econometric analysis is in order. First, the model does not account for unpaid work in one's family home. Home-based housework is an activity that absorbs the majority of the time of many female children and adolescents, that is incompatible with schooling under some circumstances, and that may make it difficult to reenter the labor force (Knaul 1999). The exclusion of unpaid housework biases the analysis in this chapter, particularly with respect to females.[4] Since retrospective information on hours spent on housework is not available in the data, it is difficult to speculate about the sign of the bias. Still, it is likely that if unpaid, home-based housework were to be incorporated into the model as a form of child labor, it would also show a penalty in terms of educational and future employment opportunities that would be much more articulated among females. It is important to note that the sample selection correction, discussed below, will help to adjust for the effects of having a large proportion of adult women out of the labor force.

Second, the age at entry into the labor force and educational attainment are endogenous variables. Given the limitations of data used herein, it is not possible to account for the endogeneity of these two variables. Therefore the empirical analysis proceeds as if both variables were exogenous.

Self-Selection

Self-selection may also be a problem for the analysis presented in this chapter. It may be that the only children who begin working at an early age are those who come from households in extreme hardship, are from "abusive" families, or do not succeed at school for reasons such as having an inadequate diet. Further, it is impossible, based on available data, to know what the effect of working as a child would have been on the people who did not undertake these activities, or what the adult wage would have been for the working children if they had not worked. As a partial test of these issues, the regressions were expanded by including controls for state of birth as a measure of individual heterogeneity and demand conditions; physical characteristics of the dwelling as indicators of family wealth and poverty; occupational choice; and municipality-level[5] fixed effects, such as the local labor market demand. The findings presented below are generally robust to these re-estimations. Neither the findings regarding the tradeoffs between returns to education and early work experience, nor the gender differentials, are likely to be driven by individual heterogeneity or variability in labor demand, nor solely by a correlation between child labor and poverty in the family.

The summary statistics (means and standard deviations) of the dependent and independent variables are given in Table 2.1. Summary statistics reveal that self-selection bias could be a potentially important problem with both the wage and earnings equations, especially for women. Among males, approximately 72 percent are economically active and earning a positive wage, while for females the figure is 34 percent. To correct for selectivity bias, the regressions models are run using the Heckman selection correction model (Heckman 1979).[6] Given the instability of sample selection models (Mroz 1987; Falaris 1995), and the fact that the data used for the analysis do not include more appropriate identification variables such as unearned income, the regressions were also run using simple least squares regressions. Only the results using the sample selection corrected models are presented in the chapter, given that the Heckman equations indicate there is a significant sample selection bias for both males and females in all of the regressions. The conclusions presented in this chapter hold, using either the sample correction version or the ordinary least squares regressions. The tables include only the regression coefficients for the wage functions.[7]

Descriptive Findings: Early Labor Force Entry and School Dropout

The retrospective pattern of age at entry into the labor force among adult Mexicans that have ever worked suggests that a large proportion began to work at an early age (Table 2.2). Thirty percent of males and 15.6 percent of females first worked by age 11. It is also important to note that a large group of women began to work as adults. Approximately 24 percent of females who have ever worked entered the labor force after age 20, compared to 11 percent of males.

Table 2.2 Age First Worked, by Gender (%)
(adults aged 18 to 59)

Age first worked	Male	Female	All
Less than 4	0.3	0.1	0.2
5 to 8	9.8	4.8	7.5
9 to 11	20.1	10.9	16.0
12 to 14	24.4	18.5	21.7
15 to 17	24.9	27.3	26.0
18 to 19	9.9	14.9	12.2
20 to 24	8.6	14.6	11.3
25 to 29	1.6	4.1	2.7
30 to 34	0.3	2.0	1.1
35 to 39	0.1	1.3	0.7
40 or more	0.1	1.5	0.7
Total %	100	100	100
n	35,425	31,371	66,796

Source: ENECE, 1995.

Furthermore, 31 percent of women report never having worked, compared to only 3.6 percent of males.

The trends in age at entry into the labor force suggest important changes over time and by cohort. Consistent with patterns that have been observed in other Latin American countries and in the developed world, market-based child labor in Mexico has shown a tendency to decline over time. While 55.5 percent of males over age 60 began work before age 11, the figure is only 40.8 percent among males age 40 to 59, and 24.1 percent among males age 18 to 39. For women, the rates are substantially lower, but the trends are the similar. The figures are 19.0 percent, 15.3 percent, and 9.6 percent, respectively.

Among adults who began working between ages 5 and 15, the distribution of occupations is quite narrow and differentiated by gender. Using the four-digit occupation codes, it is possible to distinguish the most commonly held occupations. Agriculture is the predominant activity—21 percent of females and 51 percent of males worked in this sector. For women, 6 percent began work in a factory manufacturing textiles or foodstuffs, 10 percent worked in commerce, and 33 percent worked in domestic service. Among males, 6 percent worked in factory jobs including woodwork and machinery manufacture, 7 percent worked in construction, and 5 percent worked in commerce. Occupational mobility appears to be more limited in agriculture than in other occupations. For males, 55 percent of those who began work in agriculture declare agriculture as their current occupation. The figure is 39 percent for factory work, and 27 percent for commerce. For females, the figure is 38 percent in agriculture, 14 percent in factory work, and 17 percent in domestic service. On the other hand, for females one of the most common paths after working as a youngster is to exit the labor force. Over 50 percent of women who began work as children are not working in market activities as adults. By comparison, only 37 percent of women who began working after age 15 are out of the labor force. For males, the proportion out of the labor force is less than 5 percent and is similar among the group that began to work before or after age 15.

The distribution of the age at school dropout shows that a large proportion of adults left school at an early age. By age 11, 27 percent had abandoned the school system, compared to 58 percent by age 14 (Table 2.3). The proportion of children who drop out of school is slightly higher among females. Further, and as in the case of age at entry into the labor force, important changes in age at school dropout are evident over time. According to retrospective data, the age at dropping out of school has increased steadily and substantially among both females and males. While almost 55 percent of adult males over age 60 report having dropped out of school before age 11, this is the case for only 15 percent of those aged 18 to 39. For females the figures are 54 percent and 18 percent, respectively. Early school dropout appears to have been, and continues to be, more common in rural areas.

There is a strong correlation between age at entry into the labor force and age at school dropout among Mexican adults (Table 2.4). Still, in-school work was quite common among this sample of adults, particularly at the primary school level. This is evident from the pattern of age at school dropout compared to age at entering the labor force. The age at school dropout rises steadily with the age of first work for all males and for females who began work before age 25. Average age at school dropout exceeds age at entry into the labor force for those who began to work before age 12.[8]

Empirical Findings: The Effects of Combining School and Work

The estimates of the effects of combining school and work on returns later in life using the continuous measure of in-school work are presented in Table 2.5. For both males and females, the coefficient of years of in-school work experience on returns is negative and significant in both the least squares and the selection corrected regressions. For males the coefficient is –2.4 percent, while for females it is –2.7 percent, using the selection corrected equations. These results show that there is a "penalty" for doing work at the primary or secondary levels. This can be explained as a trade-

Table 2.3 Age at School Dropout of School, by Gender (%) (adults aged 18 to 59)

Age at dropout	Male	Female	All
Less than 4	0.3	0.4	0.4
5 to 8	5.8	6.2	6.0
9 to 11	19.4	22.0	20.7
12 to 14	30.6	31.0	30.8
15 to 17	21.7	20.6	21.2
18 to 19	7.4	8.8	8.1
20 to 24	10.2	8.0	9.1
25 or more	4.7	3.0	3.9
Total %	100	100	100
Sample size	38,106	41,677	79,783

Source: ENECE, 1995.

Table 2.4 Age at School Dropout by Age First Worked and Gender
(adults aged 18 to 59)

	Age at dropout					
Age first	Male			Female		
worked	Mean	Median	Std. dev.	Mean	Median	Std. dev.
5 – 8	13.3	12	6.1	12.2	11	6.2
9 – 11	12.9	11	5.1	12.1	11	4.7
12 – 14	13.8	13	4.5	13.0	12	4.3
15 – 17	15.6	15	4.3	15.2	15	4.2
18 – 19	17.4	18	4.5	16.9	17	4.2
20 – 24	20.6	21	4.5	18.1	19	4.9
25 – 29	23.7	25	4.9	17.4	15	6.5
30 – 34	25.5	28	8.0	14.9	13	6.9
35 – 39	27.1	33	10.5	14.3	13	6.5
40 or more	29.1	32	13.4	12.8	11	6.9

Source: ENECE, 1995.

off between specializing in schooling as a full-time activity versus combining school and work, which is likely to imply devoting less time to education. Thus, there are positive returns to both schooling and work, but these are less than the returns to specializing in either activity and less than the returns to working after completing school.

Table 2.5. Returns to Human Capital: Combinations of Work and Schooling, by Gender (using Heckman Sample Selection Correction)

Dependent variable: hourly wages or earnings

Measures of experience and combination of work and school	Males		Females	
	Total years worked during life	*Total years worked and work and studies*	*Total years worked during life*	*Total years worked and work and studies*
Independent variables Total years worked during life:				
Linear	0.0577	0.0601	0.0889	0.0952
	(18.27)	(19.10)	(12.67)	(13.23)
Squared	–0.0010	–0.0010	–0.0016	–0.0017
	(14.63)	(15.15)	(12.00)	(12.51)
Years of education	0.0869	0.0923	0.1107	0.1158
	(82.61)	(83.20)	(30.90)	(30.56)
Years combining education and work	–0.0236 (13.99)			–0.0273 (7.98)
Dummy rural– urban area	–0.3448	–0.3279	–0.2691	–0.2660
	(23.76)	(22.88)	(12.45)	(12.27)
Constant	0.2696	0.2367	–0.5302	–0.6418
	(5.11)	(4.51)	(3.21)	(3.86)
Inverse mills ratio	0.5240	0.5056	0.6625	0.7100
	(8.46)	(8.30)	(7.25)	(7.80)
Adjusted R^2	0.2938	0.2985	0.3022	0.3043
F Statistic	2240.91	1910.55	1233.11	1037.96
Sample size	37,288	37,288	41,250	41,250

Note: The correction uses full-information maximum-likelihood, and the standard errors are White, heterocedasticity corrected using LIMDEP.
Source: ENE and ENECE, 1995.

The returns to each schoolwork combination differ. One way of sum-marizing these patterns is through time-use earnings profiles. Such pro-files are presented for males and females in Figure 2.1. The results are pre-sented for six possible combinations of school and work separately. The first profile refers to a person who did not attend school and worked from age 5. The next three profiles refer to combinations of schooling, in-school, and out-of-school experience. In each case it is necessary to assign a somewhat arbitrary adult-experience equivalent, which in these profiles is the same as a full year of experience. The second line refers to a person who completed high school (12 years of education), worked during the last 6 years of school, and then dropped out and entered the labor force. The third profile corresponds to a person who has 12 years of education, worked through their entire school career, and gained 12 years of work experience. The next line describes a person who combined school and work during primary school, then dropped out of school. The last line considers the case of a person who completed primary and high school and then dropped out to work.[9]

The most striking result is that additional schooling quickly outweighs any benefits to dropping out of school. The profiles for the people who never went to school, or who dropped out of school early, are below the profiles for those who remained in school.

There is also an important gender dimension to the findings. The female profiles differ substantially from the male profiles and reflect the high returns to postprimary education for females, which are in turn key to explaining low gender wage gaps in Mexico (Parker 1998). Again, these results are likely to be very sensitive to the use of the sample selection procedure.

Figure 2.1 Time Earnings Profiles: Varying the Investment of Time between School and Work Using Sample Correction, Adults Ages 18 to 59 (corresponds to Table 2.5)

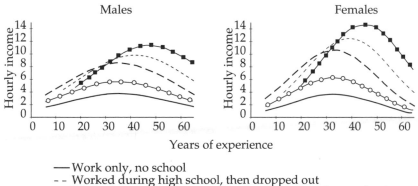

Note: Years of experience is equal to (age minus 5).
Sources: ENE and ENECE, 1995.

The next set of regressions model the fact that the combination of work and school may have different effects depending on the stage of schooling, the probability of proceeding to a higher level, and the type of work that is undertaken (Table 2.6). For example, the costs of combining primary school with work may be higher because of the age of the child. Yet, higher levels of schooling may be more challenging and leave less time for the additional pressures of working.

Table 2.6. Returns to Human Capital:
Combinations of Work and Schooling by Level and by Gender, Ages 18 to 59
(using Heckman Sample Selection Correction)

Dependent variable: hourly wages or earnings

Measures of experience and combination of work and school by ;evel	Males Total years worked, and work and studies by level (model 5)	Females Total years worked, and work and studies by level (model 5)
Independent variables		
Total years worked during life:		
Linear	0.0634	0.1009
	(18.79)	(13.02)
Squared	-0.0011	-0.0019
	(16.13)	(12.70)
Education categories:		
Some or completed primary school	0.4451	0.4109
	(15.04)	(9.74)
Some or completed jr. high school	0.7025	0.7953
	(21.52)	(14.09)
Some or completed high school	0.8441	1.2205
	(25.62)	(19.91)
Some or completed college-level degree	1.4466	1.7560
	(47.47)	(25.40)
Combination of work–study by categories:		
Combined work and primary, then dropped out	-0.0988	-0.2666
	(5.75)	(7.63)
Combined work with primary, went to jr. high school	-0.2561	-0.4159
	(8.61)	(5.86)
Combined work and jr. high, then dropped out	-0.0542	-0.2389
	(2.29)	(5.37)

Table 2.6 (continued)

Measures of experience and combination of work and school by level	Males Total years worked, and work and studies by level (model 5)	Females Total years worked, and work and studies by level (model 5)
Combined work and jr. high, then went to high school	-0.0904 (2.52)	-0.4416 (7.48)
Combined work and high school	0.0521 (1.86)	-0.1170 (4.14)
Dummy rural–urban area	0.0004 (25.80)	0.0003 (13.39)
Constant	0.2706 (4.01)	-0.5459 (2.99)
Inverse mills ratio	0.5838 (8.65)	0.7416 (7.71)
Adjusted R^2	0.2800	0.2600
F Statistic	806.23	455.00
Sample size	37,288	41,250

Note: The correction uses full-information maximum-likelihood and the standard errors are White, heterocedasticity corrected using LIMDEP.
Source: ENE and ENECE, 1995.

The five interaction terms in these regressions that refer to the stage at which work was combined with school were enumerated in the section on the empirical framework. The signs on these coefficients are all negative and significant, except the coefficient on working only during high school for males.

The gender dimensions of these results are also revealing. The returns to postprimary education are higher for women than for men. Further, the coefficients on the interaction terms are much larger for females, even at the level of high school, suggesting that there are important gender differences in the implications of combining school and work. Specifically, the penalties to combining work and school are more severe for females, and returns to early work experience are too low to offset the substantial losses associated with reducing the educational career. The spread in the returns to education may also be a reflection of the types of jobs that are available to women with no education or only primary schooling.

The returns to experience and the returns to education at each level are summarized in Figure 2.2. To calculate the returns to the allocation of time across school and work at each level of schooling, overall returns to experience are added to the returns to education and in-school work. This provides an estimate of the net return to the investment of time when school and work are combined. To do the calculation, it is necessary to make assumptions about the adult equivalent of part-time experience. Children who begin work between ages 5 and 11 are thus assumed to have worked half of the period, or on average 3 years. Those who start work during primary school and continue on to junior high school and high school are assumed to gather the equivalent of 9 years of full-time labor market experience. Those who worked during junior high and high school worked for 4.5 years. Finally, individuals who began work during high school are assumed to have 1.5 years of full-time equivalent experience.

Figure 2.2 Combinations of Education and Work
By Level of Education, Ages 18 to 58 (corresponds to Table 2.6)

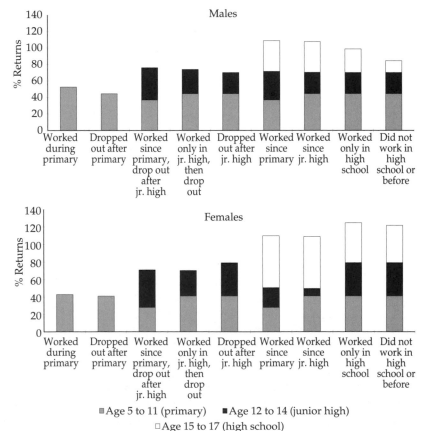

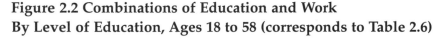

The profiles are given separately for males and females. The height of each bar corresponds to the returns to the allocation of time across school and work at each level of schooling. Starting from the left-hand side, the first two bars correspond to the primary level of schooling, the next three to junior high school, and the last four to high school. The last bar, which may be taken as a point of reference, corresponds to the case of a youth who has at least some high school education and did not work at any time during his or her educational career.[10]

The first result to note from the figures is that, consistent with the findings discussed above, dropping out of school to work never provides a higher return than continuing in school. Further, the profiles for females are slightly higher than for males, presumably reflecting the high returns to upper levels of education. The gender dimension of the results is that dropping out involves a greater penalty for girls than for boys. This could reflect several factors, including the greater likelihood of being out of the labor force, the poor job opportunities available to women with little education, and an association with early childbearing.

Another key finding is that for women, the penalties for combining school and work or for dropping out of school are not compensated by the returns to experience. For males the total returns to combining work and school may sometimes exceed those of devoting youth time exclusively to schooling. This suggests there may be a complementarity between the schooling and work undertaken by males. In contrast, for females the bars for combining work and schooling tend to be lower than those for specializing in school. This implies that while the net return to combining school and work is positive, it is lower than the return to concentrating on schooling.

Conclusion

This chapter evaluated how employment during childhood and adolescence and school dropout affect returns to human capital later in life. The availability of retrospective data about age at entry into the labor force and of school dropout makes it possible to pursue this analysis.

The main econometric results of the chapter suggest that there are positive returns to early labor market experience, but that they depend on continued progression through the school system. The penalty to shortening the educational career substantially outweighs the returns to early experience. In addition, while there is a positive net return to in-school work, it is often lower than the return to specializing in schooling.

There are important gender dimensions to the results. For women, the returns to experience are lower, the returns to postprimary education are higher, and the penalties for dropping out of school and for combining school and work are more severe. While there is evidence of complementarity between youth work and education among males, for females the returns to working only or to combining work and school tend to be lower than devoting time only to schooling.

A number of factors may contribute to explaining the high penalty to early work experience and school dropout for women compared to men. First, the type of jobs undertaken by women during school-age years may be particularly incompatible with combining school and work. Second, the returns to postprimary education are high relative to males and relative to the returns to primary education. Third, there could be low returns to accumulating experience in the types of work young women pursue during school years. Fourth, the skills that are attained by women who enter the labor market at an early age may not be transferable to other jobs, and young women who begin in these occupations may find it difficult to look for and be accepted in other types of work. Fifth, these gender differences could also reflect self-selection. It is possible that the women who begin to work at an early age are those who are less likely to do well in school. Finally, labor force exit is more common among women and could be associated with school dropout and early work experience. Other outcomes such as early childbearing could also be associated with early labor force participation and school dropout, compounding the impact on long-term educational and labor market success.

These alternate explanations require further research. Of particular interest would be further analysis of gender differentials in the occupational distribution of young workers, and in particular the impact of different types of work on educational and labor market outcomes through the life course. More detailed studies of particular occupations may also lead to increased information on the roles and responsibilities of employers. Within the range of occupations undertaken by girls and young women, one type of work that is common and deserves particular attention is domestic service. Available evidence on domestic service suggests that the women are often quite young, work long hours, and have few opportunities to attend school, and that they play an important role in explaining the differences in the returns to education and experience by gender (Knaul 1999; Flórez, Knaul, and Méndez 1995; Tenjo 1992, 1993). Further research is also required on domestic work undertaken by children in their own homes. This is often an activity that is more common among young women, that is likely to be incompatible with school attendance, and that offers only limited training for future paid work. Another area of work that requires further analysis is agricultural labor, much of which is undertaken by children without remuneration, and which is likely to interfere with school attendance.

The work of children and youth is very heterogeneous in terms of hours worked, job content, age at entering the labor force, and continuity between school and summer months. These differences have an important impact on the degree of compatibility with school attendance and progress in school, and in turn on future labor market outcomes. This implies that the negative effects of early labor force participation may not be evident from comparing workers to nonworkers, but rather rest on the unequal distribution of this work across children based on gender, poverty, and age.

Gender differentials in child labor are evident not only in the distribution of occupations, but also in the ways in which early labor market experience affects educational and future employment opportunities. Information on differentials in the nature of the work performed by girls and boys will be especially relevant to policies and programs that seek to improve educational attainment and reduce poverty. One of these is PROGRESA, the goals of which include maintaining children in school and targeting poverty at the family and community level. The gender differentials in child work also need to be incorporated into the process of developing national and international legislation in support of child workers.

Appendix 2.1

How Large Is the Bias in Child and Youth Employment Rates from Ignoring Housework?

This Appendix, a summary of Knaul (1999), draws attention to the need to take account of home-based work in addressing the issue of child labor, despite the fact that housework does not fall within a standard definition of employment. It is relevant to the knowledge regarding the undervaluation and undercounting of the work of women, and to the specific sphere of the activities of young people. Most estimates of labor force participation, including the ones in this chapter, fall short of accounting for unpaid housework activities. Traditional calculations of labor force participation tend to understate both the extent and the intensity of the work undertaken by young women. The existence of detailed data on time use from the ENE allows an assessment of the size of this bias.

Child and youth labor force participation are first evaluated using a traditional definition of employment—one that includes work undertaken inside or outside of the home, with or without remuneration, for at least one hour per week, in the production of marketable goods. Essentially, this definition excludes work undertaken in "nonmarket" activities, such as housework. The results under this definition are then contrasted to an inclusive definition. This approach adds domestic work undertaken in the child's own home to the traditional measure of child employment. The terms "home-based domestic work," "housework," "household work," and "household chores" are used to refer to this form of labor.[11]

Traditional definitions of labor force participation suggest that in all of Mexico, 12.6 percent of children aged 8 to 17 work in market activities (Table 2.A.1). Further, the incidence of work is more than twice as high for boys than for girls. Among all children and youth aged 8 to 17, 7.6 percent of girls compared to 16.8 percent of boys are employed in market-based work.[12]

Adding home-based work to traditional definitions of labor force participation generates an inclusive measure of child work. The results for children and youth aged 12 to 17 are presented in Table 2.A.2. Children and youth, in both the urbanized and less urbanized areas of Mexico, are commonly involved in household work when undertaken on a part-time basis. While a larger proportion of young women do housework, it is important to note that it is also a common activity among boys. As a result, the inclusive labor force participation rates are substantially higher than the rates based on market work. For females, the rates are approximately twice as high as the traditional labor force participation rates. For

Appendix Table 2.A.1 Employment Status among Children and Youth, Traditional Definition of Work that Excludes Domestic Labor in Own Home, by Age Group and Gender

Proportion, (N)

All age group	Male	Female	All
8–11			
%	2.6	1.6	2.1
N	105,299	65,967	171,266
12–14			
%	13.1	5.8	9.4
N	403,895	185,398	589,293
15–17			
%	36.9	17.9	28.2
N	1,285,388	530,108	1,815,496
All			
%	16.8	7.6	12.6
N	1,794,582	781,473	2,576,055
Sample size	1,624	648	2,272

Notes: Figures calculated using expansion factors. N denotes the magnitude (population) estimated with expansion factors.
Source: ENPF, 1995.

15 to 17 year olds in urban areas, for example, the market-based participation rate is 20 percent, compared to 40 percent using a definition that includes home-based work undertaken 21 hours or more per week.

Time-use patterns are presented by gender in Table 2.A.3. Young women in each age group and in both rural and urban areas spend more hours in home-based domestic work than young men do. Still, it is interesting to note that young men also spend a considerable number of hours each week doing home-based work. The differences in the average number of hours spent on market work are very small. The same is true for hours spent studying. Still, summing up market and home-based work, young women work between 5 and 7 hours more than their male counterparts each week.[13]

Adding home-based domestic work into the categories of activities that children and youth undertake provides additional insight into the time use of young people (Table 2.A.4). The activities of children and youth may be divided into exclusive categories of those who do only home-based domestic work, those who do only market work, those who

Appendix Table 2.A.2 Rates of Labor Force Participation and Home-Based Domestic Work by Age, Gender, and Rural–Urban Areas[1]

		More urbanized areas					Less urbanized areas			
	Market	Home work		Market + home work		Market	Home work		Market + home work	
Age	work	1+ hours	21+ hours	1+ hours	21+ hours [2]	work	1+ hours	21+ hours	1+ hours	21+ hours
12–14										
Female	4.8	86.3	8.1	87.0	12.7	15.6	2.1	18.3	75.4	30.1
Male	11.0	68.5	2.0	73.8	12.8	37.4	33.2	1.5	61.4	38.5
15–17										
Female	20.2	88.3	22.4	91.1	39.8	24.3	80.6	36.0	86.2	53.5
Male	31.8	63.1	3.6	80.1	34.7	61.6	26.1	1.9	74.3	62.9

1. 100,000 or fewer inhabitants.
2. Refers to minimum hours of home-based domestic work and any number of hours of market-based work.
Note: Figures calculated using expansion factors.
Source: NES, 1995.

Appendix Table 2.A.3 Weekly Hours Spent in Home-Based Domestic Work, Market Work, and Study, By Age Group, Gender, and Rural–Urban (mean and median weekly hours)

	More urbanized areas				Less urbanized areas[1]			
	12–14		15–17		12–14		15–17	
	Female	*Male*	*Female*	*Male*	*Female*	*Male*	*Female*	*Male*
Home-based domestic work								
Mean	13.7	10.2	18.9	11.0	19.6	11.5	24.7	12.1
Median	14	8	14	10	15	10	21	10
Market work								
Mean	29.7	27.6	37.9	38.8	25.9	28.2	33.2	36.9
Median	28	24	42	44	18	26	30	40
Studying								
Mean	24.2	34.3	34.8	34.5	31.8	31.5	33.1	33.7
Median	35	35	35	35	30	30	35	35
Home and market work								
Mean	41.4	34.8	53.4	46.1	45.5	38.0	51.0	43.1
Median	36	31	55	49	42	36	49	43
Home work and market work and study								
Mean	65.1	60.5	71.3	66.5	65.2	64.0	69.9	63.7
Median	63	60	72	66	67	64	69	64

1. 100,000 or fewer inhabitants.
Note: Figures are calculated using expansion factors.
Source: NES, 1995.

combine home-based domestic and market work, those who combine
market work and schooling, those who combine home-based work and
schooling, those who combine both types of work with schooling, those
who only attend school, and those who spend no time on any of the three
activities. Home-based domestic labor of one hour or more per week is
considered. A higher proportion of young women in both age groups and
in urban and rural areas spends time only on household work. The differences are higher for females aged 15 to 17. Further, it is more common
for women to combine home and market work, or school and home-
based work. A smaller proportion of females devote their time exclusively to schooling. A large proportion of males divide their time between
school and home-based work. A higher proportion of males combine
market work with schooling, while a substantially larger proportion
devote their time exclusively to schooling.

A crucial factor in evaluating the likelihood that a young person can
combine schooling with their home- or market-based work is the number
of hours spent on each activity (Table 2.A.5). Those who spend 20 hours
or less per week on home-based domestic work are quite likely to be
attending school. Further, the rates are similar for men and women. In
urban areas, approximately 95 percent of children aged 12 to 14 are
attending school, compared to over 70 percent of those aged 15 to 17. In
less-urbanized areas, the rates are close to 90 percent in the younger age
group and just over 60 percent for older youth. Young people who work
more than 20 hours per week either in the market or at home are less likely to be attending school.

The inclusive definition of child and youth work suggests not only
that young women are as likely to undertake work activities as young
men, but also that the phenomenon of child and youth work is much
more prevalent than suggested by estimates based on traditional definitions of employment. The inclusive definition implies a doubling of
work activity rates among female children and youth. This suggests that
for Mexico the number of children and youth who are economically
active is approximately 25 percent larger than figures using standard
definitions. These figures include home-based work undertaken as a primary activity or for more than 20 hours per week. It is likely that these
findings would hold true in many developing countries, and suggests
the need to reevaluate existing figures on the work activity rates of children and youth.

In terms of policy, the implications of using the inclusive definition of
child and youth work are important. The inclusive definition substantially increases the work activity rates among female children and youth.
Hence, this definition presents a much more widespread picture of the
phenomenon of child and youth labor and much higher absolute num-

Appendix Table 2.A.4 Combinations of Home-Based Domestic Work, Market Work, and School, by Age Group, Gender, and Rural–Urban

| | More urbanized areas | | | | Less urbanized areas[1] | | | |
| | 12–14 | | 15–17 | | 12–14 | | 15–17 | |
	Female	Male	Female	Male	Female	Male	Female	Male
None	0.4	0.9	1.2	3.1	0.5	1.6	1.4	5.2
Home work only	5.0	2.6	18.1	9.2	12.3	1.5	32.8	3.1
Market work only	0.4	2.8	1.4	13.1	1.2	10.7	4.3	36.2
Market and home work	1.2	1.6	12.8	9.7	4.9	2.1	13.4	7.5
School and market work	0.3	2.6	1.3	3.8	2.1	16.3	1.5	11.1
School and home work	77.4	60.4	52.9	39.4	47.8	22.9	29.4	10.0
School, market, and home work	2.6	4.1	4.6	5.1	6.4	7.4	4.3	6.2
School only	12.7	25.1	8.7	16.7	24.9	37.5	12.9	20.8
Sample size	3,792	4,011	3,928	3,830	1,148	1,138	999	1,034

1. 100,000 or fewer inhabitants.
Note: Figures are calculated using expansion factors.
Source: NES, 1995.

Appendix Table 2.A.5 School Attendance by Work Activity, Age Group, Gender, and Rural–Urban, 1995 (% attending, n)

	More urbanized Areas				Less urbanized areas[1]			
	12–14		15–17		12–14		15–17	
	Female	Male	Female	Male	Female	Male	Female	Male
Home-based work								
1–20 hours	95.7	94.7	76.9	72.2	87.7	89.7	62.8	63.1
	2,694	2,368	1,962	1,576	571	340	262	158
21+ hours	61.0	68.0	30.0	34.5	39.4	—	16.2	—
	181	61	238	58	67		53	
Market work								
1–20 hours	85.5	90.3	63.8	67.8	71.6	87.8	41.1	68.2
	78	168	192	154	67	181	29	94
21+ hours	43.6	40.0	21.4	18.1	37.9	46.2	15.1	15.6
	51	98	125	174	25	102	155	68

Notes: Figures are calculated using expansion factors.
— = less than 20 observations.
1. 100,000 or fewer inhabitants.
Source: NES, 1995.

bers of children and youth who devote long hours to activities that are likely to impair the possibility of attending school.

Notes

1. See among others, Patrinos and Psacharopoulos (1994); Flórez, Knaul, and Méndez (1995); and Grootaert and Patrinos (1999).

2. Since recall from memory can get worse with time, this bias would be positively associated with age, and in particular with the time elapsed since the respondent was school-going age at the time of the survey.

3. This suggests additional caveats for the analysis. Salaried and nonsalaried income earners are grouped together, implying that the returns to physical capital may be included in the returns to human capital for business owners. Further, the use of hourly wages masks to some extent the reduced earnings that come as a result of only being able to work part-time, which may be more common for women. Finally, the exclusion of in-kind wages may generate a bias that is particularly strong for females because a large proportion work as domestic servants and part of their salary is paid in room and board. See Knaul (1995) for a detailed analysis of the differences in returns to human capital using a variety of measures of wages and earnings.

4. This issue is discussed in detail in the Appendix to this chapter.

5. The sample includes just over 300 municipalities.

6. The Heckman procedure is performed using full maximum likelihood techniques with corrected standard errors. The probit equations are modeled using a series of variables describing the physical characteristics of the home as a proxy for wealth. In order to respect identification restrictions, these variables are excluded from the earnings and wage functions. They consist of sets of dummy variables to indicate the predominant building materials of the dwelling; the roofing materials; the flooring material; and, whether the dwelling lacks an indoor bathroom, electricity, sewerage connection, or a telephone.

7. The results for the OLS regressions are presented and compared in Knaul (2000).

8. This finding is also likely to reflect a cohort effect related to factors such as improvements in school supply, or possible changes in the compatibility between child work and schooling.

9. Note that the profiles are shifted to the right for individuals who start working later in life as the axis refers to years of experience.

10. Each individual bar summarizes a particular combination of school and work. Each of the first two bars refers to individuals who have attained only some or complete primary education, and did not go on to the junior high school level. The individuals who combined primary school and work and did not continue to secondary are represented in the first bar. The second bar includes those who went to primary school without working, but dropped out after primary. The third through fifth bars apply to individuals who completed some or all of junior high, but did not go on to further studies. The fourth bars refer to the individuals who combine work and school at the level of junior high, in the first case also combining primary and work. The fifth bar summarizes the returns to those who did not work during primary or junior high school. The sixth through ninth bars summarize the returns for individuals who have some high-school education.

11. Home-based domestic work, or housework, does not include employment as a "domestic worker," which refers to household work undertaken in the home of an employer. Strictly speaking, employment as a "domestic worker" should already be a part of the traditional definition of employment.

12. Although not presented in the table, the rates of labor force participation are approximately three times higher in rural areas than in urban areas for both girls and boys.

13. This is also true among male and female adults (INEGI 1997).

References

Abler, David, José Rodríguez, and Hector Robles. 1998. *The Allocation of Children's Time in Mexico and Peru*. Population Research Institute, Pennsylvania State University, Working Paper 98–08.

Alessie, R., P. Baker, and R. Blundell. 1992. "The Working Behavior of Young People in Rural Cote d'Ivoire." *The World Bank Economic Review* 6(1).

Becker, Brian, and Stephen Hills. 1983. "The Long-Run Effects of Job Changes and Unemployment Among Male Teenagers." *Journal of Human Resources* 17(2).

Becker, Gary S. 1993. *Human Capital: A Theoretical and Empirical Analysis with Special Reference to Education. Third Edition.* Chicago: University of Chicago Press in conjunction with the National Bureau of Economic Research, Cambridge, Mass.

Behrman, Jere R., and Nancy Birdsall. 1983. "The Quality of Schooling: Quantity Alone is Misleading." *American Economic Review* 73(5).

_____. 1985. "The Quality of Schooling: Reply." *American Economic Review* 75(5).

Beneria, Lourdes. 1992. "The Mexican Debt Crisis: Restructuring the Economy & the Household." In Lourdes Beneria and Shelley Feldman, eds., *Unequal Burden: Economic Crisis, Persistent Poverty, and Women's Work.* Boulder, Colo.: Westview Press.

Binder, Melissa, and David Scrogin. 1999. "Labor Force Participation and Household Work of Urban Schoolchildren in Mexico: Characteristics and Consequences." *Economic Development and Cultural Change* 48 (1):123–54.

Brizzio de la Hoz, Araceli. 1996. "El trabajo infantil en México: Una realidad a superar." En Araceli Brizzio, comp., *El trabajo infantil en México.* UNICEF, México.

Chant, S. 1994. "Women, Work and Household Survival Strategies in Mexico, 1982–1992: Past Trends, Current Tendencies and Future Research." *Bulletin of Latin American Research* 13(2).

Christenson, Bruce A., and Fatima Juarez. 1987. "Household Economy and the Labor Force Participation of Male and Female Children in Mexico." CEDDU–El Colegio de México. Mexico, D.F.

Cos-Montiel, Francisco. 2000. p. 7

Eaton, Peter J. 1985. "The Quality of Schooling: Comment." *American Economic Review* 75(5).

Falaris, Evangelos M. 1995. "The Role of Selectivity Bias in Estimates of the Rates of Return to Schooling." *Economic Development and Cultural Change* 43(2).

Flórez, Carmen Elisa, Felicia Knaul, and Regina Méndez. 1995. *Niños y jóvenes: ¿Cuántos y dónde trabajan?* Bogotá: Tercer Mundo Editores. Ministerio de Trabajo y Seguridad Social y CEDE/Facultad de Economía, Universidad de los Andes.

Gómez de León, J., D. Hernández, S. Parker, and M. Orozco. 2000. "PROGRESA: A Description and a Review of Initial Results." Mimeo. Poster Session. 2000 Annual Meeting of the Population Association of America. Mexico, D.F.

González de la Rocha, M. 1988. "Economic Crisis, Domestic Reorganisation and Women's Work in Guadalajara, México." *Bulletin of Latin American Research* 7(2).

_____. 1995. "The Urban Family and Poverty in Latin America." *Latin American Perspectives* 22:12.

Grootaert, C., and H. Patrinos. 1999. *The Policy Analysis of Child Labor: A Comparative Study.* New York: St. Martin's Press.

Heckman, J. J. 1979. "Sample Selection Bias as a Specification Error." *Econometrica* 47(1):153–62.

INEGI (Instituto Nacional de Estadística, Geográfica e Informática) and Programa Nacional de la Mujer. 1997. *Mujeres y hombres en México.* Aguascalientes: INEGI.

Knaul, Felicia. 1993. "Menores en circunstancias especialmente difíciles: Su vinculación escolar." *Planeación y Desarrollo* 24:201–224, Edición Especial, diciembre. Bogotá: Departamento Nacional de Planeación.

_____. 1995. "Young Workers, Street Life and Gender: The Effect of Education and Work Experience on Earnings in Colombia." Ph.D. dissertation. Department of Economics, Harvard University.

_____. 1999. "Incorporating Home-Based Domestic Work into Estimates of Child and Youth Labor: The Mexican Case." Processed.

_____. 2000. "Age at Entry into the Labor Force, Schooling and Returns to Human Capital in Mexico." Presented at the meeting of the Population Association of America, Los Angeles.

Knaul, Felicia, and Susan Parker. 1998. "Patterns over Time and Determinants of Early Labor Force Participation and School Drop Out: Evidence from Longitudinal and Retrospective Data on Mexican Children and Youth." Presented at the 1998 meeting of the Population Association of America, Chicago. Processed.

Lam, David, and Deborah Levison. 1992. "Age, Experience, and Schooling: Decomposing Earnings Inequality in the United States and Brazil." *Sociological Inquiry* 62(2).

Levison, Deborah. 1991. "Children's Labor Force Activity and Schooling in Brazil." Ph.D. dissertation. University of Michigan.

Levison, D., K. Moe, and F. Knaul. 2001. "Youth Education and Work in Mexico." *World Development* 29(1).

Mincer, J. 1974. *Schooling, Experience and Earnings.* New York: Columbia University Press.

Mroz, Thomas A. 1987. "The Sensitivity of an Empirical Model of Married Women's Hours of Work to Economic and Statistical Assumptions." *Econometrica* 55(4).

Parker, Susan W. 1998. "Wage Levels of Male and Female Salaried and Self-Employed Workers in Urban Mexico 1986–1992: A Micro-Econometric Approach." El Colegio de México, Mexico, D.F. Processed.

Parker, Susan, and Carla Pederzini. 1998. "Gender Differences in Education in Mexico: Patterns, Trends and Determinants." Processed.

Patrinos, Harry Antony, and George Psacharopoulos. 1994. "Educational Performance and Child Labor in Paraguay." *International Journal of Educational Development* 14(3).

Post, David, and Suet-link Pong. 1999. "Employment During Middle School: The Effects on Academic Achievement in the U.S. and Abroad." Working Paper 99–15. Population Research Institute, The Pennsylvania State University, University Park, Pa.

_____. 2000. "International Policies on Early Adolescent Employment: An Evaluation from the U.S. and TIMSS Participant Nations." Working

Paper 00–01. Population Research Institute, The Pennsylvania State University, University Park, Pa.

Rich, Lauren. 1993. *The Long-Run Impact of Early Nonemployment: A Reexamination.* Research Report No. 93–300. Population Studies Center, University of Michigan. Ann Arbor, Mich.

Steinberg, Laurence, E. Greenberger, L. Garduque, and S. McAuliffe. 1982. "High School Students in the Labor Force: Some Costs and Benefits to Schooling and Learning." *Educational Evaluation and Policy Analysis* 4:363–72.

Steinberg, Laurence, E. Greenberger, L. Garduque, M. Ruggiero, and A. Vaux. 1982. "Effects of Working on Adolescent Development." *Developmental Psychology* 18(3):385–95.

Tenjo, Jaime. 1992. "Labor Markets, the Wage Gap and Gender Discrimination: The Case of Colombia." In George Psacharopoulos and Zafiris Tzannotos, eds., *Case Studies of Women's Employment and Pay in Latin America.* Washington, D.C.: The World Bank.

_____. 1993. "Cambios en diferenciales salariales entre hombres y mujeres 1976–1989." *Planeación y Desarrollo*, Edición Especial, diciembre.

3

Breadwinner versus Caregiver: Labor Force Participation and Sectoral Choice over the Mexican Business Cycle

Wendy Cunningham

This chapter examines labor force entry and sectoral choice in periods of economic fluctuation in urban Mexico to determine (a) whether gender or household role is the primary determinant of labor force participation patterns in response to a change in the household's income needs, and (b) how adult men and women with distinct roles in the household use the labor market as a safety net during periods of economic uncertainty. We also seek to better understand the role of the informal sector.

Labor supply studies recognize that men and women are different from each other, but they assume that the defining characteristic of each group's labor supply decisions is their biological composition and the socially ascribed roles that emerge from them (Smith 1983; Psacharopoulos 1992), thereby treating each group as homogeneous. In other words, gender is a primary explanatory variable of differential labor supply patterns between men and women. Such an assumption forces "gender" parameters on the model and, not surprisingly, studies find that men and women are intrinsically different (Ashenfelter and Layard 1986). This chapter challenges the assumption that women (and men) are homogeneous, and instead proposes that household roles that are formed by the interaction between gender and household composition are an important factor behind labor force participation decisions when the household experiences a shock to income.

The labor force entry decisions are studied within the context of business cycle fluctuations for two reasons. First, the decision whether to work or not is a response to a change in circumstances (when an individual chooses not to work) that induces an individual to go to work. This paper focuses on the change in work decisions when household income decreases.[1] Although this change will not fully characterize why individuals search for and accept a job, it does provide insight into how men's and women's labor is used as a safety net to cope with macroeconomic downturns and negative income shocks.

Second, considering economic shocks highlights the gender dimensions of economic downturns, whether economywide or within the household. During economic downturns, the probability of job loss increases and real wages decrease. Since Mexico does not offer labor income safety nets, the household must pull from its own resources to compensate for income losses. One strategy is to send to the labor market those household members who do not work in times of economic prosperity; that is, secondary workers. Although this reallocation of labor is theoretically reasonable, it has not been unanimously statistically proven in studies of the United States and Western Europe, regions that have strong income support programs.

Finally, with respect to the informal sector, since the mid-1980s most of the literature on this sector has assumed that it is an "employer of last resort" during difficult economic times (Thomas 1992). A competing view suggests that the labor market is well integrated, so if people enter they may do so in search of flexibility (Maloney 1997; Cunningham and Maloney 1998). This paper will contribute to the debate on the role of gender and household structure in sectoral allocation outcomes.

The study takes advantage of an urban[2] Mexican employment survey (ENEU) that followed 24 groups of individuals over five consecutive quarters during 1987–93, thereby permitting the identification of changes in labor force participation and labor income of an individual without the problem of sample heterogeneity faced in cross-sectional studies. The sample will be broken into five groups of people who identify themselves as either the household head or the spouse of the head[3]: (a) married women (wives),[4] (b) married men (husbands), (c) unmarried women with children (single mothers), (d) unmarried women without children (single women), and (e) unmarried men (single men).[5] Households headed by a married man or woman will be referred to as "couple-headed households," and those with an unmarried head are "single-headed households."

This chapter describes a simple framework to motivate the connection among labor supply, business cycle fluctuations, and household structure; describes the sample and the Mexican economy over the seven-year period; gives an overview of employment and sectoral allocation levels and transitions in a peak and a trough period for each type of head; describes methodology and examines why individuals choose to enter the labor market and to take a job in a specific sector; and summarizes the information presented.

Analytical Framework

An individual will enter the labor market if household income needs exceed the value of that person's contribution to household tasks. In the analysis, all individuals are members of a household, so labor force participation and the choice of sector will depend not only on one's own wants and needs, but also on the needs and contributions of other household members.[6]

There are several theories regarding how households decide who should work and who should not. In the classic model, the household head understands the needs and wants of all members of the household so he or she alone can efficiently decide who to send to the labor market and who should remain at home (Mincer 1962). Gender was formally incorporated into the theory in 1982 when Becker (1991) argued that the most efficient way to allocate household labor was by comparative advantage, based on the biological differences between men and women and the gender roles that emerge from these differences. Thus, biology and society dictate that women should "specialize" in housework and men in market work.[7] Women and men will tend to subscribe to these assigned roles because they receive greater happiness following society's model of their gender rather than acting contrary to their roles (Akerloff and Kranton 1999).

This theory suggests that there are two main potential roles for the head adults in households: breadwinner and caregiver. The breadwinners are those who are responsible for the economic well-being of the family. They tend to work in the labor market, but this is not a necessary condition since they may also be the recipient of nonlabor income that is used to support the household (Table 3.1). Caregivers are those who are responsible for the upkeep of the household. The breadwinner–caregiver role may be divided among household members, or both roles may be performed by one individual, depending on the composition of the household. Based on gender roles, men tend to perform the former role while women perform the latter.

Table 3.1. Income Sources of Those Who Do Not Earn Labor Income (1989:3)

	Husbands	Wives	Single mothers	Unmarried, childless women	Unmarried men
Pensions	55.84%	0.65%	4.69%	17.05%	40.0%
Rents (property or business earnings)	2.89	0	2.31	7.95	4.92
Savings	10.98	0	0	10.8	8.15
Alimony/widow benefits	0	0	8.23	3.89	0
Someone else (family or nonfamily)	28.79	99.02	81.05	58.24	44.92

Note: The question posed was, "¿Cómo le hace Ud. para sostenerse economicamente?"

The neat division of household roles along gender lines is not always possible though, for two principle reasons: (a) men do not necessarily earn all the income needed to maintain a household, and (b) not all households have adult men and women present. The probability of (a) occurring increases during business cycle downturns. A possible coping strategy is for "secondary workers"—that is, those individuals whose activities are outside of the labor force—to begin working.[8] The type of work chosen will depend on the income needs of the household and the individual's other roles in it. If earnings needs are high, a primary caregiver may sacrifice some of her home responsibilities to enter a formal sector job that pays more but has very inflexible hours. On the other hand, if homecare needs exceed earnings needs, the caregiver would choose the more time-flexible informal wage or contract/piecework jobs.

The use of the various sectors of the economy based on flexibility and earnings ability should be particularly relevant for those households with a single adult at the head, who must provide for both the economic and homecare needs of the household. Earnings needs of single-headed households should also increase as the economy slows down since they are very dependent on others' generosity (Table 3.1), so those who are not working should enter the labor force, and go into those sectors that particularly provide flexibility.

Data, Terminology, and a Historical Context

Data

The national urban employment survey (ENEU) collected by the Instituto Nacional de Estadística, Geográfica e Informática (INEGI) for the period 1987–93 is used. It is arranged such that an observation is selected into the data set, surveyed every three months, then dropped from the sample after the fifth interview, thereby following individuals and their households over 15 months. Appendix 3.1 demonstrates the sampling method.[9] The seven years consist of 24 cohorts with approximately 3,000 couple-headed households per cohort, 600 households headed by single mothers, 80 headed by unmarried women without children, and 200 headed by unmarried men, per cohort, where the head is in the 14 to 70 age range. Each household member older than age 12 is surveyed about demographics, job search, characteristics of the job, income sources, current earnings, and reasons for labor force participation decisions. For those age 11 and younger, only demographics are recorded. Individuals within households can be followed in order to identify changes in household behavior over the period. The mean characteristics of each group are presented in Table 3.2

Table 3.2. Average Sample Characteristics

		Women		Men	
	Wives	Single mothers	Unmarried, no children	Husbands	Unmarried
Demographics					
Age	38.33	49.83	42.28	41.66	43.26
	(11.04)*	(11.2)	(14.93)	(11.7)	(14.87)
Education	5.93	4.66	6.82	5.94	5.67
	(3.17)	(3.27)	(3.17)	(3.17)	(3.32)
Married	0.0014	0.011	0.018	0.0014	0
	(0.037)	(0.11)	(0.13)	(0.037)	
Divorced/separated over the period	0.0011 (0.033)	—	—	0.0011 (0.033)	—
Formed consensual union over the period	—	0.012 (0.11)	0.0052 (0.072)	—	0
Were married over the period	—	0.83 (0.38)	0.12 (0.33)	—	0.4 (0.49)
Household					
Added children over the period	0.074 (0.26)	0.034 (0.18)	0.064 (0.25)	0.074 (0.26)	0.0051 (0.071)
Lost children over the period	0.015 (0.12)	0.024 (0.15)	—	0.015 (0.12)	0.0037 (0.061)
# of young female adults (18–60)	0.34 (0.69)	0.55 (0.79)	0.46 (0.72)	0.34 (0.69)	0.52 (0.82)
# of young male adults (18–60)	0.35 (0.71)	0.54 (0.81)	0.21 (0.51)	0.35 (0.71)	0.39 (0.71)
# of older female adults (65+)	0.022 (0.18)	0.04 (0.2)	0.11 (0.33)	0.022 (0.18)	0.1 (0.31)
# of older male adults (65+)	0.0071 (0.084)	0.0075 (0.086)	0.018 (0.14)	0.0071 (0.084)	0.012 (0.11)
Children age 1–5	0.5 (0.73)	0.11 (0.37)	—	0.5 (0.73)	0.014 (0.14)
Children age 6–11	0.71 (0.92)	0.28 (0.62)	—	0.71 (0.92)	0.057 (0.31)
Daughters age 12–17	0.36 (0.65)	0.26 (0.55)	—	0.36 (0.65)	0.069 (0.3)
Sons age 12–17	0.38 (0.67)	0.27 (0.57)	—	0.38 (0.67)	0.085 (0.35)
Total adults in household	2.71 (1.16)	2.14 (1.26)	1.8 (1.02)	2.71 (1.16)	2.03 (1.22)

*Standard errors in parentheses.

—— = Variable not included in the estimation since, by definition, it is not relevant to the subgroup.

Both labor force entry and sectoral allocation patterns of household heads who were out of the labor force in period 1[10] but in the labor force by period 5 are considered. A person is identified as "in the labor force" (ILF) if he or she is working at the time of the survey or looked for a job in the month prior to the survey. Conversely, being "out of the labor force" (OLF) indicates that the person is neither working nor actively looking for a job.

Terminology

The terminology for sectoral choice is controversial due to different institutions, data availability, and theoretical biases regarding the existence of the informal sector.[11] Using the International Labour Office's "firm size" indicator and the popular "benefit receipt" indicator, [12] we identify six sectors based on characteristics of the firms and remuneration (Davila 1997): formal wage, informal wage, unpaid, informal entrepreneur, formal entrepreneur, and contract employment. The formal wage jobs are defined as those that pay wages/salaries[13] and (a) pay for their workers' social security (IMSS or ISSSTE) or health insurance,[14] or (b) are in firms with more than six employees. The informal wage sector is composed of those jobs in firms with fewer than six employees that pay wages or salaries but do not pay the benefits described above. Unpaid sector jobs do not provide any remuneration or benefits to the workers. The informal entrepreneur sector is comprised of firm owners who do not collect benefits and employ fewer than six workers, although 95 percent of these firms have three or fewer workers. Formal entrepreneurs are those who own large firms and/or pay their own benefits. Since the ENEU does not ask whether benefits are paid to the employees in these firms, only the size and the benefit receipt of the owner criteria can be used. Contract workers are those who are pieceworkers or have a short-term contract with a termination date.[15] Table 3.3 summarizes the labor force participation and sector of participation terms.

HISTORICAL CONTEXT. During 1987–93 the Mexican economy moved through a complete (trough-to-trough) business cycle. In 1987 Mexico was still plagued with high inflation rates and periodic devaluations that limited trade and foreign investment. The massive devaluation in 1987, financial deregulation, privatization, cuts in public expenditures, and the Economic Solidarity Pact helped to bring inflation under control and build confidence in the economy again, and economic growth increased (Ros 1996). However, by the early 1990s, the recession in the United States and the overvalued exchange rate led to an economic slowdown. Figures 3.1 and 3.2 show that over the period, male employ-

Table 3.3. Labor Force and Sectoral Terminology

Labor force participation status

Out of the labor force	Not employed and not looking for a job
In the labor force	Either wage or nonwage employed or looking for a job
Unemployed	Searched for a job for at least one hour in the previous week

Informal employment

Unpaid	Performed market work for at least one hour in the last week without compensation
Informal entrepreneur	Owner of a firm with fewer than six employees and not collecting social security or health insurance benefits
Informal wage	Salaried employee or shift worker in a firm with less than 6 employees and benefits are not collected
Contract/piece	A worker paid by the piece or contracted for a period of time or a quantity of output

Formal employment

Formal wage	Salaried employee or shift worker who collects benefits or works in a firm with more than six employees
Formal entrepreneur	Owner of a firm who pays social security or health benefits or who employs more than five workers

Figure 3.1 GDP Growth Rates and Male Labor Force Participation, 1987–93 (%)

Figure 3.2 GDP Growth Rates and Female Labor Force Particpation, 1987–93 (%)

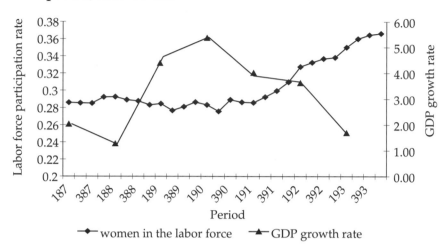

women in the labor force   GDP growth rate

ment was somewhat countercyclical, but female labor force participation did not follow a clear pattern, particularly after 1990.

Stylized Facts: Labor Force Patterns during Macroeconomic Fluctuations

Participation in the Labor Force and by Sector: Levels

A traditional breakdown by gender obscures the importance of household role and intragender heterogeneity in both labor force participation and sectoral choice. Using all 24 cohorts, Table 3.4[16] shows that over 70 percent of women and 6 percent of men are out of the labor force. However, while 76 percent of wives are out of the labor force, only half of the single mothers in the sample and 30 percent of single women without children are neither working nor looking for jobs, compared to 6 percent of husbands and 13 percent of single men. Thus, wives, 92 percent of whom have working husbands, drive the female participation statistic and obscure the fact that a high percentage of women without spouses do work. In fact, the participation patterns of women without spouses or children are more similar to those of men with the same household structure (no spouse, no children) than they are to women who have differently structured households.

Sectoral allocation also appears more similar for those with the same household roles, in spite of gender, as shown by Table 3.5. Considering only the economically active population (EAP), that is, individuals

Table 3.4. ILF/OLF by Role, All 24 Cohorts (%)

	Women				Men		
	All	Wives	Single mothers	Single no children	All	Husbands	Single
ILF	29.29	24.31	51.26	79.25	93.32	93.92	86.97
OLF	70.71	75.69	48.74	30.75	6.68	6.08	13.03
Unemployed	0.84	0.69	1.47	2.0	1.59	1.52	2.19
Sample size	90,239	77,192	13,787	1,997	80,239	77,192	4,021

who are not out of the labor force (OLF), over 13 percent of the working wives are in unpaid jobs, while less that 0.65 percent of all other groups are in unpaid jobs.[17] In fact, all unmarried people, whether male or female, have approximately the same level of participation in the unpaid sector. This difference occurs because all unpaid wives have another source of labor income—the breadwinner (husband); but for those who are the primary earners in their households, unpaid employment does not seem to be an option.

Informal paid jobs are often characterized as employing the most vulnerable workers, usually single mothers (Standing 1989). However, single mothers, who are the primary breadwinners of the family, have informal sector attachment patterns that are closer to men with similar economic responsibilities. While 34.9 percent of single mothers are informal entrepreneurs, 30 percent of men, who are also the primary breadwinners, are informal entrepreneurs; however, only 24 percent of wives,

Table 3.5. Sectoral Allocation, All Cohorts (%)

	Women				Men		
	All	Wives	Single mothers	Single no children	All	Husbands	Single
Unemployed	2.86	2.85	2.86	2.89	1.71	1.62	2.52
Unpaid	9.21	13.01	0.6	0.65	0.25	0.23	0.46
Informal entrepreneur	26.36	23.72	34.86	21.19	30.33	30.01	31.31
Informal salary	9.34	7.75	13.76	8.24	6.62	6.45	9.27
Contract/piece	4.78	4.94	4.37	3.54	7.46	7.54	5.98
Formal wage	46.92	47.06	42.74	62.84	51.61	51.73	48.73
Formal entrepreneur	0.53	0.51	0.6	0.51	2.03	2.07	1.4
N	26,386	18,766	7,066	1,383	74,627	72,496	3,497

those without primary income-generating responsibilities, are in this sector. Furthermore, informal wage employment of single mothers (13.8 percent) is more similar to that of unmarried individuals (8.5 percent) than to wives (7.8 percent). Finally, the probability of contract work is nearly equal for all groups except husbands, who are more likely to hold these quasi-entrepreneur and quasi-employee positions.

Low-risk, high-compensation formal sector jobs[18] are assumed to be the most favorable, and therefore the sector where gender discrimination is thought to be the highest. However, conditional on being in the labor force, single women without children are the most likely to enter formal sector jobs over the other sectors. Although males outnumber females in the composition of formal wage employment (51.6 percent and 46.9 percent, respectively), over 62 percent of unmarried, childless women work in large firms and collect benefits, while 47 percent of unmarried men and 51 percent of husbands hold such jobs. Employers cite a preference for women without spouses or children since their household responsibilities do not conflict with their work and women are more compliant and responsible than men, who are prone to alcoholism and absenteeism (Chant 1991). Single women with children, and wives, the most likely to have inflexible household responsibilities, are less likely to be in the formal sector (43.7 percent and 47 percent, respectively).[19] Thus, even though employers admit that they discriminate against men, their primary explanation for hiring unmarried women is an absence of household responsibility; that is, they openly acknowledge discrimination based on household role.

Transition Patterns during Economic Fluctuations

Transition patterns and trends reveal how households cope with business cycle shocks and the importance of household role in that decision. For example, just considering labor force entry patterns of those who were OLF in the first interview in cohort 11 (who were selected into the sample in the third quarter of 1989, an expansionary period), and cohort 21 (who were selected into the sample in the third quarter of 1992, a contractionary period), demonstrates the importance of the economy on labor supply.[20]

Table 3.6 summarizes the likelihood that wives, husbands, and single mothers move from OLF to sector k over the 15-month survey period. The sample size for unmarried males and females without husbands or children was too small to include in the analysis. The top number in each cell is for movements between periods 1989:3 and 1990:3 (cohort 11), and the bottom statistic is for movements between periods for 1992:3 through 1993:3 (cohort 21).[21]

Table 3.6. Conditional Probability of Moving into Sector k by Period 5 for Those Who Were Out of the Labor Force (OLF) in Period 1

	Wives	Single mothers	Husbands
OLF	90.21*	85.82	67.5
	86.8	81.89	69.79
Unemployed	0.25*	0.38	7.5
	1.02	4.91	8.33
Unpaid	1.91	0.38	0.5
	2.56	0	2.08
Informal entrepreneur	3.15*	8.43	13.5
	4.47	7.55	8.85
Informal salary	1.41	1.53	2.0
	1.24	3.02	2.6
Contract/piece	0.83	0.38	0.5
	1.11	0.38	2.6
Formal wage	2.24	3.07	8.0
	2.68	1.89	5.2
Formal entrepreneur	0	0	0.5
	0.04	0	0.52
Sample size	2,410	261	200
	2,347	265	192

Note: The top value in each cell is the probability of moving to sector k from OLF in an expansionary period, and the bottom value is the probability of moving to sector k from OLF in a contractionary period. The expansionary period used is 1989:3–1990:3, and the contractionary period is 1992:3–1993:3.

* The sample proportion between the two transitions within the cell is statistically different from zero.

Wives demonstrate labor force entry and a propensity for informal entrepreneurship when the economy slows down, while single mothers and husbands do not. Table 3.6 shows that wives are less likely to remain OLF during bad economic times: less than 10 percent enter in expansions, but 13.2 percent enter in recessions. Although single mothers seem to show the same pattern, the difference in proportions is not statistically significant.

Considering the states of entry, wives are more likely to be unemployed when the economy contracts, but single mothers and husbands do not have statistically different rates of unemployment in the two periods. Perhaps this is because single mothers and husbands have to work, but wives, who may enter the labor force as a type of "insurance" against job loss of the spouse, may spend more time searching for jobs since their income has not (yet) been negatively affected. Wives are more likely to start their own small firms when the economy gets bad, whereas others are not. Perhaps because they are not the primary breadwinner, wives may enter the risky informal entrepreneurship sector when they need to work (while also providing homecare), but husbands, the primary bread-winners, cannot take such risks. Interestingly, single mothers do not increase the likelihood of informal entrepreneurship in crisis, although this is assumed to be the refuge of the most vulnerable groups. Instead, salary work seems to be the preferred job type, although the difference in proportions is not significant.

Methodology

The above transitions are suggestive, but they do not control for other characteristics that determine labor force participation and sectoral choice. Controlling for them reveals transition patterns and the impor-tance of household role, in spite of gender, for labor supply decisions.

Statistical Models

The decision to enter the labor force is distinct from the choice of sector. Ideally we would model sectoral choice conditional on labor force entry, but statistical methodologies are not readily available.[22] Instead, a labor force participation decision model is estimated (probit), and then a sec-toral choice model is estimated (multinomial logit) separately for exit from OLF to formal, informal wage, informal entrepreneurship, and con-tract work. Unpaid workers and formal entrepreneurs are dropped from the sample due to their small sample size. The interpretation of the sec-toral choice model should take into account the biases of the working sample, as identified in the first former estimate.

We are primarily interested in whether the head enters the labor force when (a) economic conditions deteriorate, (b) other household members lose their jobs, and/or (c) household labor income falls. To identify whether the entry probabilities differ along household roles or gender lines, each household role–gender group is analyzed separately. Only those who were OLF in the first period are in the sample.[23] Following a methodology used by Valletta (1993) and Maloney (1999), we will treat the data as a cross-section but include dummies (changes) for those dis-crete (continuous) variables that change over the five periods. The method is fully outlined in Appendix 3.2 and the control variables are defined in Table 3.7.

Table 3.7. Explanatory Variables Used in Labor Force Participation Equation

Variable	Definition
Shock	
Unemployment rate*	Male national unemployment rate by quarter
Fall in household income*	Difference in household income (less own) between periods 1 & 5
Spouse involuntarily OLF*†	Dummy = 1 if husband was ILF‡ in period 1 but was forced out of his or her job by period 5
Others involuntarily OLF*	Count of nonspouse in household who involuntarily left their jobs
Fall in household income*	Dummy = 1 if household income (less own) is lower in period 5 than period 1
Fall in household income by 0–9%, 10–24%, 25–49%, 50–74%, 75–100%*	Dummy for each category corresponding to the amount of the decrease in household income between periods 1 and 5
Demographics	
Age	Reported age
Years of education	Reported years of formal education
Household Structure	
Married	Dummy = 1 if married and = 0 if in a consensual union
Separated*	Dummy = 1 changed from married or consensual union to single between the periods
Consensual union*	Dummy = 1 if changed from single to consensual union between the periods
Marry*	Dummy = 1 if changed from unmarried to married between the periods
No. children aged 1–5	Number of own children in the household aged 1–5
No. children aged 6–11	Number of own children in the household aged 6–11
No. daughters aged 12–17	Number of daughters in the household aged 12–17
No. sons aged 12–17	Number of sons in the household aged 12–17
Additional child*	Dummy = 1 if there are more own children in period 5 than 1
Fewer children*	Dummy = 1 if there are fewer own children in the household in period 5 than 1
No. females aged 18–64	Number of women in the household aged 18–64
No. females aged 65+	Number of women in the household aged 65+

(Table continues on the following page.)

Table 3.7 *(continued)*

Variable	Definition
No. males aged 18–64	Number of men in the household aged 18–64
No. males aged 65+	Number of men in the household aged 65+
Labor demand	
Regional dummies	North Central, Northeast, North, North–Northeast, Central, Gulf Central
% of labor force females	Calculated as the percentage of the municipal level labor market that is female
City size	Population calculated from 1990 census data
Search resources	
Household labor income	Total labor income of the household in period 1
Spouse was an informal entrepreneur	Dummy = 1 if spouse was an informal entrepreneur in the last job
Spouse was informal wage	Dummy = 1 if spouse was an informal wage employee in the last job
Spouse was formal wage	Dummy = 1 if spouse was a formal wage employee in the last job
Spouse was contract	Dummy = 1 if spouse was a contract worker in the last job

* Indicates a variable that measures change over the five periods.
† OLF = out of the labor force.
‡ ILF = in the labor force.

Potential Determinants of Labor Force Participation and Sectoral Choice

The estimated models will control for five basic groups of variables: potential and realized income shocks, personal characteristics, household structure, labor demand, and search resources.

Potential and Realized Income Shocks

Three measures of income shocks will be used: the national unemployment rate, involuntary job loss, and the change in household labor income. The first measure is a proxy for risk created by macroeconomic instability because as the economy slows down and the unemployment rate increases, the probability of job loss increases, so households are more likely to experience a negative shock to household income. Furthermore, since high unemployment rates are correlated with slow economic growth, the unemployment rate may proxy a fall in income from other (investment) sources. Thus, as the risk of a fall in income increases, due to macroeconomic circumstances, nonworking household members may enter the labor force as a form of "insurance" in the risky period.

Job loss of others in the household is a proxy for realized negative shocks to household income. The variable is potentially endogenous, so it is necessary to confine the loss in income to *unexpected* negative shocks. Thus, only job loss due to being fired, plant closure, or illness is identified as an involuntary job loss.

The fall in household income (less own earnings) directly measures the negative income shock, but it is potentially endogenous. However, most of the decrease of income is due to a decrease in real wages, not a fall in hours worked, which is likely to be exogenous. Both a continuous variable to measure the change in income and a set of dummies to measure the percentage fall are used in the analysis. The latter will highlight at what point the negative shock to household income is too great to be ignored or compensated by nonlabor resources.

Personal Characteristics

An individual will begin to work if his or her value in the workplace, measured by wages, is higher than that in the home. As Knaul, Parker, Pagan, and Sánchez demonstrate in this volume, wages are positively correlated with education level and experience. Since experience is difficult to measure for women, "age" will be used as a proxy. Furthermore, those with more human capital tend to be more efficient at household tasks, thus decreasing the time needed to fulfill household tasks.

With respect to sector of choice, the formal labor market is more likely to reward age and experience since they are signals to employers of high productivity. Those who do not have the signals are more likely to be in the informal entrepreneurship or informal wage sectors such that the market determines their returns.

Household Structure

A gendered allocation of time dictates that quality of the home is ultimately the responsibility of the female household head (if there is a female present). This workload may be increased or decreased based on the needs and contributions of the rest of the household through demands on or substitutes for domestic work and market work. In the formal model estimates, variables are included to account for the sex and age of other household members: children aged 1 to 5, children aged 6 to 11, daughters aged 12 to 17, sons aged 12 to 17, women (not head or spouse) aged 18 to 65, men (not head or spouse) aged 18 to 65, women aged 66 and older, and men aged 66 and older. The expected effects of these individuals are not clear, though, due to their potential contribution to or demand for domestic services and income.

With respect to domestic work, children and the elderly both require care that is often provided in the home, thereby increasing the value of the services that the woman provides in the household. Additionally, a married woman has to care for her husband, further increasing the value of her home time. These responsibilities are more easily balanced with labor market work if the woman has time and workplace flexibility, as offered by informal sector jobs. Thus, it is expected that those with young children and elderly adults in the household would be more likely to be informal entrepreneurs or contract workers or pieceworkers. On the other hand, older children or elderly adults who are still active may perform the household tasks that the head female would normally be responsible for, thus decreasing the value of her household time, as Knaul showed for daughters who are very likely to work in the home (see chapter 2).

Additional family members also increase money needs of the household. Thus, there may be a tradeoff between staying at home to dedicate time to the children and elderly and working to generate the additional resources required to provide for them. The highest earnings sector is the formal wage sector (Maloney 1997), so those with high earnings needs that the husband (or other financial supporter) cannot meet may enter the formal sector. However, the higher monetary needs of a household may be met by older children and other adults who live in the household, since they may enter the labor force to provide the needed earnings. This decreases the need for the head female to enter, or allows her to enter lower-paying, more flexible jobs. Knaul showed that 16.3 percent of boys in their teens are active in the labor market, thereby taking demands off their mothers. Finally, other household members, particularly those who are not permitted to work in the labor market, may be productively employed in the home business of the female household head or spouse, thus increasing the incentive for informal entrepreneurship of women with young children.

Labor Demand and Search Resources

The observed "working" outcome is based not only on a person's desire to work, but also on the desire of employers to hire that individual. Although the data set does not include labor demand variables, and those available from other sources are not gender disaggregated, a few proxies are included in the analysis. First, since women are more likely to find work in larger cities where there are more potential jobs (wage work) or clients (informal entrepreneurship), and in areas where females tend to be in the labor force, the size of the city and the percentage of the labor force that is female is included. In addition, regional differences, such as the minimum wage, industrial concentration, and infrastructure, will determine the ease and returns from finding a job, controlled for by regional dummies. The sector of entry will also be subject to the amount of jobs available in each sector, measured by the percentage of jobs in the regional labor market that are in each sector. Finally, networks within the home may determine sector of choice. There are barriers to entry into any sector, so having a spouse who is in one sector should increase the likelihood of participation in that sector.

Model Predictions

Taking all these factors together, it may be expected that labor force entry and sectoral allocation trends are based more on household roles than on gender. There are two hypotheses to test: (a) wives are more likely to enter the labor force when there is an expected or real shock to household income, that is, an added worker effect, but primary breadwinners (husbands, single mothers, unmarried women without children, and single men) will not; and (b) primary caregivers are more likely to enter the flexible informal sector, particularly if there are children in the household.

Estimation Results

Labor Force Participation

Labor force entry patterns are substantially different among the five groups. In particular, wives tend to act as secondary labor, entering the labor force to substitute for a fall in household income or to act as unemployment insurance. Husbands, on the other hand, are very unresponsive to changes in household employment or labor income because they have other income sources that are not subject to market fluctuations, such as pensions, that allow them the luxury of not working (Table 3.1). Single mothers fall between these two extremes, demonstrating the role of both caregiver and breadwinner. Unmarried individuals without children do not show identifiable patterns.

The LFP model is estimated three times using different sets of shock variables. The unemployment rate and the household structure, demographic, labor demand, and search resources variables are in all three models. The first estimate (model I) considers the importance of changes of employment status. The second tests if a fall in household income of any magnitude influences labor force entry, and the third considers decreases in household income of different magnitudes. Partial derivative estimates of the shock variable are presented in Table 3.8. Since the coefficient estimates of the demographic, household structure, labor demand, and search variables do not change between models, only those from model III are reported. Partial derivative estimates of household structure are presented for each model in Table 3.9; and demographic, labor demand, and search variables are presented in Table 3.10.

Labor Force Entry in Response to Economic Shocks

Wives most strongly demonstrate an added worker effect, both as a form of insurance and as a source of emergency income due to their heavy dependence on the earnings of others in the household (Table 3.1). A 1 percent increase in the unemployment rate, a proxy for increased risk of a negative shock to income, makes a wife 2.8 percent more likely to enter the labor force (Model I, Table 3.8). Furthermore, if a husband unexpectedly loses his job, there is an increased probability of 4.3 percent that his wife will begin working, but wives do not respond to sudden job losses of other household members.[24] The amount of change in household income associated with the job loss explains this pattern. A wife begins working if household labor income falls by more than 25 percent (Model III). Since husbands contribute, on average, 75 percent of household labor income and 99.3 percent of nonworking wives have working husbands, the wives are substituting their labor earnings for a fall in household income, not for a change in labor force participation status by a particular family member.

Husbands are unresponsive to economic shocks. They do not enter the labor market when the unemployment rate increases, nor do they respond to a fall in household income or unexpected job loss by other household members. This is not surprising since of the nonworking husbands, only 15 percent have working wives, while the rest are dependent on nonlabor income.

Single mothers, like husbands, are unresponsive to macroeconomic fluctuations, but like wives, they are responsive to real negative shocks to household income: they enter the labor force if household income falls by more than 50 percent (Model III). Therefore, the responsiveness of single mothers to economywide and household-level shocks is between that of husbands and wives, perhaps due to the dual role that the single mother plays as both caregiver and breadwinner. In couple-headed households where labor may be divided, nearly all nonworking wives are dependent on their husband's labor income, but only 66 percent of single mothers

Table 3.8. Partial Derivatives of Shock Variables (Estimated from Probit)

(Dependent variable = 1 if the individual enters the labor force by period 5)

| | Women | | | Men | |
	Wife	Single mother	Unmarried, no kids	Husbands	Unmarried
Model I					
Unemployment rate	0.028 (7.4)*	0.018 (1.04)	0.027 (0.84)	0.0046 (0.22)	−0.075 (−1.36)
Others involuntarily OLF†	0.0022 (0.36)	0.0048 (0.27)	−0.035 (−0.33)	−0.026 (−1.14)	0.064 (0.78)
Spouse involuntarily OLF	0.043 (3.32)	n.a.	n.a.	—	n.a.
Model II					
Unemployment rate	0.029 (0.0038)	0.017 (1.03)	0.027 (0.85)	0.0039 (0.18)	−0.07 (−1.29)
Fall, household income	0.0099 (3.84)	0.048 (3.78)	−0.034 (−0.66)	0.0027 (0.17)	0.023 (0.43)
Model III					
Unemployment rate	0.029 (7.48)	0.018 (1.06)	0.28 (0.89)	0.0047 (0.22)	−0.072 (−1.30)
% fall household income:					
1–9%	0.0059 (1.27)	0.025 (1.06)	−0.015 (0.12)	−0.048 (−1.58)	0.1 (0.96)
10–24%	0.0022 (0.53)	0.036 (1.71)	−0.11 (−1.36)	−0.012 (−0.43)	0.017 (0.18)
25–49%	0.014 (3.64)	0.031 (1.43)	−0.0043 (−0.05)	0.0036 (0.13)	−0.4 (−0.41)
50–74%	0.034 (6.41)	0.1 (3.10)	0.11 (0.77)	0.056 (1.49)	0.036 (0.35)
75–100%	0.028 (5.53)	0.087 (3.85)	−0.039 (0.47)	0.027 (1.09)	0.0077 (0.08)
Sample size	58,015	4,397	2,073	4,883	795

*z = values in parentheses.
† OLF = out of the labor force.
n.a. = Not applicable.
—— = too few responses, so variable was dropped from the model.

Table 3.9. Partial Derivatives of Demographic and Household Structure Variables (Estimated from Probit)

| | Women | | | Men | |
	Wife	Single mother	Unmarried, no kids	Husbands	Unmarried, no kids
Marital status					
Married	−0.011	—	—	−0.007	—
	(−2.13)*			(−0.23)	
Separated	−0.021	—	—	0.27	—
	(−0.53)			(1.39)	
Marry**	—	**	**	—	0.048
					(0.67)
Children					
No. children aged 1–5	−0.0065	0.015	—	0.03	—
	(−3.46)	(0.97)		(1.77)	
No. children aged 6–11	0.0023	0.017	—	−0.028	—
	(1.46)	(1.67)		(−2.35)	
No. daughters aged 12–17	0.0069	−0.00048	—	0.0025	—
	(3.39)	(−0.50)		(0.21)	
No. sons aged 12–17	0.0021	0.014	—	0.012	—
	(1.04)	(1.55)		(1.06)	
Additional children	−0.0083	−0.02	—	−0.084	—
	(−0.61)	(−0.42)		(−1.20)	
Fewer children	0.016	−0.038	—	0.14	—
	(1.2)	(−0.88)		(2.0)	
Nonhead adults					
No. females aged 18–64	−0.0084	−0.016	−0.33	0.0096	0.0035
	(−3.82)	(−2.16)	(−1.40)	(1.12)	(0.14)
No. males aged 18–64	−0.0097	−0.013	−0.029	0.01	−0.059
	(−4.46)	(−1.88)	(−0.78)	(1.16)	(−1.90)
No. females aged 65+	0.14	−0.0037	0.048	0.0081	−0.11
	(1.73)	(−0.13)	(1.04)	(0.20)	(−1.79)
No. males aged 65+	−0.0039	−0.018	−0.14	0.047	−0.083
	(−0.28)	(−0.30)	(−0.92)	(0.62)	(−0.64)

Note: The coefficient estimates were very similar among models, and the significance levels were identical. Thus, only the estimates from model III, the model with the best fit, are reported here.

*z = values in parentheses.

**Variable was dropped due to a small sample size.

—— = variable not included in the estimation since, by definition, it is not relevant to the subgroup.

Table 3.10. Partial Derivatives of Other Variables (Estimated from Probit)

	Women			Men	
	Wife	Single mother	Unmarried, no kids	Husbands	Unmarried, no kids
Demographics					
Age	0.0051	0.0049	0.14	0.03	0.018
	(5.8)*	(1.05)	(2.61)	(5.02)	(2.23)
Age^2	−0.000076	−0.00012	−0.00024	−0.00033	−0.00023
	(−7.4)	(−2.54)	(−4.13)	(−5.50)	(−2.42)
Years of	0.00085	0.0074	−0.0077	−0.0038	−0.0015
education	(2.4)	(0.72)	(−3.14)	(−2.38)	(−0.38)
Wealth					
Household labor	−0.00013	−0.0055	−0.00074	−0.004	−0.00054
income	(−4.2)	(−2.32)	(−0.64)	(−1.48)	(−0.553)
Labor demand					
Regional:					
North Central	−0.023	0.075	−0.095	−0.032	0.26
	(−3.1)	(1.68)	(−1.38)	(−0.76)	(1.59)
Pacific	−0.014	0.097	−0.053	0.053	0.31
	(−1.91)	(2.32)	(−0.74)	(1.27)	(1.94)
Northeast	0.001	0.0087	−0.065	0.016	0.28
	(0.15)	(0.26)	(−0.96)	(0.41)	(1.89)
North	−0.016	0.019	−0.12	−0.012	0.23
	(−2.50)	(0.60)	(−1.75)	(−0.35)	(1.64)
North–Northeast	−0.012	0.041	−0.12	0.0055	0.34
	(−1.7)	(1.04)	(−1.94)	(0.13)	(0.17)
Central	−0.0052	0.067	−0.10	0.064	0.33
	(−0.8)	(1.84)	(−1.65)	(1.69)	(0.15)
Gulf Central	−0.0049	0.024	−0.04	−0.019	0.35
	(−0.61)	(0.60)	(−0.57)	(0.041)	(2.08)
% local labor	0.017	0.63	−0.21	−0.25	−0.40
market female	(0.042)	(3.41)	(−0.63)	(−1.12)	(−0.67)
City size	6.88×10⁻¹⁰	−1.68×10⁻⁹	−1.28×10⁻⁸	−1.44×10⁻⁹	2.22×10⁻⁸
	(0.69)	(−0.35)	(−1.21)	(−0.26)	(1.19)
Sample size	58,015	4,397	2,073	4,883	795
Log likelihood	−1,7756.14	−1,691.31	−922.38	−2,759.15	−443.88
Chi^2	570.30	360.43	354.74	112.24	34.3

Note: The estimates are from model III, the model that had the best fit. The coefficient values for Models I and II differ slightly, but the sign and magnitude of the coefficient estimates is very similar among the three models.

*z = values in parentheses.

who do not work depend on someone else to provide resources. The remaining receive income from alimony, widow support, pensions, and rents (Table 3.1). Therefore, a larger percentage of single mothers are supported by income that is not subject to market fluctuations, explaining why they do not enter the labor force when unemployment rates increase. However, single mothers are more dependent than husbands on the support of others' labor income, explaining why a shock to the earnings of others in the household induces them to go to work. Only 15 percent of nonworking men rely on labor income (55.8 percent receive pensions and 11 percent live off savings), but two thirds of single mothers rely on it (Table 3.1). Furthermore, since a large portion of nonworking single mothers are of working age, while many nonworking men are already retired, single mothers have more of an option to enter when economic need dictates.

Household heads without spouses or children do not respond to the state of the economy, shocks to household labor, or shocks to household income. Since labor force participation rates among these groups are high, we would not expect the few who are out of the labor force to enter the labor force under the risk of labor-income shock since they depend on other sources of nonlabor income (pensions, financial instruments, rents). In addition, if they are living in communal (not familial) arrangements, they are likely to be self-sufficient and thus not responsive to earnings of roommates.

These results show that wives are the most responsive to labor-income shocks, single mothers are less responsive, and women without families are the least responsive, demonstrating high heterogeneity among women. However, single mothers behave somewhat like husbands and single women do not differ from single men, suggesting that gender roles alone do not drive labor supply decisions, but instead the combination of gender and household structure, that is, household role, is important. It is not the fact of being a woman that leads to entry, but rather the fact of having to substitute for the primary breadwinner that induces her to enter.[25]

Household Structure

The importance of household structure is tested directly by considering the influence that children or other adults have on labor force entry, controlling for economic shocks. Household structure is a black box that is often used to explain women's, and to a lesser extent, men's labor force participation decisions (Nakamura and Nakamura 1992). In particular, lower female participation is tied to the presence of young children, but higher participation is explained by the presence of daughters or other adult females in the household who can perform the household tasks. These trends strongly appear in wives' labor force participation patterns, but less so for single mothers and husbands. The partial derivatives and significance levels of the household structure variables are listed in Table 3.9.

CONSTRAINTS TO LABOR FORCE ENTRY. The presence of young children (aged 1 to 5) [26] discourages a wife's entry into the labor force by 0.65 percent for each additional child. On the other hand, the number of school-aged children (aged 6 to 11) is not correlated with labor force participation, indicating that school serves as daycare for these children, so they no longer impede the wife's labor force entry.

Husbands have opposite patterns, though; they are 3 percent more likely to work for each additional young child in the household. Since they tend to be the primary breadwinner with few caregiver responsibilities, they generate the resources that capital-intensive children impose on the household (Nakamura and Nakamura 1992). They are less likely to work if there are school-aged children, however.

The breadwinner role seems to conflict with the caregiving role for single mothers since their labor force entry is neutral to the presence of children. On one hand, the income needs of the family may exceed the opportunity cost of staying home to care for the children, so we may expect these women to enter the labor force when there are more young children in the household. On the other hand, young children cannot simply be left alone, so they may impede labor force entry. However, it is likely that when single mothers need to work, a need that is somewhat independent of the marginal child in the household, they find other childcare arrangements. These arrangements are not preferred alternatives, though, since married women do not use them, but they do allow labor force entry by women who need to work.

Marital status does influence labor force entry for wives and unmarried women without children, since it alters their roles. Married women are 1.1 percent less likely to go to work than are those who are in a consensual union since the latter, who have greater risk for separation, are more willing to enter the labor market to invest in themselves in preparation for a breakdown of the household (Fleck 1983). Marital status does not affect husbands' work decisions, and a change in the status does not significantly explain labor force entry by men without children or by those who were husbands in the first period.

AIDS TO LABOR FORCE PARTICIPATION. Teen-aged girls and elderly women seem to be a substitute for wives' homecare activities and allow labor force entry, while young adults in the household substitute for wives' labor force entry. An additional teenage daughter increases the probability that the wife enters paid market work by 0.69 percent, and additional elderly women increase the likelihood by 14 percent, because their work in the home lowers the value of the wife's home time relative to market work time. Young adults have the opposite influence because their presence decreases the likelihood of married mothers' labor force entry by nearly 1 percent, since they may substitute for the wives in the labor force.

Conversely, the presence of teenagers or elderly adults in the household does not induce single mothers or husbands to enter the labor force. Young adults do somewhat substitute for single mothers' work (0.16 percent decrease in the probability of labor force entry), but their influence, especially young men's, is not strong. The nonresponsiveness to household aids is explained by household roles since as heads of household, they are less substitutable by secondary labor and thus remain little constrained or aided by other potential labor market substitutes or homecare givers.

In summary, household structure does not constrain labor force entry by single mothers or husbands, but it is highly influential in wives' entry. If single mothers enter the labor force, they do so because they must work. They cannot be, and are not, constrained by their role as caregiver.

Personal Characteristics and Demand Variables

Older, more educated individuals are more likely to enter the labor force, regardless of gender or household role, similar to findings by Pagán in chapter 6 of this volume. Women with spouses and/or children who live in households with higher labor income are less likely to work since the additional resources in the household make entry less necessary. Finally, a more feminized labor force increases the likelihood that single mothers will begin working, but does not increase the likelihood of entry for other types of women, nor decrease the likelihood for men, and the size of the local market, proxied by city size, does not necessarily increase the chances of getting a job.

Sectoral Choice

Traditional development theory cites the purposes of the informal sector as an employer of last resort (Thomas 1992). If, indeed, it is a source of jobs when economic times are difficult, then the probability of exit to informal entrepreneurship, informal wage jobs, and contract work, relative to formal sector jobs, should increase if household employment or income falls. However, the sector of entry is also subject to household structure. If the wife needs to work, she may prefer a flexible job, such as informal wage or contract work, rather than the more restrictive formal sector, to allow her to continue to fulfill her household roles. Single mothers and husbands, on the other hand, are likely to go to the highest-paying sectors, formal wage, or informal entrepreneurship, that give less flexibility for homecare activities. In this section, the sectoral choice decision is empirically examined for wives, husbands, and single mothers only since the sample size is too small for single women without children and for unmarried men.

The model is estimated three times. The first model examines the effect of changes in employment status of household members on the sectoral choice of the observation. The second model determines the importance of a change in the earnings of other household members on the observation's choice of sector, and the third model considers decreases of others' labor income of various magnitudes. The relative risk ratios of the changes in the employment and earnings status of other household members are given in Table 3.11. The relative risk ratios of the control variables are given in Tables 3.12 (household structure) and 3.13 (other controls). [27]

Labor Force Entry in Response to Economic Shocks

Wives that enter the labor force select a sector based on household income needs. As the unemployment rate increases, wives are more likely to enter informal entrepreneurship or contract work rather than formal sector jobs. However, if her husband unexpectedly loses his job, the wife is not more likely to enter an informal sector rather than a formal sector job, although she does tend to enter informal entrepreneurship (and, to a lesser extent, informal wage employment) if there is a fall of more than 50 percent in household labor income. Thus, a job loss that results in a negative blow to income is offset by wives' entry to the higher-paying informal entrepreneurship sector (Maloney 1999), rather than the traditional "sponge" jobs, while the contract/piecework sector seems to play an insurance role by employing wives when the risk of negative income shocks increase.

Husbands are sector specific when their entry plays an insurance role, but not when responding to falls in income. Similar to wives, husbands who enter the labor force are more likely to go into contract work and, to some extent, the informal wage sector rather than the formal sector when unemployment rates are higher. These findings directly support the assumption that informal work arrangements are the employers of last resort when the economy is tight. However, informal entrepreneurship does not serve as a sponge sector, supporting

(Text continues on page 117.)

Table 3.11. Multinomial Logit Estimates of Shock Variables (in relative risk ratios)

Pr(exit to formal over)	Wife			Single mother			Husband		
	Informal entrepreneurship	Inf. wage employment	Contract/piecework	Informal entrepreneurship	Inf. wage employment	Contract/piecework	Informal entrepreneurship	Inf. wage employment	Contract/piecework
Model I									
Unemployment rate	1.27 (1.77)*	1.2 (1.09)	1.67 (2.69)	1.02 (0.06)	1.77 (1.18)	1.03 (0.04)	0.89 (−0.44)	2.23 (2.23)	2.81 (2.23)
Others OLF† involuntarily	0.75 (−1.2)	0.78 (−0.87)	1.17 (0.52)	1.99 (1.15)	3.07 (1.77)	1.86 (0.74)	0.65 (−1.51)	0.89 (−0.31)	0.83 (−0.33)
Spouse OLF involuntarily	1.25 (0.62)	2.42 (1.35)	1.54 (0.89)	—	—	—	2	2	2
Model II									
Unemployment rate	1.24 (1.60)	1.12 (0.19)	1.63 (2.53)	1.01 (0.033)	1.76 (1.17)	1.03 (0.046)	0.88 (−0.47)	2.25 (2.25)	2.83 (2.24)
Fall in hh income	1.14 (1.47)	1.05 (0.48)	1.0 (0.02)	1.33 (0.89)	1.43 (1.00)	0.50 (−1.34)	0.93 (−0.39)	0.82 (−0.73)	0.67 (−1.05)
Model III									
Unemployment rate	1.19 (1.37)	1.23 (1.31)	1.64 (2.68)	1.03 (0.073)	1.81 (1.21)	0.99 (−0.003)	0.86 (−0.55)	2.22 (1.22)	2.7 (2.14)
Fall in income by: 1–9%	1.26 (1.45)	1.09 (0.46)	1.24 (0.98)	1.75 (0.88)	2.33 (1.22)	0.47 (−0.63)	0.69 (−0.95)	0.63 (−0.84)	0.41 (−1.05)

10–24%	0.98	1.04	0.89	1.19	1.11	0.58	0.74	0.77	0.87
	(−0.25)	(0.25)	(−0.53)	(0.36)	(0.19)	(−0.69)	(−0.86)	(−0.52)	(−0.21)
25–49%	0.86	0.85	0.88	1.22	1.37	0.29	1.2	1.0	1.17
	(−1.18)	(−1.03)	(−0.71)	(0.32)	(0.45)	(−1.06)	(0.57)	(0.012)	(0.28)
50–74%	1.78	1.49	1.32	1.31	0.99	2	1.38	0.94	1.38
	(3.28)	(1.88)	(1.1)	(0.44)	(−0.005)		(0.75)	(−0.10)	(0.40)
75–100%	1.44	1.19	0.99	1.39	1.62	0.86	0.90	0.82	0.39
	(2.26)	(0.85)	(−0.033)	(0.67)	(0.89)	(−0.21)	(−0.36)	(−0.48)	(−1.62)
Sample size	2,917	1,046	577	356	152	43	1,176	329	178

*z = values in parentheses.
† OLF = out of the labor force.
— = Variable not included in the estimation since, by definition, it is not relevant to the subgroup.
2Variable dropped from model because of small sample size.

Table 3.12. Multinomial Logit Estimates of Household Structure Variables (in relative risk ratios)*

Pr(exit to formal)	Wife			Single mother			Husband		
	Informal entrepreneurship	Inf. wage employment	Contract/piecework	Informal entrepreneurship	Inf. wage employment	Contract/piecework	Informal entrepreneurship	Inf. wage employment	Contract/piecework
Marital status									
Married	1.32 (1.8)*	1.07 (0.39)	1.67 (2.08)	—¹	—¹	—¹	1.11 (0.27)	1.03 (0.066)	0.71 (−0.61)
Separated	1.73 (0.47)	—²	—²	—¹	—¹	—¹	—²	—²	—²
Children									
No. children aged 1–5	1.14 (2.01)	0.97 (−0.43)	1.15 (1.57)	0.99 (−0.006)	0.78 (−0.74)	0.97 (−0.059)	0.92 (−0.41)	1.39 (1.33)	1.13 (0.67)
No. children aged 6–11	1.16 (2.81)	1.13 (1.91)	1.23 (2.81)	1.18 (0.81)	1.22 (0.85)	1.67 (1.77)	0.79 (−1.61)	0.68 (−1.72)	1.32 (1.36)
No. daughters aged 12–17	1.06 (0.79)	1.12 (1.31)	0.93 (−0.68)	1.21 (0.92)	1.13 (0.85)	1.23 (0.70)	1.05 (0.36)	0.99 (0.00)	1.39 (1.51)
No. sons aged 12–17	0.99 (−0.069)	1.03 (0.4)	0.85 (−1.52)	0.53 (−3.36)	0.51 (−3.1)	0.72 (−1.23)	0.93 (−0.51)	1.09 (0.46)	0.83 (−0.72)
Increase no. children	0.68 (−0.81)	0.71 (−0.59)	0.29 (−1.68)	2.2 (0.59)	0.79 (−0.15)	—**	2.09 (0.64)	1.98 (0.46)	—²
Decrease no. children	1.46 (0.78)	2.17 (1.46)	—²	—**	—**	—**	0.99 (−0.005)	1.24 (0.23)	1.74 (0.47)
No. females	1.15	1.05	1.11	0.93	0.81	0.90	0.82	1.04	0.9

aged 18–64	(1.43)	(0.38)	(0.79)	(−0.40)	(−0.96)	(−0.36)	(−1.88)	(0.36)	(−0.52)
No. males	1.06	1.14	1.09	1.11	0.88	0.85	0.93	0.87	0.96
aged 18–64	(0.59)	(1.16)	(0.71)	(0.54)	(−0.55)	(−0.53)	(−0.67)	(−0.89)	(0.20)
No. females	0.81	1.09	0.78	2.29	0.74	1.26	0.62	0.59	1.14
aged 65+	(−0.73)	(0.28)	(−0.56)	(1.15)	(−0.30)	(0.19)	(−0.98)	(−0.73)	(0.15)
No. males	0.93	0.93	0.22	—**	—**	—**	0.21	2.82	2.26
age 65+	(−0.15)	(−0.12)	(−1.35)				(−1.24)	(0.99)	(0.59)

Note: The estimates are from model III, the model that had the best fit. The coefficient values for models I and II differ slightly, but the sign and magnitude of the coefficient estimates are very similar among the three models.

*z = values in parentheses.

**Dropped because the variable predicted failures perfectly.

—¹ not relevant for category.

—² dropped due to small sample size.

Table 3.13. Multinomial Logit Coefficient Estimates of Remaining Control Variables (in relative risk ratios)

Pr(exit to formal over)	Wife			Single mother			Husband		
	Informal entrepreneurship	Inf. wage employment	Contract/piecework	Informal entrepreneurship	Inf. wage employment	Contract/piecework	Informal entrepreneurship	Inf. wage employment	Contract/piecework
Demographics									
Age	1.04 (1.14)*	0.98 (-0.46)	1.05 (0.92)	1.02 (0.19)	1.01 (0.10)	1.25 (1.05)	1.14 (1.76)	1.0 (0.002)	1.04 (0.34)
Age²	1.0 (0.47)	1.00 (0.81)	0.99 (-0.19)	1.00 (0.56)	1.0 (2.3)	0.99 (-0.88)	0.99 (-1.51)	1.0 (0.02)	0.99 (-0.31)
Years of education	0.87 (-11.44)	0.83 (-12.16)	0.89 (-6.61)	0.87 (-3.90)	0.78 (-5.55)	0.84 (-2.7)	0.93 (-1.01)	0.86 (-5.23)	0.93 (-1.99)
Wealth									
Household labor income	1.0 (0.54)	0.99 (-0.29)	1.00 (0.78)	0.98 (-2.35)	0.99 (-0.95)	1.00 (0.31)	1.00 (0.86)	0.99 (-0.023)	0.99 (-0.81)
Labor Demand									
Regional:									
North Central	0.93 (-0.28)	0.97 (-0.07)	0.55 (-1.52)	0.19 (-1.38)	0.63 (-0.33)	0.10 (-1.57)	0.46 (-1.55)	1.38 (0.43)	0.48 (-0.77)
Pacific	0.79 (-0.87)	0.89 (-0.34)	0.36 (-2.79)	0.21 (-1.40)	0.42 (-0.64)	0.09 (0.07)	0.66 (-0.89)	1.20 (0.24)	0.87 (-0.16)
Northeast	0.92 (-0.33)	1.1 (0.31)	0.92 (-0.28)	0.17 (-1.7)	0.62 (-0.37)	0.12 (-1.63)	1.95 (1.29)	3.62 (1.74)	4.30 (1.85)

	(1)	(2)	(3)	(4)	(5)	(6)	(7)	(8)	(9)
North	0.55 (−2.65)	0.99 (−0.017)	0.43 (−2.84)	0.16 (1.70)	0.72 (−0.25)	0.099 (−1.89)	0.75 (−0.70)	1.39 (0.49)	0.57 (−0.73)
North–Northeast	1.00 (0.033)	1.45 (1.1)	0.45 (−2.05)	0.15 (−1.64)	0.54 (−0.44)	0.054 (−2.02)	0.66 (−0.87)	0.88 (−0.16)	0.72 (−0.36)
Central	0.83 (−0.77)	1.13 (0.43)	0.46 (−2.36)	0.18 (−1.64)	0.91 (−0.072)	0.12 (−1.71)	0.47 (−1.79)	1.20 (0.27)	1.23 (0.28)
Gulf Central	1.99 (2.29)	1.71 (1.42)	0.84 (−0.42)	0.22 (−1.24)	0.91 (1.16)	0.12 (−1.44)	0.44 (−1.58)	2.20 (0.99)	0.97 (−0.031)
% local labor market female	0.88 (−0.082)	1.06 (0.03)	0.0083 (−2.09)	105.28 (1.062)	0.51 (−0.14)	0.12 (−1.35)	3.95 (0.49)	0.074 (−0.68)	0.0006 (−1.53)
City size	1.0 (−0.26)	1.0 (0.56)	1.0 (0.96)	0.99 (−1.24)	1.0 (0.11)	0.99 (−1.35)	0.99 (−0.83)	1.0 (0.97)	1.0 (1.24)
Search									
Spouse was an informal entrepreneur	1.6 (2.68)	1.44 (1.68)	1.1 (0.43)	—	—	—	1.06 (0.33)	0.94 (−0.14)	1.96 (1.43)
Spouse was informal wage	0.96 (−0.19)	1.55 (0.40)	0.95 (−0.18)	—	—	—	1.15 (0.25)	0.85 (−0.22)	2.92 (1.48)
Spouse was formal wage	0.99 (−0.086)	1.05 (0.23)	0.86 (0.20)	—	—	—	0.96 (−0.15)	0.51 (−1.33)	1.24 (0.39)
Spouse was contract	1.01 (0.046)	1.27 (0.89)	0.79 (−0.76)	—[1]	—[1]	—[1]	1.60 (0.68)	1.26 (0.24)	1.74 (0.57)
% self-employed	1.08 (0.079)	0.059 (0.072)	0.018 (−2.81)	3.12 (0.39)	1.95 (0.19)	0.094 (−0.50)	0.26 (−0.72)	0.72 (−0.12)	0.0030 (−1.74)
% formal	0.14 (−3.04)	0.058 (0.046)	0.013 (−4.66)	0.78 (−0.13)	8.19 (18.40)	0.18 (−0.63)	0.18 (−1.53)	1.05 (1.67)	0.03 (−1.82)

(Table continues on the following page.)

115

Table 3.13 (continued)

Pr(exit to formal over)	Wife			Single mother			Husband		
	Informal entrepreneurship	Contract/ piecework	Inf. wage employment	Informal entrepreneurship	Contract/ piecework	Inf. wage employment	Informal entrepreneurship	Inf. wage employment	Contract/ piecework
Sample size			4,060			589		1,778	
Log likelihood			−4,606.74			−603.07		−1,943.42	
Chi²			901.56			170.71		315.04	
(d.o.f.)			(111)			(78)		(102)	

Note: The estimates are from model III, the model that had the best fit. The coefficient values for models I and II differ slightly, but the sign and magnitude of the coefficient estimates are very similar among the three models.

*z = values in parentheses.

—[1] dropped because not relevant for sample.

Maloney's (1999) findings that men's participation in informal entrepreneurship is procyclical. Furthermore, husbands do not appear to
select specific sectors in response to negative employment or income
shocks in the household.

Single mothers are not more likely to enter any particular sector in
response to an increase in risk or family earnings losses, although the
informal wage sector is used to compensate for an unexpected shock to
household employment. Thus, only one subsector of the informal sector
is (marginally) an employer of last resort for single mothers when the
economy is tight since the probability of entry into the formal sector is not
different from entry into informal entrepreneurship or contract work for
this group. This pattern is distinct for wives, indicating that all women do
not use the informal sector in the same way to respond to economic
shocks. Instead, single mothers have patterns that are very distinct from
wives but somewhat similar to husbands.

Household Aids and Impediments to Labor Force Entry

Only wives seem to take into consideration household constraints when
selecting a sector, as shown in Table 3.12. Wives with young children are
more likely to be informal entrepreneurs, but those with school-aged children will enter any of the informal sectors rather than formal wage jobs.
This may be due to the flexible work shifts, convenient location of informal firms, and the ease of using their children in their work. The presence
of teenaged children or adults does not influence sectoral choice one way
or the other, indicating that their labor is not a factor in the sectoral choice
decision.

Others members of the household tend to increase the husband's and
single mother's formal market attachment rather than impede it, as in
the case of wives. The primary breadwinners with young children do not
select any particular sector, and school-aged children actually increase
the probability of the father being in the formal sector rather than in the
informal wage sector. Single mothers with school-aged children have a
propensity for contract work rather than formal sector jobs. Since these
children do not need the intensity of care that their younger siblings do,
they are possibly used as unpaid workers to help supplement family
income in a covert manner. The presence of an adult female in households headed by fathers, and the presence of teenage sons in single-
mother households, decrease the probability of informal entrepreneurship or informal wage employment with respect to formal wage work.
This is due perhaps to their value elsewhere (teenage sons in the wage
labor market, adult women in the household) such that they are not useful in the home firm.

Comparing the sectoral allocations of wives and single mothers demonstrates the importance of household roles, despite gender. If a single mother must enter the labor force to support household income, she does not have the option of selecting lower-paying informal sector jobs, that is, contract or informal wage work, in order to care for children. Instead, she must have other childcare arrangements.

The strength of the marital contract and its implication for future household roles affect contemporaneous sectoral allocation patterns. Women who are married rather than in a consensual union are more likely to participate in piecework than in any other sector, and more likely to enter informal entrepreneurship rather than wage employment. A higher likelihood of entry to nonwage employment may be due to the lower risk of economic hardship provided by the rigid marital contract, an informal source of financing, and/or gender roles. Those in a consensual union do not have a formal contract to guarantee a long-term relationship between the partners, so there is a higher risk that the union will end and the woman will have to support herself. Thus, investment in the formal labor market is as important as investment in the home market since there is a high probability that she may need the labor market skills and connections. In addition, a husband who is married may be more likely to supply his wife with capital for piecework or informal entrepreneurship since he knows his wife's earnings and capital are more likely to benefit him than if the couple were in a weaker consensual union arrangement (Zabludovsky 1998). Finally, the flexibility that piecework offers allows the woman to invest in her job as a housewife while contributing to family income. A change in marital status does not induce entry to any particular sector by husbands.

Personal and Demand Characteristics

Age does not matter for women, but husbands who are older (and therefore have more work experience) are more likely to enter informal entrepreneurship. More educated individuals of both sexes are more likely to enter formal sector work rather than any type of informal work. Household linkages are important for wives because those with an informal entrepreneur husband tend to become an informal entrepreneur as well. This relationship is asymmetric, however, since husbands with informal entrepreneur wives are drawn to any informal sector job. Finally, a higher proportion of formal sector work in the municipality is correlated with formal sector rather than informal sector jobs for wives, and formal rather than contract work for husbands. Single mothers, however, do not integrate into this larger formal market and instead gravitate toward informal wage jobs. Again, city size does not enter significantly.

Conclusion

An analysis of the data shows that labor patterns may be more similar for those with the same role in the household than for those who are of the same sex, implying that it is necessary to take into consideration household structure and the various responsibilities of the household head to better understand labor force entry patterns of primary adults. Of course, gender does affect labor market entry decisions, but our results suggest that it has an indirect effect, entering through constraints imposed by household members, rather than directly, since women who do not have spouses or children to care for behave more similarly to men than they do to married women. In fact, women without a spouse or children are more likely than any other group to be in the higher-paying, inflexible, formal sector jobs, bringing into question whether employers discriminate based on sex or on household role. Married women, on the other hand, have labor force entry and exit patterns that are distinct from other women. They are very responsive to homecare needs and the presence (or absence) of labor income from other household members. While unmarried women are the primary breadwinners, married women are often the social safety net to catch the household when the primary breadwinner cannot fully satisfy the household's needs.

Programs that are designed to ease the difficulties associated with negative income shocks will differ among women with varying household structures. Ignoring these differences such that there is a single program that targets all women will not efficiently aid those in need. Instead, it is important to take into consideration that wives do serve as secondary labor when there is a potential or realized shock to household income, while unmarried women who enter the labor force during such periods are entering not in response to a shock, but in response to other factors. Thus, regardless of the state of the Mexican economy or the income needs of the household, labor market programs such as training in job search methods, job search assistance, and a quality education system will benefit all of Mexico's workers, regardless of their gender or household structure. However, single mothers and wives have additional needs when economic growth stagnates, since their labor is a form of insurance when the risk of a negative shock to income increases, such as during economic downturns or in response to actual falls in household income.[28] Thus, in the short term, they would benefit from unemployment assistance programs (for their husbands), job-matching services, or short-term income-generating opportunities.

The data also show that household composition is important. Although it is well established that wives and mothers are less likely to work than are women without spouses or children, this analysis shows that the arrangement is based on the division of labor in the household. When a woman splits from her partner, she is more likely to work, so there is not something "about" wives that leads them to not work. Instead, it is their household situation that requires them to not work when they do have a partner but to join the labor force when they become the primary breadwinner. Furthermore, the presence of children seems to diminish the labor supply of wives, but not single mothers, so we cannot conclude that children alone lead to lower labor supply. Instead, the sole breadwinning responsibility of the single mother is likely to lead to other childcare arrangements that are a substitute for a "stay-at-home mom." All these factors regarding the structure of the household are very important in the determination of labor supply patterns, so any analysis of and interventions to support individuals in times of economic hardship should use the household, rather than the individual, as the unit of analysis and target.

The sectoral allocation estimates show that the informal entrepreneurship and contract sectors are employers of last resort during economic downturns, but the entry patterns are very specific to household role. In particular, wives use the informal entrepreneurship sector as insurance or as a response to real decreases in household income; that is, entry to informal entrepreneurship is countercyclical, in contrast to Maloney (1997), who finds that for men, it is procyclical. For both men and women, contract work is a form of insurance when the economy slows down. Thus, emergency programs for economic downturns may provide resources to women for self-employment or simply provide unemployment insurance to support consumption levels during the short-term income loss.

Finally, household composition does have an effect on sector of choice. Flexible informal sector jobs seem to be more feasible for women with young children, perhaps because the nature of the work, hours, and location allow mothers to care for their children while also participating in the labor force. More rigid formal sector jobs do not allow this. However, formal sector jobs are higher paying, so policies that would decrease the cost of household care constraints, such as daycare, flexible work hours, and cheap market goods and services to substitute for home-produced goods, would allow higher participation of mothers in the higher-paying formal sector, while still providing the homecare for their families.

Appendix 3.1.

Sampling Design (interview number for each cohort in the cells below the cohort number)

Year	Quarter	Cohort																							
		1	2	3	4	5	6	7	8	9	10	11	12	13	14	15	16	17	18	19	20	21	22	23	24
1987	1	1																							
	2	2	1																						
	3	3	2	1																					
	4	4	3	2	1																				
1988	1	5	4	3	2	1																			
	2		5	4	3	2	1																		
	3			5	4	3	2	1																	
	4				5	4	3	2	1																
1989	1					5	4	3	2	1															
	2						5	4	3	2	1														
	3							5	4	3	2	1													
	4								5	4	3	2	1												
1990	1									5	4	3	2	1											
	2										5	4	3	2	1										
	3											5	4	3	2	1									
	4												5	4	3	2	1								
1991	1													5	4	3	2	1							
	2														5	4	3	2	1						
	3															5	4	3	2	1					
	4																5	4	3	2	1				

(Table continues on the following page.)

Appendix 3.1 (continued)

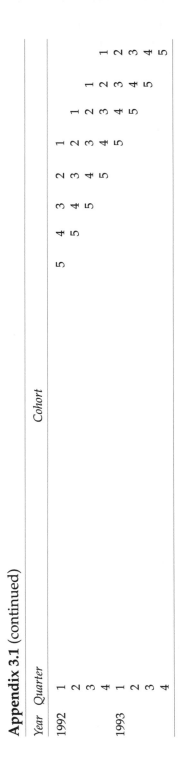

Year	Quarter	Cohort				
1992	1					5
	2				4	5
	3			3	4	5
	4		2	3	4	5
1993	1	1	2	3	4	5
	2	1	2	3	4	5
	3	1	2	3	4	5
	4	1	2	3	4	5

Appendix 3.2
Methodology

Labor Force Participation—Logit

The sample consists of all 24 cohorts. The entry decision is estimated as a probit model, corrected for heteroscedasticity, that estimates the probability of labor force entry of individual i by period 5 conditional on being out of the labor force in period 1:

$$Pr\ (P_{olf->ilf}) = \phi\ [\alpha + X_i\ \beta_1 + (UNEMP)\ \beta_2 + (INVOLF)\ \beta_3 + (HHINV)\ \beta_4$$

$$+ (FALLHHY)\ \beta_5 + (FALLH10)\ \beta_6 + (FALLH25)\ \beta_7 + \qquad\qquad (A1)$$

$$(FALLH50)\ \beta_8 + (FALLH75)\ \beta_9 + (FALLH100)\ \beta_{10} + \varepsilon]$$

where ϕ is the normal distribution function, X_i is a vector of control variables for individual i, UNEMP is the unemployment rate in each cohort's first period, INVOLF is a dummy that takes a value of 1 if the spouse involuntarily left his or her last job over the five periods, and HHINV is the number of workers in the household (less the spouse) who involuntarily lost their jobs between periods 1 and 5. FALLHHY is the change in family labor income between periods 1 and 5, net of the head's earnings, and the dummies FALLH10, FALLH25, FALLH50, FALLH75, and FALLH100 take a value of 1 if the fall in household labor income is in the range 1 to 9 percent, 10 to 24 percent, 25 to 49 percent, 50 to 74 percent, and 75 to 100 percent, respectively, and 0 otherwise.

There are three specifications of equation (2). In the first model, the change in income variables (those associated with $\beta_5 - \beta_{10}$) are dropped so we may focus on the impact of unexpected shocks to household *employment*. However, involuntary job losses may not accurately capture an increased need for household income for two reasons. First, the labor market in Latin America may adjust through wages, so a decrease in real wages rather than employment is more likely (Marquez 1994). Second, household members are heterogeneous and thus have different earnings potential, so entry and exit by multiple household members probably affects household income. Thus, model II tests the response of household heads to a fall in *total household labor income less own income* by including the control variables (*X*), the unemployment rate (*UNEMP*), and the change in the household income variable (*FALLHHY*). To account for nonlinearities in the continuous variable *FALLHHY*, the third model drops all variables except the control variables, the unemployment rate, and the five dummies that identify the magnitude of the income fall to identify the labor supply responses to different *levels of household labor income* decreases. If an added worker effect exists, we expect a positive coefficient on each of the independent variables that are not included in vector *X*.

The control variables include characteristics that would influence the reservation wage and expected market wage through household structure, labor demand variables, and productivity indicators. Each is described and their reasons for inclusion are stated in Table 3.7.

Sector of Participation—Multinomial Logit

To identify which sector workers enter, only those household heads who were OLF in period 1 and became employed by period 5 are included in the sample (4,060 wives, 589 husbands, and 1,778 single mothers). The sample size of unmarried individuals without children was not large enough to estimate sectoral choice. A multinomial logit framework is employed where the sector of exit may be formal wage, informal wage, informal entrepreneurship, or subcontracting. The same independent variables as above will be used.

Appendix 3.3
Labor Force Exit Estimates

(Dependent variable = 1 if the individual exited the labor
force by period 5)

| | Women | | | Men | |
	Wife	Single mother	Unmarried, no kids	Husbands	Unmarried
Model I					
Unemployment rate	−0.34* (0.057)	−0.35* (0.11)	−0.46 (0.35)	0.19* (0.069)	0.1 (0.21)
Fall household income	−1.76×10⁻⁶ (4.65×10⁻⁷)	−8.68×10⁻⁶ (1.75×10⁻⁶)	3.85×10⁻⁶ (9.01×10⁻⁶)	2.61×10⁻⁶ (8.04×10⁻⁷)	−3.95×10⁻⁶ (4.59×10⁻⁶)
Model II					
Unemployment rate	−0.34* (0.057)	−0.34* (0.11)	−0.44 (0.36)	0.19* (0.069)	0.088 (0.22)
% fall household Y:					
1 to 9%	−0.31* (0.081)	−0.19 (0.22)	2.2** (0.79)	−0.13 (0.13)	−1.51* (0.76)
10 to 24%	−0.24* (0.064)	−0.22 (0.16)	−0.83 (1.18)	−0.028 (0.098)	−0.61 (0.42)
25 to 49%	−0.41* (0.05)	−0.29* (0.12)	−0.21 (0.67)	−0.14 (0.078)	−0.7* (0.31)
50 to 74%	−0.52* (0.054)	−0.56* (0.14)	0.42 (0.61)	−0.19* (0.077)	−0.23 (0.28)
75 to 100%	−0.41* (0.062)	−0.57* (0.1)	0.76 (0.45)	−0.3* (0.066)	−0.68* (0.21)
Sample size	14,916	6,100	990	56,402	3,396

*Significant at the 5 percent level.
**Significant at the 1 percent level.

Notes

1. Changes in household structure are also controlled for, but due to the complicated endogenous nature of their relationship with labor supply, they are not treated in detail.

2. Urban areas are defined by the statistical agency (INEGI) as cities with 100,000 or more inhabitants. This covers approximately 45 percent of the Mexican population.

3. The use of children to smooth consumption in such periods is examined in Cunningham and Maloney (2000).

4. Wives with children and without children were analyzed as separate groups, but their behaviors are so similar that they were joined together in the same group for this analysis.

5. Single men could not be disaggregated into a "single father" and a "single men without children" category because the data do not specify the fatherhood of the children in the household. This information is recorded only for motherhood.

6. For a formal presentation of the standard theory, see, for example, Khandker (1988).

7. Recently these theories have been criticized in favor of bargaining models (Pollack 1994) that assume that all members simultaneously make their market and home labor allocation decisions based on their own utility function and the expected behavior of other family members. Since we are not concerned with intrahousehold bargaining, and work in developing countries (Haddad and Hoddinott 1997; Pradhan and Van Soest 1997) suggests that a Mincer/Becker model is still appropriate, we will use the traditional model.

8. Although the added worker effect is theoretically a sound idea, it has not been strongly supported by empirical evidence. Heckman and McCurdy (1982) and Lundberg (1985) find that there is an added worker effect for certain groups of people, but it is very small. On the other hand, Layard (1980) and Maloney (1987, 1991) do not find any evidence of an added worker effect. Gruber and Cullen (1996) suggest that the absence of an added worker effect in the above studies is expected, since the data are drawn from universes with unemployment insurance programs that dampen the need for substitute labor and decrease the likelihood that secondary workers will enter the labor force. Mexico does not have such an income support program.

9. For example, cohort 11 entered the sample in the third period of 1989, was interviewed in the forth period of 1989 and the first three periods of 1990, then dropped from the sample.

10. An individual may be selected into the data set in any of the four quarters each year, so "period 1" for cohort x is the first period that the cohort is selected into the survey. It is not a chronological term referring to the first period of a calendar year.

11. Traditional theories suggest that the presence of various sectors are characteristic of a segmented labor market where institutional barriers such as minimum wage laws (Stiglitz 1986), unions, or employment quotas force up labor costs and lead to an excess supply of labor at the offered wage. An alternative hypothesis (Hart 1972) does not view the labor markets as segmented, but instead recognizes that they are well integrated and the different sectors reveal the heterogeneity of work preferences of the labor force.

12. Maloney (1999) finds a very high correlation between firm size and firm registration with the authorities. Thus, only the firm size criterion will be used, particularly since workers are more likely to know the general size of the firm that they work for than if their employer is registered with the Finance Ministry.

13. Defined as *"trabajador a sueldo fijo, salario o jornal"* in question 3a of the ENEU.

14. Derived from question q7d in the ENEU.

15. It may be argued that contract work should be subsumed in the informal wage category (Beneria 1989). However, Maloney (1997) shows that although participation patterns in the contract and informal wage sectors move together, wages in the contract sector behave similarly to those in the informal entrepreneurship sector. Thus, contract work lies between the informal wage and informal entrepreneurship sector and should be its own category.

16. Using 24 ENEU quarterly cohorts for 1987–93, the sample consists of 77,192 couple-headed households, 13,787 households headed by unmarried women with children, 1,997 households headed by unmarried women without children, and 4,021 households with unmarried men as the head.

17. Since a large number of wives are OFL, the EAP allows us to compare proportions more accurately. The EAP sample sizes are 18,766 wives, 7,066 single mothers, 1,383 unmarried women without children, 72,496 husbands, and 3,497 men without spouses.

18. The benefits associated with formal sector jobs are estimated to increase the wage bill by 80 percent (Marquez 1994).

19. This argument does not prove that there is not discrimination against women in formal employment, because women who prefer formal sector jobs may be discriminated against in the hiring and drop out of the labor force.

20. Although the period of analysis is "summer" in Mexico, when children may be out of school and available to substitute for parents' market labor, the participation rates were nearly identical to the transition probabilities for the cohorts that entered the sample in the *second* quarter of the year. Thus, any substitution between adult and child labor does not emerge in these statistics.

21. Letting P_j represent the count of individuals OLF in period 1, and P_{jk} represent the count of individuals who moved from OLF to sector k by period 5, the conditional probability is calculated as:

$$Pr\ (sector\ k\ in\ period\ 5\ |\ OLF\ in\ period\ 1) = P_{jk} / P_j.$$

22. The error terms from a labor force entry model have a discrete rather than a normal or a logistic distribution, requiring a program is not readily available in the standard computer software econometric packages.

23. The exercise is repeated to test for the probability of labor force exit, rather than entry. This highlights the symmetry of entry and exit patterns. Thus, only those who were in the labor force in the first period are in the sample. Results are presented in Appendix 3.3.

24. We tried to include in the model an interactive term for husband's job loss and a business cycle downturn, but the interactive term and the job loss dummy were highly correlated.

25. The results are quite symmetric. The labor force exit trends of wives are even more sensitive to a change in income since wives do not exit if there is a fall in household income of any magnitude. The labor force exit of single mothers falls if the negative shock to household income exceeds 50 percent, similar to her entry decisions (Appendix 3.3). The labor force exit of husbands is less likely with large falls in household income. The increased probability of exit during downturns is likely due to older men being forced out of their jobs and collecting pensions, rather than searching for new employment in the tighter economy. The results for unmarried men and women are mixed and may be poorly estimated due to the small sample size.

26. The newborn variable may be endogenous since the decision to bear a child and the labor force participation decision may be realizations of the same factors. If a woman has low work potential, the opportunity cost of childbearing is low, so a lower propensity to enter the labor market may exist even if a child is not born. Regardless of whether the child represents a time constraint or low earnings potential, his or her presence decreases the likelihood of labor force entrance for wives. Existing children are exogenous parameters, so we do not need to be concerned with a biased estimator.

27. The relative risk ratios are defined such that if the ratio on a variable x for sector j over sector k is larger than 1, then as x increases, the likelihood of exit to sector j relative to sector k increases. This may occur due either to an increase in the numerator (probability of exit to sector j) or a decrease in the denominator (decreased likelihood of exit to sector k).

28. Probit estimates of the probability of moving from ILF to OLF show that wives and single mothers are more likely to exit the labor force when the economy improves, that is, when the unemployment rate falls.

References

Akerloff, George, and Rachel Kranton. 1999. "Economics and Identity." Manuscript.

Ashenfelter, Orley, and R. Layard, eds. 1986. *Handbook of Labor Economics, Vol. I.* New York: Elsevier Science Publishers.

Becker, Gary. 1991. *A Treatise on the Family (Enlarged Edition).* Cambridge, Mass.: Harvard University Press.

Beneria, Lourdes. 1989. "Subcontracting and Employment Dynamics in Mexico City." In Alejandro Portes, Manuel Castells, and Lauren A. Benton, eds., *The Informal Economy: Studies in Advanced and Less Developed Countries.* Baltimore: The Johns Hopkins University Press.

Chant, Sylvia. 1991. *Women and Survival in Mexican Cities: Perspectives on Gender, Labor Markets and Low Income Households.* New York: Manchester University Press.

Cunningham, Wendy, and William Maloney. 1998. *Heterogeneity among Mexico's Micro-Enterprises: An Application of Factor and Cluster Analysis.* Policy Research Working Paper 1999. Washington, D.C.: World Bank.

_____. 2000. "Child Labor and School Attendance in Periods of Economic Volatility." World Bank, Washington, D.C. Draft.

Davila, Enrique. 1997. "Mexico: The Evolution and Reform of the Labor Market." In Sebastian Edwards and Nora Lustig, eds., *Labor Markets in Latin America: Combining Social Protection with Market Flexibility.* Washington, D.C.: The Brookings Institution.

Fleck, Susan. 1983. *The Political Economy of Intrahousehold Resource Allocation: A Non-Cooperative Sequential Move Game.* Unpublished.

Gruber, Jonathan, and Julie Cullen. 1996. "Spousal Labor Supply as Insurance: Does Unemployment Insurance Crowd Out the Added Worker Effect?" Working Paper No. 5608. National Bureau of Economic Research, Cambridge, Mass.

Hart, K. 1972. *Employment, Income and Inequality: A Strategy for Increasing Productive Employment in Kenya.* Geneva: International Labour Office.

Heckman, James, and Thomas McCurdy. 1982. "Corrigendum on a Life Cycle Model of Female Labour Supply." *Review of Economic Studies* 49(49):659–60.

Khandker, Shahidur. 1988. "Determinants of Women's Time Allocation in Rural Bangladesh." *Economic Development and Cultural Change* 37(1):111–26.

Layard, R., M. Barton, and A. Zabalza. 1980. "Married Women's Participation and Hours." *Economica* (47):51–72.

Lundberg, Shelly. 1985. "The Added Worker Effect." *Journal of Labor Economics* 3(1):11–39.

Maloney, Tim. 1987. "Employment Constraints and the Labor Supply of Married Women: A Reexamination of the Added Worker Effect." *The Journal of Human Resources* 22(1):51–61.

_____. 1991. "Unobserved Variables and the Elusive Added Worker Effect." *Economica* 58(230):173–87.

Maloney, William. 1997. *The Structure of Labor Markets in Developing Countries: Time Series Evidence on Competing Views.* Policy Research Working Paper No. 1940. World Bank, Washington, D.C.

_____. 1999. "Does Informality Imply Segmentation in Urban Labor Markets: Evidence from Sectoral Transitions in Mexico." *The World Bank Economic Review* 13(2):275–302.

Marquez, Gustavo. 1994. *Regulación del mercado de trabajo en América Latina.* Chile: CINDE.

Mincer, Jacob. 1962. "Labor Force Participation of Married Women." In H. Greg Lewis, ed., *Aspects of Labor Economics.* Universities National Bureau of Economic Research Conference Series No. 14. Princeton, N.J.: Princeton University Press.

Nakamura, Alice, and Masao Nakamura. 1992. "The Econometrics of Female Labor Supply and Children." *Econometric Reviews* 11(1):1.

Pollack, Robert. 1994. "For Better or Worse: The Roles of Power in Models of Distribution within Marriage." *AER Papers and Proceedings* 84(2):148–52.

Pradham, Menno, and Arthur Van Soest. 1997. "Household Labor Supply in Urban Areas of Bolivia." *Review of Economics and Statistics* 79(2):300–11.

Psacharopoulos, George, and Zafiris Tzannatos. 1992. *Women's Employment and Pay in Latin America: Overview and Methodology.* Washington, D.C.: World Bank.

Ros, Jaime. 1996. "Prospects for Growth and the Environment in Mexico in the 1990s." *World Development* 24(2):307–23.

Smith, James P. 1983. *Female Labor Supply: Theory and Estimation.* Princeton, N.J.: Princeton University Press.

Standing, Guy. 1989. "Global Feminization through Flexible Labor." *World Development* 17(7):1077–96.

Stiglitz, J. E. 1986. "Alternative Theories of Wage Determination and Unemployment in LDCs: The Labor Turnover Model." *Quarterly Journal of Economics* 88:194–227.

Thomas, J. J. 1992. *Informal Economic Activity*. Ann Arbor: University of Michigan Press.

Valletta, Robert G. 1993. "Union Effects on Municipal Employment and Wages: A Longitudinal Approach." *Journal of Labour Economics* 11(3).

Zabludovsky, Gina. 1998. "Women Business Owners in Mexico: An Emerging Economic Force." National Foundation for Women Business Owners, Washington, D.C.

4

A Gender Perspective on *Maquila* Employment and Wages in Mexico

Susan Fleck

The labor force participation of both women and men in Mexico has risen over the past 25 years—from 33.1 percent in 1973 to 36.9 percent in 1998 for women, and from 74.6 percent to 78.7 percent for men (Fleck and Sorrentino 1994; INEGI 1999d). Although *maquila* employment for men has increased significantly more than for women in recent years, more women than men continue to work in the *maquila* export industry.[1] The *maquila* program—assembly manufacturing for export—was initiated in 1965, in part to replace lost employment opportunities due to the termination of the *bracero* program (Castillo and Ramírez Acosta 1992). Whereas the *bracero* program exported men as temporary workers to the United States from 1943 to 1964,[2] the *maquila* program started off by employing predominantly young, single women in the northern border area of Mexico (MacLachlan and Aguilar 1998). In some border areas today, married men now represent a majority of *maquila* workers. As the *maquila* export industry becomes an increasingly important segment of the Mexican economy, with *maquila* employment recently topping 1 million, men hold a minority—but ever-increasing—share of employment nationwide.

The feminization of labor has been a characteristic of free-trade zones and export-led growth strategies. On one hand, economic need and family responsibility push women into the labor force. On the other hand, possibilities of increased autonomy and bargaining position in the household, greater employment opportunities, and access to wage and non-wage benefits attract women to the labor force, outweighing costs of transportation, childcare, and other opportunity costs. An increasing proportion of men has been attracted to the work in Mexican *maquiladora* plants because they offer relatively better pay and benefits, as well as steady hours and free time on weekends, compared to other jobs (Catanzarite and Strober 1993; Sargent and Matthews 1999; Standing 1999; Tiano 1994; Wilson 1992).

The author's views do not necessarily reflect the views or opinions of the Bureau of Labor Statistics.

The transformation of Mexico's *maquila* program, begun more than 30 years ago, with its ever-decreasing limitations on location of production, type of production, and ownership of plants, has changed the type of employer, the skills required for work, and the overall attractiveness of the *maquila* labor market. The mature *maquila* program today has characteristics distinctly different from its predecessor.

The *maquila* workforce remains young, but has become increasingly male and is less likely to be single. Many of these young people come in search of better opportunities than those found in the rural areas from which they migrate (see Chapter 7, this volume). Even though some of these workers are relatively better off earning *maquila* manufacturing wages, they earn a wage that has not kept up with inflation. Options in the labor market entice workers to rotate among firms or to find other jobs besides assembly work.[3] Options in the marriage market and social expectations of married women to stay in or close to the household have in the past led women to take part-time jobs, create home-based self-employment, or opt out of the labor force altogether (Anderson and Dimon 1998). However, the share of the population under age 12 has been declining nationally, potentially freeing up women's time previously dedicated to childcare. This trend coincides with the rising labor force participation rate of nonsingle women; these are also the women who have increased their share of employment among *maquila* firms in the 1990s, according to household survey data.

The characteristics of firms have changed over time as well. Firm size has grown significantly, multinational corporations are more prevalent, and many plants are relocating to smaller, less urban, nonborder areas in search of better-educated workers and lower turnover rates (MacLachlan and Aguilar 1998; Wilson 1992). Firms with little capital base are likely to compete on a labor cost advantage, searching for the cheapest workers to engage in tasks requiring little technical skill. Advanced technology multinational firms are likely to have more sophisticated human resource policies that try to retain workers, provide training, and offer internal job ladders to promote good workers (Sargent and Matthews 1997). In either case, foreign employers maintain a significant cost advantage by locating production in Mexico compared to developed countries.

Reasons behind the phenomenon of defeminization are numerous. On one hand, employers hire relatively more men every year. The literature suggests four reasons. First, employers perceive a reduced militancy of male workers (Kopinak 1995b; Sklair 1993). Second, there has been a growth in the presence of multinational firms and a shift in the perception of employers of the ideal worker from young single women to responsible family men and women (Kopinak 1995b; Stoddard 1987; Tiano 1994). Third, industries that traditionally had a greater share of men have been expanding (Catanzarite and Strober 1993). Fourth, the skewed female–male employment ratio has decreased over time in all industries (Jiménez Betancourt 1989).

On the other hand, relatively more men are looking for work in *maquiladora* plants. Some possible reasons for this are (a) wage convergence between other manufacturing jobs and *maquila* jobs; (b) decline in domestic manufacturing employment as a result of economic crisis; (c) women's self-selection bias away from the growth industries of the *maquiladora* plants; and (d) a gender division of labor that limits women's labor force participation, especially of married women (Anderson and Dimon 1998; Chapter 3, this volume).

The data analyzed in this chapter confirm the growth of multinationals, the increased importance of industries with more male workers, decreasing sex segregation of employment by industry, wage convergence between *maquila* and national manufacturing, and married women's increasing, but still low, labor force participation rate. This chapter notes three additional trends in the 1990s. First, an interindustry wage gap persists and is strongly correlated with industry characteristics, including the gender composition of the workforce. Second, a gender wage gap exists within industries. Third, the defeminization of *maquila* employment since the program's inception appears to be due to a labor supply constraint based on a rising female labor force participation rate that is nonetheless outpaced by the speed at which the sector is growing. The inability of women's participation to meet growing demand begs further investigation into the choices and constraints that affect a woman's decision to participate in the labor force.

Revisions in industry classification and lack of disaggregated data limit data analysis of establishments for years prior to 1980; from 1980 forward, data on the characteristics of employment, plant size, and hourly earnings by region and sex are available for most industries.[4] Improved labor force survey coverage of border cities with *maquila* activity made 1991 the best year from which to develop the comparative analysis of *maquila* and non-*maquila* employed. Economic and demographic data from the labor force survey were tabulated and provided by Mexico's *Instituto Nacional de Estadística, Geografía, e Informática* (INEGI) for 1991 and 1997 for the border cities covered by the *Encuesta Nacional de Empleo*.

This chapter first compares national and *maquila* hourly earnings, compensation, minimum wage, and employment from the 1970s, then analyzes three years of establishment data—1980, 1990, and 1998—to identify the major shifts within the *maquila* industry over time. Next, the significance of industry characteristics on the interindustry wage gap during 1991–98 is tested in a least squares regression. More detailed establishment data for 1997–98 are used to describe the gender wage gap and test for the significance of industry variables on the gender wage differential. Finally, the labor force survey data for border cities highlight the changes in the average characteristics of the *maquila* labor force in the 1990s and show how defeminization is partially a labor supply phenomenon.

Historical Changes in the *Maquila* Industries

National Comparisons

In a few years' time, the *maquila* export promotion program will be folded into the North American Free Trade Agreement (NAFTA) with the United States and Canada. Mexico will apply *maquila*-type tax incentives to all U.S. and Canadian imports and exports,[5] and *maquiladora* plants will be more like other Mexican manufacturing industries.[6] The small beginnings of an employment-generating border development plan have grown into an important source of Mexican export revenue in an export-led regime (Gambrill 1995). Since 1994, *maquiladora* plants have contributed between 38 percent (1996) and 45 percent (1998) of the value of all Mexican exports (INEGI 1999a).

Maquiladora plants had a minimal impact on employment in their initial years, but their importance has increased over time. The growth was particularly acute in the years following peso devaluations. In 1975, the devaluation, coupled with the recovery of the U.S. economy, led to an expansion of *maquila* employment. After the 1982 devaluation, as the peso devaluation accelerated in 1986 and after the peso crisis in January 1995, employment in the sector grew dramatically, even though there was a slowdown in the rest of the economy (Arroyo del Muro 1997; Sklair 1993; Figures 4.1 and 4.2).

Just as employment growth in *maquiladora* plants is countercyclical to trends in the value of the peso and the growth of the overall economy, so is the trend in hourly earnings, nonwage labor costs, and hourly compensation. In the past 20 years, this countercyclical tendency has been accompanied by faster average annual growth of *maquila* hourly earnings and labor costs relative to national manufacturing, thus contributing to wage convergence. (See Chapter 3 for a discussion of economic growth.)

As can be seen in Table 4.1, the annual growth rate of manufacturing hourly earnings in *maquiladora* plants for production-line workers was greater than that of national manufacturing for all wage workers from 1980 to 1988. This paralleled a period of slow recovery from a recession.[7] Relatively slower growth of *maquila* hourly earnings in the early 1990s paralleled a period of positive growth in the national economy. With the signing of NAFTA in 1994, *maquila* hourly earnings' growth outpaced that

Figure 4.1 Border Employment by Gender and Industry, Production Workers 1980–98

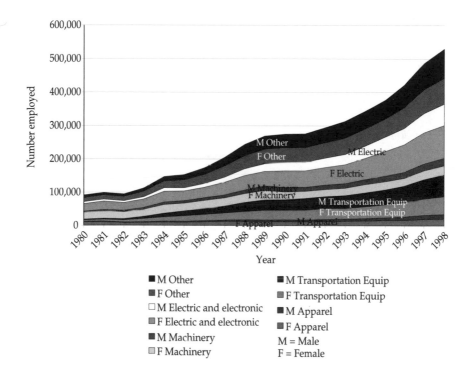

of national manufacturing again; this faster growth of hourly earnings has continued, particularly with the national recession that followed the peso crisis of January 1995.

The nonwage labor costs as a share of hourly earnings in *maquiladora* plants did not even equal one third of hourly earnings in 1980 (28.3 percent), but peaked to nearly one half of hourly earnings by 1996 (49.8 percent). Nonwage labor costs are contributions paid to the state (for items such as social security) and other nonwage benefits provided directly to workers, such as housing and work clothes. These labor costs, representing nonwage benefits, fluctuated around one third of hourly earnings through 1988, but rose dramatically in the early 1990s as multinational firms invested more and labor supply in border areas tightened. In national manufacturing, the labor costs reflect business cycle fluctuations, declining after 1983, recovering in the early 1990s, and falling again after 1995.

Figure 4.2 Nonborder Employment by Gender and Industry, Production Workers 1980–98

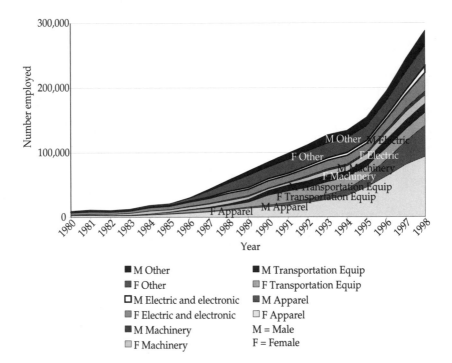

In the *maquila* export program, hourly compensation of production-line workers—estimated as hourly earnings of production-line workers and hourly nonwage labor costs paid by the employer[8]—followed the hourly earnings trends and reached 85 percent of national manufacturing hourly compensation in 1997. Hourly compensation of all wage workers in *maquiladora* plants was actually higher than national manufacturing compensation since 1997, the first year in which wage and hour data were collected for all wage and salary *maquila* employees.

Over the past two decades, *maquila* manufacturing hourly earnings and nonwage labor costs have risen relatively more than manufacturing nationally, causing wage convergence. The closing gap in wages between the two sectors reflects tighter regional labor markets, changes in the *maquila* industry composition, and a relatively greater decline in real hourly earnings in national manufacturing.

The positive picture of *maquila* employment growth and relative improvement in wages is offset by the reality of declining real wages.

Table 4.1 Mexican Manufacturing: Hourly Earnings and Compensation Costs of Wage Workers, in Current Pesos, and Nonwage Labor Costs as Percent of Earnings 1980–98

| | National manufacturing | | | Maquila manufacturing[1] | | | | |
| | All employees | All wage workers | | All employees | All wage workers | | Production-line workers | |
Year	Nonwage labor costs[2] (in percent)	Hourly earnings	Hourly compensation[3]	Nonwage labor costs[2] (in per-ent)	Hourly earnings	Hourly compensation[3]	Hourly earnings	Hourly compensation[3]
1980	33.5	38	51	28.3	—	—	25	32
1981	35.7	51	69	28.6	—	—	32	41
1982	37.2	81	111	30.1	—	—	53	69
1983	41.7	120	170	29.8	—	—	84	109
1984	37.9	190	262	29.7	—	—	136	176
1985	36.7	299	409	29.0	—	—	214	276
1986	37.5	485	667	30.9	—	—	374	490
1987	34.4	1,069	1,437	31.8	—	—	845	1,114
1988	35.8	2,087	2,834	32.9	—	—	1,684	2,238
1989	39.3	2,526	3,509	40.1	—	—	2,024	2,836
1990	39.2	3,190	4,440	41.8	—	—	2,496	3,539
1991	39.7	3,966	5,541	43.5	—	—	3,057	4,387
1992	40.0	4,797	6,716	47.1	—	—	3,432	5,048
1993[4]	41.2	5.30	7.48	46.3	—	—	3.78	5.53
1994	42.0	5.87	8.34	47.5	—	—	4.16	6.14
1995	43.6	6.75	9.69	47.6	—	—	5.08	7.50
1996	41.2	8.27	11.68	49.8	—	—	6.18	9.26

(Table continues on the following page.)

Table 4.1 (continued)

	National manufacturing			Maquila manufacturing[1]				
	All employees			All employees				
		All wage workers			All wage workers		Production-line workers	
Year	Nonwage labor costs[2] (in percent)	Hourly earnings	Hourly compensation[3]	Nonwage labor costs[2] (in percent)	Hourly earnings	Hourly compensation[3]	Hourly earnings	Hourly compensation[3]
1997	40.1	10.08	14.12	48.0	9.71	14.37	8.08	11.96
1998	39.6	12.02	16.78	47.3	11.70	17.23	9.68	14.26

— Data not available.

1. Excludes *maquila* services.

2. Nonwage labor costs include costs to the employer that are not earnings received by the employee. These costs include direct and indirect benefits to the employee, payroll taxes, etc.

3. The estimate of hourly compensation costs for all wage workers and production-line workers uses hourly earnings of workers and the ratio of nonwage labor costs of all employees.

4. Mexico's currency was converted in January 1993 to new pesos; 1 new peso is equivalent to 1,000 pre-1993 pesos. The new peso was renamed the peso in 1996.

Source: Bureau of Labor Statistics, 1995, 1999, 2000; author's calculations based on BLS and INEGI (1998b and 1998c).

Over the 18-year period studied, wages in *maquiladora* plants were relatively better than the minimum wage (see Table 4.2). As the minimum wage was maintained at a rate below inflation for the past decade (influenced by the *Pacto Social* of the Salinas presidency that began in 1987 and expired under Zedillo's term), *maquila* wages (and national manufacturing wages) rose more quickly than the minimum wage, but more slowly than inflation (Gambrill 1995). *Maquila* production workers' real wages have fallen over time, but have improved relative to the minimum wage. In dollar terms, *maquila* daily earnings in 1998 were roughly equivalent to those of 1980, whereas the minimum wage halved its dollar value over the same period.[9]

The *maquila* sector has been a source of employment, hourly earnings, and benefit growth for many years. Since 1980, *maquila* earnings in dollar

Table 4.2 Mexico: *Maquila* Average Earnings and Legislated Minimum Wages, Daily Rates, in Current and Constant Pesos and U.S. Dollars (Recent Selected Years)

	Maquila *production workers*			Entire *country*		
	Average *daily earnings*[1]			Average *daily minimum wage*		
Year	(Current pesos)[2]	(1994 pesos)	(U.S. dollars)[3]	(Current pesos)[2]	(1994 pesos)	(U.S. dollars)[3]
1980	0.20	51.20	8.92	0.14	35.25	6.14
1985	1.71	40.02	6.67	1.04	24.21	4.03
1990	20.00	33.27	7.11	9.41	15.66	3.35
1991	24.37	33.04	8.07	10.95	14.85	3.63
1992	27.30	32.05	8.82	12.08	14.18	3.90
1993	30.16	32.26	9.68	13.06	13.97	4.19
1994	33.20	33.20	9.84	13.97	13.97	4.14
1995	40.56	30.04	6.29	16.43	12.17	2.55
1996	49.36	27.21	6.49	20.41	11.25	2.69
1997	64.64	29.54	8.16	24.30	11.10	3.07
1998	77.36	30.50	8.45	28.32	11.16	3.09

1. Average daily earnings were calculated by estimating average hourly earnings (production worker earnings divided by production worker hours worked) and assuming an eight-hour workday.

2. Mexico's currency was converted in January 1993 to new pesos; 1 new peso is equivalent to 1,000 pre-1993 pesos. The new peso was renamed the peso in 1996. All figures in 1996 currency units.

3. Before 1995, converted using IMF annual average of monthly exchange rate; for 1995 and later, converted using Federal Reserve annual average of daily exchange rate.

Source: Author's calculations based on INEGI 1991b, 1994b, 1998b, 1998c, 1999c; IMF 1996, 1987; US 1999a; Fleck and Sorrentino 1994, Table 10, p. 25.

terms have fluctuated within a narrow margin, never rising above US$10 a day. The greater importance of *maquiladora* plants as a source of manufacturing employment, the expansion of geographic coverage, and the increasing share of male employment highlight how the export program has become integrated into the national economy, but remains an important source of countercyclical growth.

As the importance of *maquiladora* plants has grown over the past three decades, three significant trends have occurred in *maquila* employment: (a) overall *maquila* employment has become an increasingly significant part of manufacturing employment, (b) the share of employment generated by *maquiladora* plants along the border has fallen, and (c) the percentage of female employment has fallen as the total number of men and women employed in *maquiladora* plants has risen (see Table 4.3).

First, *maquila* employment was just over one half of 1 percent of total employment in 1979. By 1998, 2.6 percent of all employed worked in *maquiladora* plants; these workers made up 14.6 percent of manufacturing employees. Beginning in the 1980s, previously protected domestic industries became subject to competitive pressures, reducing employment opportunities in domestic manufacturing (López 1999). The recessions of 1982–83 and 1995, and economic slowdowns in 1988 and 1993, contributed to the restricted growth of domestic manufacturing and the expansion of *maquila* manufacturing (Aguayo Ayala 1998; Arroyo del Muro 1997).

Second, there has been a significant shift in the location of *maquila* industries away from the border. When the program started, most *maquiladora* plants were built along the border with the United States. A number of factors have contributed to the movement of firms and employment away from the border. Relatively lower wages, less competitive labor markets, better living conditions, loosening restrictions on location of firms, and changing regulations that allow an increasing portion of sales to domestic markets have all influenced firms to move toward the interior (Salomón 1998; Sklair 1993; Wilson 1992). In 1998 the portion of firms located in border areas had fallen to 62.2 percent, and 64.8 percent of employment was in border areas. This compares to 88.9 percent of firms and 90.7 percent of employment along the border in 1979 (INEGI 1991b, 1998c).

Third, growth of both women's and men's employment has been vigorous, even as employment is increasingly male. From a total of nearly 74,000 female production workers representing 77.1 percent of *maquila* workers in 1979, six times that number of women were employed in 1998. By 1998, men's employment had grown 16 times the 1979 level to 354,000 workers. Men were 43 percent of *maquila* production workers in 1998.

Table 4.3 Mexico: Number of Employed Persons, by Selected Industry Characteristics, 1967, 1970, 1975, 1980–98

	Entire economy Total		Manufacturing		Maquiladora plants[1] All employees				Production-line workers		
Year	Total	Percent female	Total	Percent female	Total	Percent of entire economy	Percent of manufac-turing	Percent female	Total	Percent female	Percent border region
1967	—	—	—	—	4,000	—	—	—	—	—	—
1970	—	—	—	—	20,327	—	—	—	—	—	—
1975	—	—	—	—	67,214	—	—	—	57,850	78.2	92.6[2]
1979	19,177,000	—	—	—	111,365	0.6	—	—	95,818	77.1	90.7
1980	—	—	—	—	118,546	—	—	—	101,020	77.1	90.4
1981	—	—	—	—	130,973	—	—	—	110,684	77.4	89.4
1982	—	—	—	—	127,048	—	—	—	105,383	77.2	89.6
1983	—	—	—	—	150,867	—	—	—	125,278	74.5	89.8
1984	—	—	—	—	199,684	—	—	—	165,505	70.9	88.8
1985	—	—	—	—	211,968	—	—	—	173,874	69.0	87.9
1986	—	—	—	—	249,833	—	—	—	203,894	68.2	85.1
1987	—	—	—	—	308,253	—	—	—	248,638	66.0	82.5
1988	28,128,000	—	5,547,936	—	369,489	1.3	6.7	—	301,379	63.2	80.8
1989	—	—	—	—	418,533	—	—	—	340,508	61.6	79.0
1990	—	—	—	—	446,436	—	—	—	360,358	60.9	76.3

(Table continues on the following page.)

143

Table 4.3 (continued)

	Entire economy		Manufacturing		Maquiladora plants [1]						
					All employees				Production-line workers		
Year	Total	Percent female	Total	Percent female	Total	Percent female	Percent of entire economy	Percent of manufacturing	Total	Percent female	Percent border region
1991	30,534,083	34.8	4,805,943	—	467,352	—	1.5	9.7	374,827	60.3	73.6
1992	—	—	—	—	505,698	—	—	—	406,879	60.4	72.4
1993	32,833,000	33.6	5,077,678	—	542,074	—	1.7	10.7	440,683	59.5	71.1
1994	—	—	—	—	583,045	—	—	—	477,032	59.5	71.9
1995	33,881,068	30.2	5,066,909	—	648,263	—	1.9	12.8	531,729	59.1	70.9
1996	35,226,036	33.8	5,721,717	—	749,857	—	2.1	13.1	612,069	57.7	68.9
1997	37,359,758	36.2	6,176,525	—	898,785	53.1	2.4	14.6	731,470	57.7	66.6
1998	38,617,511	36.2	6,921,601	—	1,008,032	52.1	2.6	14.6	817,877	56.6	64.8

— Data not available.

1. Maquila program includes some services.

2. Based on employment data by municipality, which slightly undercounts border employment.

Source: Fleck and Sorrentino 1994, Tables 3 and 4; INEGI 1988, 1989, 1991a, 1993, 1994a, 1994b, 1996, 1997a, 1998a, 1998b, 1998c, 1999d; Sklair, 1993.

Industry-Level Trends

To understand the changing face of the *maquila* program, this section presents a three-year historical snapshot of the trends in employment, plant number and size, and hourly earnings by industry and region.

The major shift in employment is that women's share of production-worker employment in all *maquiladora* plants has fallen steadily from 77 percent in 1980 to 57 percent in 1998, even as overall employment opportunities in *maquiladora* plants mushroomed. More significantly, women's share of all wage and salary employment in *maquiladora* plants was less than half—48.3 percent—in border areas in 1998. Table 4.4 and Figures 4.1 and 4.2 provide a descriptive background on the shifts in the gender composition of production-worker employment by industry and region since 1980.

The reduction in female employment in all *maquila* industries is influenced by a number of factors. First, the importance of sectors with greater shares of male workers has grown. These sectors have maintained their below-average share of female workers, despite the reduction in the relative disparity in the male–female employment ratio. Most significant of these is transportation equipment, whose share of all *maquila* workers grew from 6.2 percent in 1980 to 18.7 percent in 1998. Second, women's share of employment within each industry has been lower on average in border *maquiladora* plants, which continue to comprise the majority of employment, compared to nonborder *maquiladora* plants. The third factor is the continually declining share of women's employment among the *maquila* sectors that were overwhelmingly female in 1980. The reasons for this decline, arguably, are due to constraints on women's labor supply and a low, yet rising, women's labor force participation.

Figures 4.1 and 4.2 clearly illustrate the growth in men's and women's employment, the expansion of men's employment by region over the complete time period, and the spikes in employment after the 1982 and 1995 devaluations. One can see the ever-increasing importance of the transportation equipment industry along the border and the dominance of apparel and textile production in the nonborder *maquiladora* plants.[10] The sharp rise in nonborder employment in Figure 4.2 tracks the growth of the nonborder region's significance in *maquila* employment, particularly after NAFTA lifted restrictions on Mexican textile imports to the United States, and on the heels of the 1995 peso devaluation.

The primary factor to consider in expansion of plant number and size is the growing importance of multinational corporations and the increasing capital intensity of production. This historical snapshot of *maquila*

Table 4.4 Mexican *Maquila* Manufacturing and Services; Production-Line Worker Employment and Female Share, by Industry and Region, 1980, 1990, 1998

| | 1980 | | | | | | 1990 | | | | | | 1998 | | | | | |
| | Total | | Border | | Nonborder | | Total | | Border | | Nonborder | | Total | | Border | | Nonborder | |
Industry category[1]	No. of workers	Percent women	No. of workers	Percent women	No. of workers	Percent women	No. of workers	Percent women	No. of workers	Percent women	No. of workers	Percent women	No. of workers	Percent women	No. of workers	Percent women	No. of workers	Percent women
Total	101,020	77	91,308	77	9,712	83	360,358	61	274,909	57	85,449	73	817,877	57	529,732	52	288,145	64
Food	1,260	74	1,260	74	—	—	6,725	61	3,205	60	3,520	62	10,002	56	4,102	40	5,900	67
Apparel	15,736	84	12,771	83	2,965	88	36,107	76	17,453	66	18,654	85	175,266	65	34,116	60	141,150	66
Footwear	1,571	48	1,355	48	216	49	5,990	53	5,037	56	953	38	7,772	55	5,499	52	2,273	64
Furniture	2,839	13	2,779	13	60	0	19,838	29	18,695	28	1,143	48	39,670	26	34,540	27	5,130	22
Chemicals	66	30	66	30	—	—	5,536	53	4,842	54	694	50	16,124	55	13,628	55	2,497	53
Transportation	6,310	68	5,981	67	329	88	82,987	53	60,606	47	22,381	67	152,793	48	118,815	45	33,978	59
Assembly of tools	1,541	32	1,541	32	(1)	(1)	4,051	39	3,935	36	116	22	8,583	33	7,839	36	745	2
Machinery	24,879	86	24,000	85	879	92	40,810	63	36,784	63	4,026	65	69,436	58	50,407	55	19,028	66
Electric	32,272	80	28,393	80	3,879	79	89,734	68	75,410	66	14,324	76	200,739	63	162,251	61	38,488	74
Toys	2,517	86	2,517	86	(1)	(1)	8,348	66	7,972	67	376	63	11,271	49	10,256	48	1,015	59
Other	6,525	60	6,250	61	275	44	39,968	60	28,139	58	11,829	64	92,504	54	64,201	52	28,303	58
Services	5,504	88	4,395	87	1,109	92	20,264	75	12,831	67	7,433	88	33,716	64	24,078	62	9,638	67

— Data are available for border areas only.

[1] The 13 categories are: Total manufacturing & services; Food & related products; Apparel & other textile products; Footwear & leather products; Furniture & fixtures; Chemicals & chemical products; Transportation equipment; Assembly of tools, equipment, & parts, excl. electric; Machinery & equipment, & electric & electronic articles; Electric & electronic materials & accessories; Toys & sporting goods; Other manufacturing; Services.

Source: Author's calculations based on INEGI 1991b, 1994b, 1998c.

establishments not only shows the effect of changes in legislation on plant number and size, but also reveals the importance of the restructuring of two industries and the concomitant introduction of technological innovations in the 1980s. First, the U.S. automobile manufacturing industry at that time was facing stiff competition from foreign-made small cars, and in an effort to cut costs, the large U.S. automakers moved further south. The Ford Motor Company had established five *maquila* auto parts plants in Mexico by the end of the 1980s, and many other auto parts plants were also formed, primarily with U.S. investment (United Nations 1996). Second, Japanese electronics firms were expanding their presence in the United States and also expanded their investment in *maquila* assembly of electronics inputs to maintain competitiveness (United Nations 1996). Investment in capital-intensive technology accompanied the expansion of these two sectors. Firm size in the transportation equipment industry expanded considerably from 1980 to 1990 and stayed high, and the electronics sector has consistently maintained a large average number of employees (see Table 4.5).

In 1980, the average number of workers per plant, or plant size, was lower than in later years. The number of plants grew more slowly than the number of employees because average plant size grew over the period. Comparing the data on gender composition with that of plant number and size, the plants in 1980 can be classified into two groups. The first group consists of small plants with a large share of male workers, such as furniture, footwear, chemicals, and tool assembly. The others are medium- and large-size plants with a larger share of women workers employed in light assembly. By 1990, plant size had grown significantly, more men were employed in previously female-concentrated *maquiladora* plants, and more women were employed in previously male-concentrated *maquiladora* plants. However, smaller plants maintained a relatively greater share of men's employment. By 1998, average plant size had increased in 9 of 12 sectors, while only furniture maintained a high concentration of male workers and a small plant size. The growth of the transportation equipment sector—with the largest plant size and an increasing but still minority share of female workers— redraws the picture of the average plant. This growth was a result of a concerted effort by the *Secretaría de Comercio y Fomento Industrial* (SEC-OFI, the Mexican ministry that administers the *maquila* program) to attract large multinational firms into *maquila* production since the mid-1980s (Sklair 1993).

Two important aspects of changes in *maquila* hourly earnings over the 18 years studied are the significant shift in interindustry wage differentials between 1980 and 1990 and the dampening effect of nonborder wages on average hourly earnings. Box 4.1 examines these factors.

Table 4.5 Mexican *Maquila* Manufacturing and Services; Number of Plants and Average Number of Production-Line Workers per Plant, by Industry and Region, 1980, 1990, 1998

Industry category[1]	1980 Total Plants	1980 Total Avg. no. workers	1980 Border Plants	1980 Border Avg. no. workers	1980 Nonborder Plants	1980 Nonborder Avg. no. workers	1990 Total Plants	1990 Total Avg. no. workers	1990 Border Plants	1990 Border Avg. no. workers	1990 Nonborder Plants	1990 Nonborder Avg. no. workers	1998 Total Plants	1998 Total Avg. no. workers	1998 Border Plants	1998 Border Avg. no. workers	1998 Nonborder Plants	1998 Nonborder Avg. no. workers
Total	620	163	551	166	69	141	1,703	212	1,298	212	405	211	2,983	271	1,857	285	1,127	256
Food	12	105	12	105	—	—	45	149	28	114	17	207	80	125	48	85	32	184
Apparel	117	134	94	136	23	129	276	131	147	119	129	145	837	209	255	134	583	242
Footwear	21	75	18	75	3	72	47	127	38	133	9	106	58	134	37	149	21	108
Furniture	59	48	56	50	3	20	219	91	200	93	19	60	343	116	286	121	57	90
Chemicals	4	17	4	17	—	—	75	74	60	81	15	46	128	126	97	140	31	81
Transportation	53	119	50	120	3	110	155	535	115	527	40	560	209	731	150	792	60	566
Assembly of tools	16	96	16	96	—	—	39	109	33	119	6	54	42	204	34	231	8	93
Machinery	66	377	63	381	3	293	103	396	82	449	21	192	139	500	100	504	39	488
Electric	157	206	137	207	20	194	374	240	317	238	57	251	473	424	386	420	86	448
Toys	21	120	21	120	—	—	32	254	26	307	6	24	59	191	43	239	17	60
Other	63	104	53	118	10	28	264	151	194	145	70	169	447	207	325	198	122	232
Services	31	178	27	163	4	277	78	260	58	221	20	372	169	200	97	248	73	132

— Data are available for border areas only.

[1] The 13 categories are: Total manufacturing & services; Food & related products; Apparel & other textile products; Footwear & leather products; Furniture & fixtures; Chemicals & chemical products; Transportation equipment; Assembly of tools, equipment, & parts, excl. electric ; Machinery & equipment, & electric & electronic articles; Electric & electronic materials & accessories; Toys & sporting goods; Other manufacturing; Services.

Source: Author's calculations based on INEGI 1991b, 1994b, 1998c.

Box 4.1 Interindustry Wage Differentials and the Effect of Nonborder Wages on *Maquila* Hourly Earnings

The shift in the interindustry wage gap over the decade of the 1980s is worth studying, given that differentials are expected to be stable over time (Goux and Maurin 1999). It is likely that the expansion of multinational corporations influenced the shifts in wage differentials from 1980 to 1990. Multinationals pay more than smaller, Mexican-owned plants (Stoddard 1987). Whereas footwear, furniture, and services were well-paid sectors in 1980, relative hourly earnings fell in these sectors throughout the decade. By 1990, the growing sectors of transportation equipment, machinery, and tool assembly became the better-paying sectors and have remained so. In 1998, the sectors with low wages compared to other maquila sectors were food, apparel, and footwear; transport and machinery jobs were relatively better paid.

Table 4.6 compares average hourly earnings, or wages, in *maquiladora* plants by industry and region in U.S. dollars.[11] In 1980, the wage in apparel—the lowest-paid industry—was 80 percent of the wage for footwear and leather products—the highest-paid. Tool assembly had the highest relative wage 10 years later, and apparel and food the lowest, at 59 cents to the dollar. This relative relation from 1990 persisted in 1998, but did not broaden. In the 1990s, only two industries saw relative shifts in the interindustry wage gap; these were in toys (a relative decline) and electrical and electronic equipment (a relative improvement).

The breakdown of *maquila* wages by region shows that, on average, the nonborder region wages are approximately one fourth less than the border region. Within each industry, border plants paid greater wages for the years studied, except for footwear and tool assembly. The nonborder wages as a percentage of border wages fluctuate between 50 and 90 percent, depending on the industry. For footwear, wages were higher for nonborder workers in 1980 and 1990, although they had fallen by 1998. By 1998, wages in assembly of tools and equipment were the same between regions and had shifted from being one of the lowest-wage sectors to being the highest.

Comparing all three characteristics of employment, plant size, and hourly earnings over time and space, one can gain a better understanding of industry changes. In recent years, transportation equipment, machinery, and assembly of tools have been the wage leaders in *maquiladora* plants. The transportation equipment sector has less than 50 percent women workers and larger-than-average plant size, and two and a half times more plants at the border.[12] Machinery has an average share of women workers, larger-than-average plant size, and just more than twice as many plants and employment on the border. Tool assembly has

Table 4.6 Mexican *Maquila* Manufacturing and Services; Production-Line Worker Average Hourly Earnings by Industry and Region, in U.S. dollars, 1980, 1990, 1998

Industry category	1980			1990			1998		
	Total	*Border*	*Nonborder*	*Total*	*Border*	*Nonborder*	*Total*	*Border*	*Nonborder*
Total manufacturing & services	1.12	1.14	0.89	0.89	0.94	0.72	1.06	1.17	0.86
Food & related products	1.10	1.10	(2)	0.71	0.76	0.66	0.81	0.93	0.72
Apparel & other textile products	1.03	1.07	0.83	0.70	0.79	0.62	0.80	1.01	0.75
Footwear & leather products	1.33	1.32	1.34	0.82	0.80	0.91	1.02	1.18	0.67
Furniture & fixtures	1.30	1.31	1.07	0.90	0.91	0.78	1.09	1.10	0.98
Chemicals & chemical products	1.28	1.28	—	0.89	0.91	0.75	1.05	1.08	0.92
Transportation equipment	1.16	1.19	0.64	0.99	1.06	0.77	1.22	1.27	1.05
Assembly of tools, equipment, & parts, excl. electric	1.06	1.06	—	1.20	1.20	1.01	1.39	1.39	1.39
Machinery & equipment, & electric & electronic articles	1.10	1.11	1.06	0.93	0.93	0.87	1.18	1.20	1.13
Electric & electronic materials & accessories	1.09	1.14	0.83	0.86	0.90	0.69	1.11	1.17	0.89
Toys & sporting goods	1.24	1.24	—	1.06	1.08	0.57	1.10	1.16	0.66
Other manufacturing	1.13	1.14	0.99	0.87	0.90	0.80	1.06	1.08	1.01
Services	1.30	1.33	1.19	0.87	0.95	0.73	1.03	1.12	0.82

— Data are available for border areas only.

Note: Before 1995, pesos were converted to dollars using IMF annual average of monthly exchange rate; for 1995 and later, they were converted using Federal Reserve annual average of daily exchange rate.

Source: Author's calculations based on INEGI 1991b, 1994b, 1998c; IMF 1987, 1996; US 1999a.

only 33 percent women and 10 times more workers on the border than in the interior, but it has a smaller-than-average plant size. The transportation equipment and machinery sectors in general represent large multinational companies that want to retain workers and are willing to pay more to entice workers to stay, and also attract more men to their workforce. Assembly of tools—despite below-average plant size—is also a wage leader and has a majority male workforce.

Food and apparel sectors have smaller-than-average plant size, average to higher-than-average share of women, and higher-than-average share of employment in nonborder areas. All of these factors are expected to lower wages. These sectors are not only the lowest paid in border regions, they are even more poorly paid in nonborder regions and have a greater share of women employees. Apparel's dramatic growth since NAFTA has overwhelmed other nonborder *maquila* production.[13]

In summary, this snapshot of the *maquila* industry for 1980, 1990, and 1998 shows that the industry has grown—number of plants, employment, and average number of employees have all had dramatically positive growth. Wage differentials among industries have also shifted over time, but have not widened in recent years. These differences are the focus of the next section.

Interindustry Wage Gap

Most of the literature on the interindustry wage differential considers the differences of hourly earnings between industries on the basis of job and individual worker characteristics and technological change. However, results have also been reported on the effect of firm characteristics on the gap in a given industry (Goux and Maurin 1999). The wealth of industry-level data representing all Mexican *maquiladora* plants allows us to look at the differential from this labor demand perspective, despite the drawbacks associated with excluding worker characteristics. The interindustry wage gap model presented below analyzes the effect of gender composition, location, plant size, capital intensity, and time on hourly earnings between the 12 manufacturing and service industries that comprise *maquiladora* plants.

In a regression analysis of industry-level real average hourly earnings of production-line workers,[14] using data for 1991 to 1998, the five characteristics mentioned above are considered as having a possible effect on the level of hourly earnings for each industry, and thus the interindustry differential. These variables, their definition, and the reason for their consideration are listed below.

- **Female Production-Line Workers as a Share of All Production-Line Workers.** This variable measures the gender composition of the labor force and is calculated as a continuous variable ranging from 0 to 1. It is expected that the female share of employment should be negatively related to hourly earnings levels, due to a gender wage gap that favors male workers (this gap is discussed in the following section). Employers' perceptions that categorize employees as either heads of household (men) or extra workers (women), and as either skilled (men) or unskilled (women), can affect wages offered (Tiano 1994). Perception of workers is complicated by employers' sex preferences. Human capital characteristics may also differ. Combined, these characteristics may not only affect the gender composition of labor, but also the wage level of the workers. In an analysis of jobs advertised in the Nogales daily newspaper throughout the 1980s, Kopinak (1995a) notes that a fourth of the jobs advertised requested female applicants, of which 11 percent were for secretarial jobs and 89 percent were for unskilled production jobs. Only one eighth of the jobs requested male applicants.

- **Border Employment as Share of All Employment.** The location of a firm affects the wages it offers. This variable measures the different labor market conditions in border and nonborder regions. It is calculated as a continuous variable ranging from 0 to 1. The share of border employment is expected to have a positive sign, because *maquila* firms located along the border area are competing in tight local labor markets where unemployment rates are generally lower than the national average. Because of their proximity to the United States, border cities are a point of emigration as well as a point of production. *Maquila* wages along the border are thus competing with emigration to the United States and the potential for greater hourly earnings found there, despite the costs associated with illegal border crossing.

- **Natural Log of Plant Size.** Plant size is defined as number of line workers per establishment. The annual average of the monthly number of workers per plant for each industry is calculated and converted to its natural log in order to address problems of scale and to create a continuous variable. The plant size is a proxy for firm characteristics that could influence hourly earnings. Firms with more workers are likely to be well established and in demand of a reliable workforce, for which they are willing to pay a wage premium (Sargent and Matthews 1997). They also probably have a competitive edge in the market and are able to take advantage of cost savings in other areas due to economies of scale to pay their workers more. On the other hand, firms with fewer workers focus on cutting all costs to establish a competitive position. These firms are not only likely to have less capital-intensive production compared to larger firms in the same industry, but are also likely to pay workers as little as possible.

- **Natural Log of Capital Intensity.** Capital intensity is a measure of technological change and innovation. Value-added output excluding compensation is a proxy to measure capital intensity, given that data on flows of capital services or profits are not available. It is calculated as the industry's value added minus employee compensation adjusted by the producer price index to produce a constant price value, and then divided by production-line worker hours worked to normalize across industries. This measure of capital intensity per hour worked is then converted to its natural log. The coefficient for the capital intensity variable is expected to have a positive sign, because capital intensive firms are likely to employ complex production processes requiring skilled manual labor and are expected to pay more. Labor-intensive production is expected to pay lower average wages (Bartel and Sicherman 1999).

- **Time.** Real wages have fallen over the past two decades in Mexico. Furthermore, the 1995 economic crisis was a turning point in the economy in the 1990s. Including a dummy variable addresses the effect of time on real average hourly earnings. A value of 0 is assigned to all data observations for 1991–94. A value of 1 is assigned to all data observations for 1995–98. Given the trend over time of declining real wages, the sign of the coefficient for the dummy is expected to be negative, despite gains in real wages in 1997 and 1998.

Multicollinearity exists between the independent variables—capital intensity and the female–male employment ratio are negatively correlated with border employment and are positively correlated with size of plant. Capital intensity is positively correlated with the employment ratio. The instrumental variable technique, which addresses modeling problems due to multicollinearity, would not be easily applied given the interaction among the variables. Even though the values of the coefficients are difficult to interpret due to correlation between the independent variables, the signs of the coefficients do not change when each variable is regressed separately against real hourly earnings. There are likely to be problems of omitted variable bias as well, given that other differences among industries may not be included, and labor supply variables that match firm data are not available.

The results of the regression are shown in Table 4.7. The mean of real hourly earnings is 3.92. All five of the variables explain a significant por-

Table 4.7 Mexican *Maquila* Manufacturing and Services, Interindustry Wage Gap Model, 1991–98

Variables	Coefficients (standard error)	t Statistic	P value	Mean
Intercept	3.53094 (0.5306)	6.65465*	2.16E-09	
Share female emp.	−1.77784 (0.35405)	−5.0215*	2.58E-06	0.553
Share border emp.	1.45410 (0.21539)	6.75096*	1.39E-09	0.733
ln of plant size	0.46716 (0.08629)	5.41374*	5.08E-07	5.235
ln of capital intensity	−0.14349 (0.04505)	−3.18547*	1.99E-03	13.228
Year (pre-1995)	−0.48786 (0.07325)	−6.66044*	2.11E-09	0.5

Multiple R	84.1%
R square	71.8%
Adjusted R square	69.2%
Standard error	0.339549
Observations	96

ANOVA

	df	SS	MS	F	Significance F
Regression	5	25.1333	5.0267	43.5988	1.292E-22
Residual	90	10.3764	0.1153		
Total	95	35.5097			

*1 percent significance level.

tion of the difference in hourly earnings between industries at the 1 percent level. A rise in the share of female workers leads to a decrease in real average hourly earnings. An increase in border employment has a positive effect on real average hourly earnings. The natural log of plant size also has a positive correlation with hourly earnings. The time variable is negatively correlated with real average hourly earnings. The log of capital intensity is a significant determinant of real average hourly earnings, but not in the expected direction.

Three possible explanations for the negative correlation between workers' hourly earnings and capital intensity, in addition to the problems with using a proxy, are that (a) inflation of inputs is greater than the rise in wages; (b) more capital-intensive industries employ less-skilled labor (a counterintuitive explanation); and (c) workers do not share in productivity gains expected in more capital-intensive industries. With an R^2 of 69.2 percent, the interindustry wage differential model offers a plausible explanation of wage differences.

Gender Wage Gap

The regression model above shows how the gender composition, among other factors, affects the interindustry wage gap. This section analyzes the observed differences in hourly earnings of male and female production workers within industries. As of 1997 more detailed data allow average hourly earnings to be calculated by gender and industry for *maquila* production-line workers, among other variables. These disaggregated data allow us to answer the question, do men earn more than women?

The descriptive data in Table 4.8 clearly show that men earn more than women. Women production-line workers earn 92.4 percent of what men in similar positions earn for all industries. This inequality holds for each industry as well. The industry with the greatest differential in hourly earnings is tool assembly—the highest-paid and mostly male sector—in which women earn 79 centavos for every peso earned by men. Food and footwear—both with lower-than-average hourly earnings—also have significant wage gaps; compared to men, women earn 80 and 84 centavos to the peso, respectively. The industry with the least hourly earnings difference by gender is transportation equipment, with near parity between men and women (and a predominance of international corporations).

It is possible that tasks (assembler, solderer, packer, forklift operator) are both segregated by gender and offer different pay scales, a characteristic observed in earlier studies of the Mexican labor market (Rendon 1993). This could explain part of the gender wage gap. Yet these differentials in average hourly earnings between male and female production workers in all but transportation equipment beg further investigation into the character of these differences. The transportation equipment industry sector, which reports near equal wages for men and women, leads one to consider that establishment or firm characteristics may reflect personnel practices and thus directly impact wages.

To determine whether industry characteristics of gender composition, location, plant size, and capital intensity have an effect on the ratio between women's and men's wages, a regression is estimated using the industry-level data for the two years[15] (see section on "Interindustry Wage Gap" for definition of these four variables). The results are presented in Table 4.9. The mean of the ratio is .912. The three variables of

Table 4.8 Mexican *Maquila* Manufacturing and Services; Earnings by Industry and Type of Employee, in Current Pesos, 1998

| | *Average hourly earnings* | | |
| | *All* | *Production-line workers* | |
Industry category	*employees*	*Men*	*Women*
Total manufacturing & services	14.15	10.10	9.33
Food & related products	9.89	8.28	6.66
Apparel & other textile products	9.03	7.61	7.14
Footwear & leather products	11.45	10.23	8.66
Furniture & fixtures	13.80	10.23	9.17
Chemicals & chemical products	13.98	9.90	9.40
Transportation equipment	16.53	11.24	11.18
Assembly of tools, equipment, & parts, excl. electric	17.19	13.64	10.79
Machinery & equipment, & electric & electronic articles	16.89	11.18	10.54
Electric & electronic materials & accessories	16.13	10.54	10.00
Toys & sporting goods	15.30	10.53	9.69
Other manufacturing	13.84	10.07	9.36
Services	12.69	9.73	9.21

Source: Author's calculations based on INEGI 1998c.

gender composition, natural log of capital intensity, and location are statistically significant in estimating the ratio of hourly earnings of women to men. Multicollinearity reduces the ability to interpret the coefficients; the capital intensity variable is correlated with border and plant size variables. Increases in the share of women employed in a specific industry increase the difference between the hourly earnings of women and men, as do increases in the natural log of capital intensity. On the other hand, an increase in the share of employment being located away from the border region leads to a decline in the difference between the hourly earnings of men and women. Plant size showed no significant effect.

That is to say, a greater concentration of women in an industry and an increase in capital intensity expand the gender wage gap, while location in nonborder areas reduces it. A plausible explanation for lower hourly earnings in industries with a greater share of female

Table 4.9 Mexican *Maquila* Manufacturing and Services; Gender Gap in Earnings Model, 1997–98

Variables	Coefficients (standard error)	t Statistic	P value	Mean
Intercept	0.2424 (0.1295)	1.8719	0.0767	
Share female emp.	0.2637 (0.09625)	2.7393*	0.0130	0.528
Share border emp.	0.1102 (0.05509)	2.0002*	0.0600	0.718
ln of plant size	−0.0127 (0.02216)	−0.5722	0.5739	5.387
ln of capital intensity	0.0380 (0.01074)	3.5398*	0.0022	13.680

Multiple R	78.3%
R square	61.4%
Adjusted R equare	53.2%
Standard error	0.042214
Observations	24

ANOVA

	df	SS	MS	F	Significance F
Regression	4	0.053812	0.0135	7.5492	0.0008114
Residual	19	0.0338587	0.0018		
Total	23	0.0876708			

*1 percent significance level.

employment is overcrowding in a segmented labor market; that is, employer discrimination against women in some sectors creates an oversupply of women in other sectors, pushing down wages in those sectors. As for location, an abundant labor supply of men in nonborder regions can explain the reduction in the gap. However, the effect of capital intensity on the gender gap begs explanation. It would appear that men benefit from industries with greater capital investment (which generally connotes more productive industries) more than women do.

The sample size is based on 12 *maquila* industries over two years. Despite the limited years of data available and multicollinearity, the model's adjusted R^2 of 53.2 percent does signal that the model is not without merit.

Labor Markets in Border Cities

The labor force data for four border cities for 1991 and 1997 offer a richer explanation for some of the changes described earlier in the chapter. In particular, the changes in labor force participation of married women, the relative differences in schooling between men and women, and the differences in hourly earnings between *maquiladora* plants and other employment add to the analysis of defeminization and the interindustry wage gap.

The four cities of Ciudad Juarez, Matamoros, Nuevo Laredo, and Tijuana comprised 64.9 percent of national *maquila* employment in 1991 (using the proxy definition of *maquila* employment in the household survey) and 48.4 percent in 1997, and an even larger share of border *maquila* employment.[16] The labor force data show how the defeminization of the *maquila* industry is a supply-driven phenomenon, at least in the border areas. Despite the dramatic growth of women's participation and an increased absorption of women into *maquila* employment, new jobs in the *maquila* industry absorbed nearly twice as many men as women. One of the major factors that has restricted women's labor supply is married women's low labor force participation. Nonetheless, women's labor force participation rose significantly over the six-year period.

This phenomenon of the increasing labor force participation of women has been a national trend over the past two decades in Mexico. Looking at the data for the four cities, one can see that participation of single women did not change, although the participation of married and divorced women rose. Given that the participation rate is measured for the population that is age 12 and older, the participation rate of single women quite likely includes a number of girls who are continuing their schooling and thus are unlikely to work. The slight increase in educational levels from 1991 to 1997 also would indicate that generally the labor supply of young single women is inelastic, given that girls and young women are in school for more years. The fact that women with children—married, divorced, separated, and widowed—have increased their participation rates could possibly be due to their declining childcare responsibilities; a declining share of the national population is under age 12. These trends in the labor force participation rate of women and the dependency ratio are shown in Table 4.10. The national labor force participation rate of women was 32.3 percent in 1988, while the percent of the population under age 12 was 30.8 percent. Ten years later, the labor force participation rate had risen by 4 percentage points and the dependency ratio had fallen by 3 percentage points.

The data in Table 4.11 show that a greater percentage of all employed women work in *maquiladora* plants than all employed men. However, a

Table 4.10 Mexico, Selected Population Characteristics

Year	Women's labor force participation rate	Percent population < 12 years
1988	32.3	30.8
1991	31.5	30.0
1993	33.0	29.6
1995	34.5	29.0
1996	34.8	28.3
1997	36.8	27.9
1998	36.9	27.5

Source: INEGI 1991a, 1993, 1994a, 1996, 1997a, 1998a, 1999d.

larger number of men are employed in the *maquila* industry in the four cities, Cuidad Juarez, Matamoros, Nuevo Laredo, and Tijuana. From 1991 to 1997, the importance of *maquiladora* plants as a source of employment for both men and women rose; men's dependence on *maquila* employment grew from 30.9 percent to 38.3 percent, and women's employment in the sector grew from 48.8 percent to 53.4 percent.

Single men were more dependent on *maquila* employment than other men in 1991, depending on *maquiladora* plants for more than one third of their jobs. By 1997, single men's share of *maquila* employment rose to 44.5 percent of all single men's jobs, and married men had increased their employment in *maquiladora* plants from one fourth to one third of all employment. Approximately half of single, formally married, and common-law married women depended on employment in *maquiladora* plants in 1991, but by 1997, the share of single and common-law married women was around 60 percent. Employment in *maquiladora* plants accounted for nearly half of formally married, divorced, and separated women's employment that year. Labor demand grew faster than the working-age population, employing people who were not previously employed.

The greater availability of *maquila* jobs had little impact on single women's flat participation rate of 42 to 43 percent, but participation rates rose from 24 percent to 32 and 36 percent for formally and common-law married women over the six years. For the two years, although *maquila* employment absorbed the greatest share of single women, it also accounted for half of married women's employment and an increasing share of single mothers' employment.[17]

For the past decade, the typical *maquila* worker in these four large cities has not been a woman. More men than women worked in the *maquila* industry in both years. As *maquila* employment opportunities expanded, men increasingly filled the gap. The labor force participation rate of men

Table 4.11 Mexico: Socioeconomic Characteristics of the Working-Age Population, 1991 and 1997, Four Border Cities

	1991			1997		
	Total	Men	Women	Total	Men	Women
Working-age population	1,605,793	763,925	841,868	1,772,144	873,400	898,744
Labor force	838,480	565,238	273,242	1,019,303	681,435	337,868
Employed	825,223	556,198	269,025	1,003,906	671,389	332,517
Employees in *maquiladora* plants[1]	303,327	172,096	131,231	434,836	257,175	177,661
Labor force participation rate						
Total	52.2%	74.0%	32.5%	57.5%	78.0%	37.6%
Single	48.7%	55.0%	42.4%	52.4%	60.1%	42.9%
Formally married	56.6%	90.4%	23.6%	61.2%	91.0%	31.7%
Common-law married	58.3%	92.4%	24.6%	66.1%	96.9%	36.1%
Divorced	63.9%	78.8%	59.1%	73.1%	87.1%	65.6%
Separated	64.4%	81.3%	59.0%	65.3%	85.2%	58.8%
Widowed	26.1%	59.6%	18.8%	28.8%	45.0%	24.8%
Share of employed working in *maquiladora* plants[1]						
Total	36.8%	30.9%	48.8%	43.3%	38.3%	53.4%
Single	43.2%	36.5%	51.9%	50.2%	44.5%	60.0%
Formally married	33.2%	29.0%	49.1%	40.6%	37.0%	50.9%
Common-law married	31.6%	25.3%	54.6%	39.2%	32.2%	57.5%
Divorced	34.7%	26.8%	38.0%	38.8%	24.0%	49.5%
Separated	36.0%	33.6%	37.0%	41.9%	29.9%	47.7%
Widowed	20.3%	14.3%	24.5%	24.9%	24.3%	25.2%
Maquila employees[1] as percent of national *maquila* employees	64.9%	n.a.	n.a.	48.4%	61.0%	37.2%

Table 4.11 (continued)

| | 1991 | | | 1997 | | |
	Total	Men	Women	Total	Men	Women
Average years of schooling						
Working-age population	7.6	8.0	7.3	8.3	8.6	8.0
Labor force	8.2	8.2	8.3	8.8	8.8	8.8
Employees in *maquiladora* plants[1]	9.0	9.4	8.5	9.5	9.7	9.2

n.a. Not available.
Note: The four cities are Ciudad Juarez, Matamoros, Nuevo Laredo, and Tijuana.
1. Employees of establishments with more than 100 employees.
Source: Except for share of national *maquila* employment, data tabulated for BLS by INEGI from the *Encuesta Nacional de Empleo*; calculations prepared by author. National *maquila* employment, INEGI 1997b, 1998b.

rose on average from 74 to 78 percent. Men's share of employment in *maquiladora* plants grew faster than women's did, but *maquila* jobs remained a relatively less important source of employment for men (Table 4.11).

The shift to a majority male *maquila* workforce had occurred by 1997 in all border regions, which was the first year sex-disaggregated establishment survey data on *maquiladora* plants were collected for all types of employees. In 1997, men comprised 50.8 percent of all *maquila* wage and salary employees in border areas, and 51.7 percent in 1998 (INEGI 1998b, 1998c).

Furthermore, the typical female *maquila* worker is no longer a single woman in these four important border cities. The distribution of employed by civil status in Table 4.12 also shows that the share of the labor force of both formally and common-law married women increased over the six years, and that their share of *maquila* employment expanded beyond that of single women. The importance of the *maquila* export industry for women's employment, particularly that of married women, is unusual. Women's primary responsibility for household production has often limited married women's involvement in full-time employment, and more so for formally married women. The greater share of women in the informal sector has often been attributed to women's desired flexibility for hours and location of work. This is considered to be a choice made by women who have children to support. However, the descriptive data in Tables 4.11 and 4.12 seem to tell a different story—one in which *maquila* employment successfully attracts an ever-increasing share of women in the labor force.

The gender difference between educational levels may offer a partial explanation for differences in hourly earnings. Compared with other employed people, men and women employed in *maquiladora* plants have on average a higher educational level for both years. Among *maquila* employees, men's educational level is slightly higher than women's. The average years of education in 1991 was 9.4 for men, and 8.5 for women. By 1997, men's average years of schooling rose slightly to 9.7, and women's rose more quickly but still lagged behind men's, at 9.2 years of schooling. The slight difference in educational levels (a few months) does not seem sufficient reason to fully explain a gender wage gap. Data on work experience—another individual characteristic that affects wages—are not available for comparison.

Table 4.12 Mexico, Distribution of Income Level and Civil Status by Labor Force Characteristics, 1991 and 1997, Four Border Cities

	Labor force		Employed		Employees in establishments with >100 workers	
	Men	Women	Men	Women	Men	Women
1991						
Total	565,238	273,242	556,198	269,025	172,096	131,231
Civil status						
Single	33.2%	51.9%	32.6%	51.4%	38.4%	54.8%
Formally married	55.7%	30.9%	56.2%	31.3%	52.6%	31.5%
Common-law married	8.0%	4.4%	8.0%	4.5%	6.6%	5.0%
Divorced	0.7%	3.6%	0.7%	3.6%	0.6%	2.8%
Separated	1.0%	4.9%	1.0%	4.9%	1.1%	3.7%
Widowed	1.4%	4.2%	1.4%	4.2%	0.6%	2.1%
Income level[1]						
No income	—	—	4.4%	2.9%	0.4%	0.2%
One or less m.w.	—	—	5.0%	4.1%	1.9%	3.2%

Table 4.12 (continued)

	Labor force		Employed		Employees in establishments with >100 workers	
	Men	Women	Men	Women	Men	Women
More than 1 to 2 m.w.	—	—	37.1%	34.1%	40.1%	51.9%
More than 2 to 3 m.w.	—	—	24.8%	24.1%	26.2%	30.1%
More than 3 to 5 m.w.	—	—	18.3%	21.7%	19.1%	10.1%
5 and more m.w.	—	—	10.5%	13.0%	12.4%	4.4%
1997						
Total	681,435	337,868	671,389	332,517	257,175	177,661
Civil status						
Single	31.6%	36.9%	31.1%	36.7%	36.1%	41.1%
Formally married	51.6%	36.6%	51.9%	36.8%	50.2%	35.1%
Common-law married	12.6%	9.7%	12.7%	9.8%	10.7%	10.5%
Divorced	1.0%	2.9%	1.0%	2.9%	0.7%	2.7%
Separated	2.3%	9.6%	2.3%	9.6%	1.8%	8.6%
Widowed	0.9%	4.1%	0.9%	4.2%	0.6%	2.0%
Income level[1]						
No income	—	—	3.3%	2.2%	0.6%	0.5%
One or less m.w.	—	—	5.3%	4.2%	1.0%	3.2%
More than 1 to 2 m.w.	—	—	35.6%	32.2%	38.6%	48.7%
More than 2 to 3 m.w.	—	—	25.4%	26.7%	27.9%	26.3%
More than 3 to 5 m.w.	—	—	14.8%	16.2%	15.3%	12.5%
5 and more m.w.	—	—	15.6%	18.6%	16.6%	8.8%

m.w. Minimum wage.

1. The distribution of income level excludes the "not specified" category.

Note: The four cities are Ciudad Juarez, Matamoros, Nuevo Laredo, and Tijuana.

Source: Data tabulated for BLS by INEGI from the Encuesta Nacional de Empleo; calculations prepared by author.

Finally, *maquiladora* plants offer less risk and possibly better opportunities compared to other employment. A review of the distribution of income for all employed and *maquila* employees shows that the income of *maquila* employees has less dispersion than the income of all employed (see Table 4.12). Looking at lower incomes, a comparison of all employed and *maquila* employees in both years shows that fewer *maquila* workers earn below the minimum wage compared to the average employed person.[18] At the higher end of the income scale, more men and fewer women in *maquila* employment earned greater than three times the minimum wage, in comparison with other employment. This reflects the gender wage gap within industry. The degree of difference was larger in 1991 than 1997. For the roughly 80 percent of women earning between one and three times the minimum wage in 1991, this share fell to 75 percent in 1997 as more women earned higher incomes. The increase in income levels in 1997 does not necessarily mean that employees are better off than in 1991, because hourly earnings of *maquila* employees have fallen in real terms.

This labor force analysis reinforces the story told with the establishment data—defeminization occurs as demand for *maquila* workers grows faster than the absorption of women into the labor force. Even so, women have responded to increased employment opportunities. In border areas, *maquila* industries have become the employer of choice because of their overwhelming presence, even though women in the labor force receive higher relative income in self-employment and as non-*maquila* employees in other sectors.

Some may wonder why the labor force participation rate of women has not risen faster, particularly because women's labor supply is considered more elastic than men's. On one hand, the inclusion of girls under age 15 in the working-age population artificially deflates the labor force participation rate, because a large share of younger adolescent girls are less likely to be in the labor force. On the other hand, there are real constraints on women interested in working due to their household roles and responsibilities. This division of labor becomes less time consuming as children under age 12 become a smaller share of the total population, freeing women to participate in paid work.

Conclusion

This historical analysis of employment and wages among *maquila* employees suggests that—although the employment share of women is falling—there continues to be a growing demand for both male and female workers. This demand flattens as the value of the peso rises, but historically has spiked after devaluations. Real hourly earnings have fallen over time, but not as quickly as the real minimum wage, and *maquila* manufacturing has become relatively more attractive than other manufacturing work over the 18 years studied. The wage convergence between national manufacturing and *maquila* manufacturing provides a partial explanation for men's increased participation in *maquila* work. The expansion of male employment has primarily been in tool assembly and transportation equipment. The first of these is a small, technical, and male-concentrated industry. The second of these is a large and growing sector of large plants run by multinational firms. The amelioration of women's declining share of *maquila* employment can be attributed to the explosive growth of nonborder employment, where the female-concentrated apparel industry makes up half of *maquila* employment.

Labor force data for four border cities complement this picture. Women have recently expanded their participation in the labor market and in *maquila* employment compared to other employment. Part of this growth depends on the participation of married women who have—compared to earlier in the decade—a greater involvement in the labor force. The overall growth is based on a smaller labor force relative to that of men. Labor force growth of men was lower than that of women, but their growth in *maquila* employment was nearly double that of women. Labor demand among *maquiladora* plants has drawn more men into *maquila* employment because the growing participation rate of women still has not kept up with job growth.

An interindustry wage gap exists among *maquila* industries; greater shares of women's and nonborder employment and capital intensity are negatively correlated with real hourly wages, while plant size is positively correlated with wages. Hourly earnings are lowest in food and apparel, both majority female industries. The best-paid workers are in the majority male industries of machines and tool assembly, and in the transportation equipment industry, which—while it has a smaller-than-average share of female employment—has both the largest plant size of all industries and the majority of its production along the border. A wage gap between male and female line workers is evident for all industries, although insufficient detail is available to determine the basis for this inequality.

The increasing importance of *maquiladora* plants as a source of employment, married women's increasing participation, falling real wages, and the gender gap between men and women working in *maquila* industries influence labor market and social policy. Examples of future research and policy implications are discussed below.

- High-paying industries have a much lower share of women compared to other industries. Although a higher concentration of women is negatively correlated with hourly earnings, expanding women's access to high-paying sectors can offer some women better hourly earnings. Research on job requirements and barriers to entry in these relatively better-paying sectors is needed to determine whether coeducational training and gender-sensitive marketing would successfully prepare more women for employment in these industries.

- The labor force participation of women has risen over time in Mexico, but is only at the level of the United States and Canada 30 years ago. One of the reasons women stay out of the labor market is their primary role in child rearing and lack of childcare options. Other women are compelled to work even though they do not find satisfactory childcare (see Chapter 3, this volume). This lack of childcare options is known to create risks for children in families who have no choice but to work. For example, older school-aged siblings may take care of younger siblings, and children may be locked inside their homes without supervision. Research into the availability and quality of childcare would be an important piece of the policy puzzle to understand how men and women respond to job opportunities, particularly in border areas of Mexico that have tight labor markets. The access to and cost of childcare is an important issue for families with members involved in the general and *maquila* workforce.

- The gender gap in production worker wages in all industries but transportation equipment needs further study. Do task and job differences explain the difference in hourly earnings? Do multinational companies in the transportation equipment sector have unique human resource policies to address differences in job descriptions, or do men and women work in the same jobs? Are there human capital differences?

These research suggestions address the gender gap and the low labor force participation of women, but do not confront the challenge of overcoming declining real wages. The devaluation of the Mexican peso has had a positive effect on *maquila* employment, while at the same time inflation has reduced the purchasing power of hourly earnings. In developed countries, the expansion of industrial employment led to the growth of a middle class, but the continuation of the Mexican model does not appear likely to follow the same trajectory. While expansive labor demand is pulling more people into employment, declining purchasing power is leading to different coping strategies that push more women, particularly married women, into the labor force.

Notes

1. The Border Industrialization Program was the original name of the *maquila* export program. The *maquila* industry has primarily been an assembly industry of foreign-owned firms. The firm posts a bond for imported capital and intermediate goods that are used for production; this bond is then released when the good is exported. The importer pays tax only on the value-added portion of production that is exported from Mexico.

2. From 1951 to 1964, annual emigration ranged between 177,000 and 444,000 workers (<www.farmworkers.org/migrdata.html>).

3. *Maquila* workers and managers were interviewed for a large study of labor turnover in Tijuana. The instability of the labor force did not appear to be related to working or living conditions. Rather, turnover was negatively correlated to demographic characteristics related to age of worker and number of children (Carrillo and Santibáñez 1993).

4. Industry classification of *maquila* firms was limited to seven categories from 1975 to 1978 and was reported by geographic region only (INEGI 1988a), 1979 data are not available by industry, and there are no data available for certain industries for both border and nonborder areas between 1979 and 1990.

5. Intermediate and capital goods imported to Mexico from the United States and Canada will not be taxed if goods are used to produce exports. However, the same goods imported from non-NAFTA countries will not be able to maintain the tax advantage established by the *maquila* program and concretized by NAFTA. This particularly affects the predominantly Japanese-owned electronics industries that import inputs and machines from Asia (United Nations 1996).

6. Changes in Mexican *maquila* legislation in 1972–73, 1983, and 1989 progressively loosened restrictions on *maquilas*—the assembly plants were allowed to spread through nearly the entire country, expand "assembly" operations to "manufacturing" operations, have 100 percent foreign ownership (except textiles), and be free to sell all products nationally. The effect of NAFTA is to steadily reduce tariffs, limits, quotas, and even value-added taxes between North American countries by 2008 (United Nations 1996).

7. The data reported for the two sectors differ in coverage of type of worker and type and size of establishment. On one hand, national manufacturing data are reported for all wage workers, which includes production-line workers, technical workers, and line supervisors. It also encompasses a wide range of estab-

lishments, including very small, labor-intensive informal sector establishments. On the other hand, the *maquila* data allow calculation of hourly earnings for production-line workers only through 1996, and for all wage workers from 1997 forward. In addition, the type of establishment shifted from assembly to including manufacturing over the two decades as Mexican legislation loosened restrictions on the export program.

8. Labor costs paid by the employer are on an all-employee basis. Data on non-wage labor costs are not available for production workers only.

9. In 1990 the lowest minimum wage (in mostly rural areas) was 83 percent of the highest minimum wage (in large urban and border areas). For 1998 the lowest minimum wage was 86 percent of the highest minimum wage (INEGI 1999b).

10. One of the effects of NAFTA was to phase out U.S. tariff and quota protection from its most protected major industry.

11. Hourly earnings are presented in U.S. dollars for ease of analysis. Mexican currency changes in 1992 make a cross-year comparison of figures in pesos difficult. Each year's figures are converted by that year's annual average exchange rate. Exchange rates fluctuate significantly between years.

12. The 1983 Mexican Auto Decree restructured the transportation and equipment industry, leading to Mexico's increased importance in engine and parts production for the U.S. market (Scheinman 1990).

13. Anderson (1990) argues that the declining importance of apparel in the 1980s was due to the restrictions on textile imports under the Multifiber Arrangement (MFA) (1990). These restrictions were lifted with NAFTA.

14. Real average hourly earnings in pesos were calculated using the national Consumer Price Index published by INEGI (1999b). The dependent variable is a continuous variable. Data for 12 industries were included.

15. The drawback of using establishment data is that individual characteristics are not accounted for.

16. There is no precise definition for *maquila* employment in the ENE survey. The proxy used here is employees working in establishments with more than 100 employees. This figure may exclude some smaller *maquilas* (of which fewer exist than in the previous decade) and thus undercount employment. Establishments with more than 100 employees that are not *maquilas* may be included.

17. Divorced and separated women are overwhelmingly single mothers.

18. These data are not adjusted for hours and thus may include individuals who work few hours. No explanation is provided by INEGI on the observations of individuals who are employees and earn no income.

References

Aguayo Ayala, Jose Francisco. 1998. "Cambio Estructural y Empleo en la Manufactura." Thesis. Universidad Nacional Autónoma de México, Facultad de Economía.

Anderson, Joan. 1990. "*Maquiladoras* in the Apparel Industry." In Khosrow Fatemi, ed., *The Maquiladora Industry, Economic Solution or Problem?* New York: Praeger.

Anderson, Joan, and Denise Dimon. 1998. "Married Women's Labor Force Participation in Developing Countries: The Case of Mexico." *Estudios Económicos* 13(1):3–34.

Arroyo del Muro, Rodolfo Hector Hugo. 1997. "Reestructuración Productiva, Localización Industrial y Empleo en México." Thesis. Universidad Nacional Autónoma de México, Facultad de Economía.

Bartel, Ann, and Nachum Sicherman. 1999. "Technological Change and Wages: An Interindustry Analysis." *Journal of Political Economy* 107(21):285–325.

Bureau of Labor Statistics. 1995. "Hourly Compensation Costs for Production Workers in Manufacturing Industries, Mexico, 1975–1994." Unpublished data. Office of Productivity and Technology. April.

_____. 1999. "Mexico, Hourly Compensation Costs for Production Workers in Manufacturing, All Manufacturing and *Maquiladora* Manufacturing, 1981–1998." Unpublished data. Office of Productivity and Technology. May.

_____. 2000. "International Comparisons of Hourly Compensation Costs for Production Workers in Manufacturing, 1975–1998." Underlying data from News Release USDL 00-07. Office of Productivity and Technology. January 11.

Carrillo V. Jorge, and Jorge Santibáñez. 1993. *Rotación de Personal en las Maquilas de Exportación en Tijuana*. Mexico: Secretaría del Trabajo y Previsión Social y El Colegio de la Frontera Norte.

Castillo, Victor, and Ramón Ramírez Acosta. 1992. "La Subcontratación en la Industria Maquila de Asia y México." *Comercio Exterior* 42(1):33–41.

Catanzarite, Lisa, and Myra Strober. 1993. "The Gender Recomposition of the *Maquila* Workforce in Cuidad [sic] Juárez." *Industrial Relations* 32(1):133–47.

Fatemi, Khosrow, ed. 1990. *The Maquila Industry, Economic Solution or Problem?* New York: Praeger.

Fleck, Susan, and Constance Sorrentino. 1994. "Employment and Unemployment in Mexico's Labor Force." *Monthly Labor Review* 117(11):3–31.

Gambrill, Monica. 1995. "La política salarial de las maquilas: Mejoras posibles bajo el TLC." *Comercio Exterior* 44(7):543–49.

Goux, Dominique, and Eric Maurin. 1999. "Persistence of Interindustry Wage Differentials: A Reexamination Using Matched Worker-Firm Panel Data." *Journal of Labor Economics* 7(3):492–533.

Instituto Nacional de Estadística, Geografia, e Informática (INEGI). 1988. *Estadística de la Industria Maquila de Exportación, 1975–1986*. Aguascalientes, México.

_____. 1989. *Estadística de la Industria Maquila de Exportación, 1978–1988*. Aguascalientes, México.

_____. 1991a. *Encuesta Nacional de Empleo, 1988*. Aguascalientes, México.

_____. 1991b. *Estadística de la Industria Maquila de Exportación, 1979–1989*. Aguascalientes, México.

_____. 1993. *Encuesta Nacional de Empleo, 1991*. Aguascalientes, México.

_____. 1994a. *Encuesta Nacional de Empleo, 1993*. Aguascalientes, México.

_____. 1994b. *Estadística de la Industria Maquila de Exportación, 1989–1993*. Aguascalientes, México.

_____. 1996. *Encuesta Nacional de Empleo, 1995*. Aguascalientes, México.

_____. 1997a. *Encuesta Nacional de Empleo, 1996*. Aguascalientes, México.

_____. 1997b. *Estadística de la Industria Maquila de Exportación, 1991–1996*. Aguascalientes, México.

————. 1998a. *Encuesta Nacional de Empleo, 1997*. Aguascalientes, México.

_____. 1998b. *Estadística de la Industria Maquila de Exportación, 1992–1997*. Aguascalientes, México.

_____. 1998c. *Estadística de la Industria Maquila de Exportación, Información Preliminar*. Aguascalientes, México. diciembre.

_____. 1999a. *Estadísticas del Comercio Exterior de Mexico*, 22(1). Aguascalientes, México.

_____. 1999b. *Cuaderno de Información Oportuna*. No. 312. March. Aguascalientes, México.

_____. 1999c. *Cuaderno de Información Oportuna*. No. 313. April. Aguascalientes, México.

_____. 1999d. *Encuesta Nacional de Empleo, 1998*. Aguascalientes, México.

International Monetary Fund. 1987. *International Financial Statistics Yearbook, 1987*. Washington, D.C.

_____. 1996. "International Financial Statistics, January 1996." Washington, D.C.

Jiménez Betancourt, Rubi. 1989. "Participación Femenina en la Industria Maquiladora." In Jennifer Cooper, Teresita de Barbieri, Teresa Rendón, Estela Suarez, and Esperanza Tuñon, eds., *Fuerza de Trabajo Femenina Urbana en México*. Vol. 2. UNAM Coordinación de Humanidades and Grupo Editorial Miguel Angel Porrua, S.A. Mexico.

Kopinak, Kathryn. 1995a. "Gender as a Vehicle for the Subordination of Women *Maquila* Workers in Mexico." *Latin American Perspectives* 22(1):30–48.

_____. 1995b. "Transitions in the Maquilization of Mexican Industry: Movement and Stasis from 1965 to 2001." *Labour, Capital and Society* 28(1):68–94.

López, Julio. 1999. "The Macroeconomics of Wages and Employment in Mexico." *Labour* 13(4):859–878.

MacLachlan, Ian, and Adrian Guillermo Aguilar. 1998. "*Maquila* Myths: Locational and Structural Change in Mexico's Export Manufacturing Industry." *Professional Geographer* 50(3):315–31.

Peña, Devon G. 1997. "The Terror of the Machine: Technology, Work, Gender, and Ecology on the U.S.-Mexico Border." Center for Mexican American Studies, University of Texas at Austin.

Rendón, Teresa. 1993. "Female Labor in Mexico within a Framework of Equitable Productive Transformation." Social Development Unit. Economic Commission for Latin America and the Caribbean. Consultant's Report. May.

Salomón, Alfredo. 1998. "Inversión Extranjera Directa en México en los Noventa." *Comercio Exterior* 48(10):804–810.

Sargent, John, and Linda Matthews. 1997. "Skill Development and Integrated Manufacturing in Mexico." *World Development* 25(10):1669–81.

_____. 1999. "Relative Attractiveness of Maquila Work: Exploitation or Choice?" *Journal of Business Ethics* 18(2).

Scheinman, Marc N. 1990. "*Maquiladoras* in the Automobile Industry." In Khosrow Fatemi, ed., *The Maquiladora Industry, Economic Solution or Problem?* New York: Praeger.

Sklair, Leslie. 1993. "Assembling for Development: The Maquila Industry in Mexico and the United States." La Jolla: Center for U.S.–Mexican Studies, University of California, San Diego.

Standing, Guy. 1999. "Global Feminization through Flexible Labor: A Theme Revisited." *World Development* 27(3):583–602.

Stoddard, Ellwyn. 1987. *Maquila, Assembly Plants in Northern Mexico*. El Paso: Texas Western Press, University of Texas at El Paso.

Tiano, Susan. 1994. *Patriarchy on the Line: Labor, Gender, and Ideology in the Mexican Maquila Industry*. Philadelphia: Temple University Press.

United Nations. 1996. *México: La Industria Maquiladora*. Santiago, Chile: Economic Commission for Latin American and the Caribbean.

Wilson, Patricia A. 1992. *Exports and Local Development; Mexico's New Maquilas*. Austin: University of Texas Press.

5

Explaining Gender Differences in Earnings in the Microenterprise Sector

Susana M. Sánchez and José A. Pagán

Over the last few years, the labor force participation rate of women in Mexico has substantially increased, particularly in less urban areas (Brown, Pagán, and Rodríguez 1999). In Mexico, as in other developed and developing countries, women have become active participants in the microenterprise sector through business ownership, job creation, and through their contribution to overall economic growth (Pagán and Sánchez 2000). Yet, despite considerable advances in the economic well-being of women, female-owned microenterprises earn less than those owned by men, are relatively smaller, and most belong to the services and retail trade sectors (Rhyne and Holt 1994; Cohen 1996).

Female-owned small businesses in rural and urban areas represent 26 to 44 percent of all of these firms in Mexico; nonetheless, women earn 36 to 50 percent of what their male counterparts earn. As a result of these substantial differences in employment and earnings across gender, policymakers and international organizations have begun to pay attention to the economic status of women entrepreneurs, given the role that microenterprises play in providing better employment opportunities for women, which ultimately fuels economic growth (World Bank 1994).

Male–female differences in microenterprise sector participation and earnings could arise from gender differences in domestic responsibilities and the allocation of labor to market activities across household members (see Chapters 1 and 2, this volume). Differentiated roles and responsibilities within the household have a significant impact on the acquisition of education and skills that could prove useful in the microenterprise sector, and that ultimately have an impact on employment choices across the life cycle.

Given the importance of the microenterprise sector in Mexico, the role of gender in explaining differences in earnings across microenterprise owners has become an area of interest to social scientists and policymakers. Although most countries have targeted programs devoted to microenterprise development and the promotion of small-firm formation, only recently have policymakers started to incorporate gender issues in the microenterprise development agenda (Wilson and Adams 1994). Researchers have recognized that effective policymaking should take into account gender roles over the life cycle, the fact that gender bias is concentrated in only some sectors, and heterogeneity in household structure (Chaves and Sánchez 2000; Parker 1995; and Correia and Katz in the introduction to this volume).

This chapter analyzes the role of gender-specific factors in explaining male-female differences in earnings in rural and urban microenterprises. It emphasizes the role of gender differences in size of operations, returns to productive factors, and the economic sector.

The determinants of gender earnings differentials are examined using the 1994 Survey of Rural Entrepreneurs and Financial Services (*Encuesta Regional de Servicios Financieros a Unidades de Producción Rural*, SREFS) and the 1992 National Survey of Urban Microenterprises (*Encuesta Nacional de Micronegocios*, ENAMIN). The results indicate that (a) gender differences in productive characteristics (including owners and businesses) are more important in explaining gender earnings differentials in rural than in urban areas, and (b) most of the gender earnings gap is explained by male–female differences in earnings within each economic sector instead of sectoral segregation. Thus, efforts to channel female entrepreneurs into sectors in which they are underrepresented would have a limited impact in increasing female earnings in the microenterprise sector.

The chapter presents a profile of microenterprises and examines male–female differences across basic descriptive statistics; investigates observable and unobservable factors that could determine gender earnings differentials in the microenterprise sector; discusses the role of the sector of economic activity on the gender earnings gap; presents the empirical methodology used to evaluate the role of inter- and intrasectoral factors in explaining gender earnings disparities, and the statistical results; analyzes gender differences in credit access; and presents a conclusion.

Profile of Urban and Rural Microenterprises

Individual-level data from the SREFS and the ENAMIN are used to analyze gender differences in net earnings for both rural and urban areas. The SREFS was conducted in the summer of 1994 in rural areas of the states of Guanajuato, Puebla, and Veracruz. Rural areas are defined as communities with a population of 1,000 to 20,000 inhabitants, and, as such, the survey universe is composed of households residing in rural communities in these three states. Households were selected through a cluster random sampling procedure (1,944 households in 54 communities). The 1992 ENAMIN contains similar data for 11,461 microenterprise owners (that is, businesses with either less than 16 employees in the manufacturing sector or 6 employees in all other sectors). The interviews were conducted in 34 urban areas of Mexico. Both surveys contain household demographic data and individual-level socioeconomic data for these microenterprises.

Female participation in Mexico's microenterprise sector rose dramatically during the first half of the 1990s. According to the Mexican National Employment Surveys, female representation in the microenterprise sector in localities with less than 100,000 inhabitants increased from 36 percent in 1991 to 44 percent in 1995, whereas female representation increased from 26 percent to only 29 percent in more urban areas. About 24 percent of microenteprises in urban areas and 39 percent of microenterprises in rural areas are owned by women. Nonetheless, female-headed microenterprises account for 16 percent of total sectoral earnings in urban areas and 27 percent in rural areas, and the former earn about 50 percent and the latter 36 percent of what male-headed microenterprises earn (Figure 5.1).

Tables 5.1 and 5.2 present descriptive statistics for urban and rural microenterprises, by gender. The categories presented differ across rural and urban areas given that the surveys are not strictly comparable. As such, the descriptive statistics presented attempt to capture the most

(Text continues on page 182.)

Figure 5.1 Female Earning as a Percentage of Male Earnings in Rural and Urban Areas

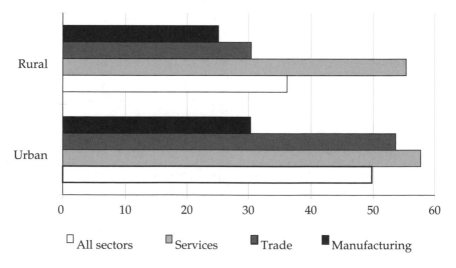

□ All sectors   ▨ Services   ■ Trade   ■ Manufacturing

Sources: ENAMIN 1992; Rural Survey 1994.

Table 5.1 Characteristics of Urban Microenterprises (% of each column heading)

	All MEs	Female	Male
All MEs (% all MEs)	100	24	76
Sector of economic activity			
Services	45.6	33.9	49.2
Trade	34.8	51.7	29.4
Manufacturing	19.6	14.3	21.3
Reasons to enter ME sector[a]			
Want to be independent	40.5	21.4	46.5
Family tradition	8.5	6.8	9.0
Complement family income	23.4	57.0	12.9
Get higher income than as a worker	19.7	7.9	23.4
Did not find salaried work	11.6	5.5	13.4
Flexible hours	4.0	6.1	3.4
Lost previous job	2.6	0.7	3.1
Other	6.4	8.0	5.9
Main problem faced			
Lack of clients	35.0	32.8	35.7
Lack of credit	2.7	1.7	3.0
Lack of economic resources	6.3	7.7	5.9
Low earnings	10.2	11.9	9.7
Problems with authorities	2.5	2.1	2.6
Excessive competition	15.5	15.2	15.7
Problems with workers/partners	0.5	0.4	0.5
Customers pay with delays	3.8	4.2	3.7
Merchandise, inputs, and raw materials	0.8	0.6	0.9
Other	3.5	2.9	3.8
No problem	19.1	20.6	18.6
Future plans			
Will not continue in business	10.9	10.8	10.9
Without important changes	66.8	68.1	66.4
Expanding line of products	7.8	9.1	7.4
Making new investments	10.7	9.1	11.2
Expanding number of employees	1.4	0.2	1.7
Other	1.7	1.8	1.7
Do not know	0.7	0.8	0.7
Place of operation			
Temporary establishment	10.0	14.9	8.5
Ambulant	4.5	2.5	5.1

(Table continues on the following page.)

Table 5.1 (continued)

	All MEs	Female	Male
Carts	3.4	0.9	4.2
Clients' home	23.3	8.8	27.9
At home	17.4	32.7	12.5
Without business premises	0.8	0.5	0.9
Fixed business premises	34.2	39.4	32.5
Transportation	6.4	0.2	8.4
Owned fixed business premises			
No	83.5	77.7	85.3
Yes	16.5	22.3	14.7
Assets/workers (pesos)			
Missing Value	0.2	0.1	0.2
0–293	25.0	29.3	23.6
294–1,590	24.9	28.2	23.9
1,591–10,275	25.0	24.8	25.0
10,276–51,000	19.9	14.5	21.6
Other	5.0	3.2	5.6
Monthly income (pesos)			
Missing value	1.8	1.6	1.9
0–345	8.2	18.1	5.1
346–2,146	50.4	50.3	50.4
2,147–15,650	36.1	28.1	38.6
Other	3.6	1.8	4.1
Monthly profits (pesos)			
Missing value	2.5	2.1	2.7
Negative	4.3	5.0	4.1
0–387	20.1	38.9	14.2
388–802	24.3	24.2	24.3
803–1,440	24.4	14.9	27.4
1,441–2,733	14.6	8.9	16.4
Other	9.7	5.9	10.9
Age			
Missing value	0	0	0
12–32	25.5	24.9	25.7
33–41	25.0	25.6	24.8
42–52	25.0	26.0	24.6
53–68	19.7	18.7	20.0
Other	4.8	4.7	4.8
Years in operation			
Missing value	0	0	0
0–2 years	31.1	42.4	27.5
2–5 years	21.9	21.2	22.1

	All MEs	Female	Male
5–12 years	23.8	20.0	25.0
12–30 years	19.7	13.9	21.5
Other	3.5	2.4	3.8
Number of workers (including owner)			
1	66.0	68.1	65.4
2–3	27.5	27.5	27.4
4–6	5.9	4.1	6.5
7–16	0.6	0.3	0.7
Monthly hours of operations			
Missing value	0.1	0.1	0.1
4–151	24.7	41.6	19.4
151–207	23.7	17.0	25.8
207–242	24.9	14.7	28.1
242–425	26.6	26.7	26.6
Type of accounting			
Formal accounting	23.1	19.7	24.1
Income & expenses notebook	6.6	8.0	6.2
Personal notes	19.8	22.3	19.0
None	50.5	49.9	50.6
Other	0.1	0	0.1
Missing value	0	0	0
Registered with SHCP			
No	57.9	58.5	57.7
Yes	42.1	41.5	42.3
Involuntary entry into self-employment			
No	86.1	93.8	83.7
Yes	13.9	6.2	16.3
Married			
No	30.2	49.2	24.2
Yes	69.8	50.8	75.8
Years of education			
Missing value	0.2	0.2	0.2
0 years	8.1	10.6	7.3
1–3 years	16.2	16.9	16.0
4–6 years	33.8	35.6	33.3
7–9 years	20.1	20.6	20.0
10–12 years	8.4	7.6	8.6
More than 12 years	13.1	8.6	14.5

ME = Microenterprise.
a. Question allows for multiple responses.
Source: Encuesta Nacional de Micronegocios 1992.

Table 5.2 Characteristics of Rural Microenterprises
(% of each column heading)

	All MEs	Female	Male
All MEs (% all MEs)	100	39	61
Sector of economic activity			
Services	27.0	31.8	24.0
Trade	43.9	51.8	38.7
Manufacturing	29.1	16.3	37.3
Place of operation			
Temporary establishment	7.2	8.6	6.4
Ambulant	4.7	4.1	5.0
Carts	0.6	—	1.0
Clients' home	13.0	10.1	14.9
At home	29.9	43.6	21.1
Without business premises	5.4	1.5	7.9
Fixed business premises	35.8	32.2	38.2
Transportation	3.4	—	5.6
Owned fixed business premises			
No	79.3	82.7	77.2
Yes	20.7	17.3	22.8
Assets/workers (1992 pesos)			
Missing value	3.1	4.5	2.1
0–293	37.0	44.2	32.5
294–1,590	27.2	27.1	27.3
1,591–10,275	22.1	16.7	25.5
10,276–51,000	10.3	7.3	12.2
Other	0.4	0.2	0.4
Monthly income (1992 pesos)			
Missing value	3.0	2.4	3.4
0–345	22.5	39.8	11.5
346–2,146	46.7	40.1	50.9
2,147–15,650	24.9	15.0	31.3
Other	2.9	2.8	3.0
Monthly profits (1992 pesos)			
Missing value	3.0	2.4	3.4
Negative	5.8	5.2	6.1
0–387	42.9	64.5	29.1
388–801	22.8	14.4	28.2
802–1,440	13.0	6.2	17.4
1,441–2,733	6.3	3.9	7.9
Other	6.2	3.4	8.0

	All MEs	Female	Male
Age			
16–32	25.6	24.2	26.6
33–41	22.3	21.9	22.6
42–52	26.9	26.0	27.5
53–68	18.8	22.6	16.3
Other	6.3	5.3	6.9
Years in operation			
Missing value	0.8	0.4	1.1
0–2 years	32.6	43.0	25.9
2–5 years	23.3	24.0	22.9
5–12 years	19.8	14.7	23.2
12–30 years	17.7	15.6	19.1
Other	5.7	2.3	7.9
Number of workers (including owner)			
1	53.4	64.1	46.5
2–3	36.6	30.8	40.3
4–6	8.4	4.2	11.1
7–16	1.6	0.9	2.0
Type of accounting			
Formal accounting	22.3	17.8	25.2
Income & expenses notebook	3.2	5.1	2.0
Personal notes	18.2	16.8	19.1
None	55.8	59.4	53.5
Other	0.5	0.9	0.3
Registered with SHCP			
No	57.6	62.2	54.8
Yes	42.4	37.8	45.3
Marital status			
Single	13.9	18.8	10.7
Married	61.6	44.5	72.5
Common-law marriage	11.6	8.0	13.9
Divorced	1.0	2.5	0
Separated	4.0	8.1	1.3
Widow(er)	8.0	18.0	1.6
Married			
No	38.4	55.5	27.6
Yes	61.6	44.5	72.5
Education index			
Illiterate	14.5	22.2	9.5
Did not go to school	2.1	2.6	1.8

(Table continues on the following page.)

Table 5.2 (continued)

	All MEs	Female	Male
Some primary	31.6	33.2	
30.6Completed primary	26.3	21.5	29.3
Some secondary	4.7	2.0	6.4
Completed secondary	11.0	11.4	10.7
High school or college	9.9	7.2	11.7
Years of education			
0 years	16.6	24.8	11.3
1–3 years	31.6	33.2	30.6
4–6 years	26.3	21.5	29.3
7–9 years	15.7	13.4	17.1
10–12 years	5.5	3.7	6.7
More than 12 years	4.4	3.5	5.1
Ethnicity			
Nonindigenous	86.1	85.8	86.3
Indigenous	13.9	14.2	13.7

ME = Microenterprise.
Source: Encuesta Regional de Sevicios Financieros a Unidades de Producción Rural 1994.

important issues related to gender and the characteristics of microenterprises in both areas.

Most male-headed microenterprises are in either the service sector (urban areas) or trade (rural areas), whereas most female-headed microenterprises are in the trade sector. In rural areas, however, female participation is more evenly distributed across sectors, but it is somewhat higher in trade and manufacturing when compared to services. The trade sector includes anything related to the purchase or sale of goods, such as food and beverages, apparel, magazines, books, and shoes. The manufacturing sector includes nondurable goods such as food, textiles, apparel, leather, paper and printing, and miscellaneous goods, and durable goods such as furniture and fabricated metals.

In urban areas, almost half of male microenterprise owners indicated that the main reason to enter the sector was to become more independent, whereas 57 percent of female owners indicated that the main reason to enter the sector was to complement family income. This result points out the substantial gender differences in goals and, hence, potential profitability, of microenterprises. Interestingly, even though men and women enter the microenterprise sector for different reasons, both face the same problems: lack of clients, lower earnings, and excessive competition; and most do not have plans for any important changes in the near future as to how they conduct business.

Most female-owned microenterprises operate from home, although substantial urban–rural differences exist. In rural areas, about 44 percent of female-headed microenterprises (21 percent of male-headed enterprises) are home based, while in urban areas 33 percent of female-headed enterprises (13 percent of male-headed enterprises) are home based. The business location seems to be closely linked to the sector of economic activity and, thus, to earnings. The manufacturing sector, which has the lowest female-to-male earnings ratio, also has a disproportionate share of home-based microenterprises among female owners in both rural and urban areas (88 percent and 81 percent, respectively; Sánchez 1998).

Although there are no substantial gender differences in the age of the owner, female-headed microenterprises have been in business for an average of 6.7 years in both rural and urban areas. In contrast, male-headed microenterprises are relatively older, with 10.8 and 9.2 years of operation in rural and urban areas, respectively. The survival rate of microenterprises—particularly those owned by women—is lower in rural areas. In urban areas, only 36 percent of female-headed microenterprises (33 percent in rural areas) have been in business for more than five years, compared to 51 percent of male-headed microenterprises (50 percent in rural areas).

Most microenterprises are operated by the owner in both urban and rural areas (66 percent and 53 percent, respectively). In urban areas, the average number of workers (including the owner) in male-headed microenterprises is 1.65 and ranges from a high of two workers in manufacturing to a low of 1.47 in the service sector (Sánchez 1998). In rural areas, microenterprises are a stronger source of employment generation—male- and female-headed businesses employ, on average, 2.11 and 1.59 workers, respectively.

In urban areas, microenterprises owned by women operate seven hours less per week than those owned by men.[1] Moreover, this gender disparity in hours of operation greatly differs across economic sectors (Sánchez 1998). In addition, about two fifths of microenterprises are registered with the *Secretaría de Hacienda y Crédito Público*. Gender differences in being registered with tax authorities arise only in rural areas, where 37.8 percent of female-owned microenterprises are registered compared to 45.3 percent of male-owned enterprises.

Gender disparities in educational attainment are greater in rural than in urban areas. About 25 percent of female rural entrepreneurs have not received any formal education compared to 11 percent in urban areas. In the case of men, however, about 11 percent of rural entrepreneurs do not have formal schooling compared to 7 percent in urban areas. Thus, urban–rural differentials are substantially greater among female than among male entrepreneurs. See Box 5.1 for a discussion of gender earnings differentials in the microenterprise sector, and Box 5.2 for a discussion of the role of the microenterprise sector in economic activity.

Box 5.1 Gender Earnings Differentials in the Microenterprise Sector

Earnings differentials between male and female microenterprise owners are a result of gender differences in both observable and unobservable factors.[2] Male–female differences in earnings can arise from, for example, differences across gender in the number of employees, capital, level of formality, firm life, human capital variables, market conditions, and household demographics. Moreover, the market return to each of these characteristics could also play a role in explaining gender differences in earnings.

Market returns also capture unobservable factors, such as entrepreneurial ability. Male–female differences in entrepreneurial ability might result in differential returns to human and physical capital (Maloney and Cunningham 1997). Further, differences in entrepreneurial ability influence the success of microenterprises, and, thus, their size (Lucas 1978). Therefore, if self-employed women have lower levels of entrepreneurial ability, then their microenterprises are likely to be smaller and their earnings lower than those of men.

Unobservable factors work their way through affecting the demand and supply of microenterprises. Labor market distortions—which influence demand—and gender-based household responsibilities—which influence supply—might also explain differing returns to measurable characteristics. For example, if women are unable to get salaried work because of employer discrimination or because of household responsibilities, then those who are not entrepreneurially talented might be forced into self-employment. Their entrance into this sector in turn reduces the mean earnings of self-employed women. Indeed, using the same rural survey in Mexico, Pagán and Sánchez (2000) found that structural supply and demand factors—such as differences in employment preferences, employer discriminatory behavior, and household constraints—induce women into self-employment.

The need to balance home and market responsibilities—which affects labor supply—is a major constraint on productivity and earnings (Blau 1998; Pagán and Sánchez 2000; Chapters 1, 2, and 6 this volume). Family responsibilities have a direct effect on earnings by reducing the amount of energy and effort available to devote to income-generating activities (Hersch 1991). Because household responsibilities generally have predetermined schedules, women's microenterprises are more likely to be home based. This arrangement allows them to have greater flexibility in hours worked, although at the expense of a lower growth rate and earnings than those firms with fixed business premises. On the other hand, accommodating work schedules might lead to lower earnings as a result of compensating wage differentials arising from favorable working conditions that allow women to combine family and job responsibilities.

Further, women and men might have different goals with respect to microenterprise activity, which influences their business strategies and, thus, their earnings. For example, many women select self-employment to supplement family income and reduce risk (Rhyne and Holt 1994; Rothstein 1995). Thus, a woman might engage in low-risk, low-return activities to provide her family with a stable source of income. In fact, in Mexico's urban areas, 57 percent of women enter the microenterprise sector to supplement family income, while 47 percent of men go into self-employment out of their desire to become independent (Table 5.1). Further evidence of gender differences in risk preferences is evident when respondents were asked the reasons for not requesting a loan. About 45.3 percent of women in urban areas did not see a need to seek credit compared to 44 percent of men. Moreover, 27.2 percent of women prefer to use their own resources instead of resorting to credit compared to 25.2 percent of men.

Finally, credit constraints might be an important impediment to microenterprise growth (Evans and Jovanovic 1989; Rhyne and Holt 1994). The presence of credit constraints affects the ability of business owners to smooth consumption over time and undertake profitable investments. Thus, the investment behavior of microenterprises—and, therefore, their growth and earnings potential—might be restrained by limited access to credit services (Tybout 1983; Nabi 1989).

In the urban areas surveyed, about 12 percent of all microenterprises have received a loan since starting their businesses. However, in rural areas only 45 percent of women have received some type of consumption–production financing during the two years prior to the interview compared to 56 percent of men (see Sánchez 1998). This shrinking difference is explained by differences in the questions regarding access to financial services between the two surveys.

Box 5.2 The Role of the Microenterprise Sector in Economic Activity

Another important source of differences in the gender earnings gap is whether women are relatively segregated into low-profit-margin sectors. If female-headed microenterprises are overrepresented in low-profit-margin sectors and underrepresented in high-profit-margin sectors, then part of the gender earnings gap could be attributed to male–female differences in sectoral distributions.

Gender disparities in sectoral distributions can be analyzed by using the index of dissimilarity (or Duncan Index), which equals $0.5\Sigma j \mid PjF - PjM \mid$ (Psacharopoulos and Tzannatos 1992). PjF and PjM represent the proportion of females and males in the jth economic sector. The index compares the sectoral distribution across gender: if men and women were equally distributed across sectors, the index would equal zero; if all sectors were

(Box 5.2 continues on the following page.)

Box 5.2 (continued)

completely dominated by one gender, the index would equal 100 percent. Using a detailed sectoral classification, the estimated Duncan Index is about 51 percent, which suggests a high level of gender segregation across sectors.

Differences between men and women on sectoral choices are likely to be influenced by many different factors: individual preferences, barriers to entry and discrimination, gender differences in household responsibilities, initial sector-specific investment requirements, and gender differences in business skills. In addition, premarket factors—such as differential treatment by parents and schools, and gender differences in educational access and business experience—also channel entrepreneurial women into confined economic sectors. As such, it is not surprising to find that female-headed microenterprises concentrate primarily in economic sectors associated with household activities, such as food processing or domestic services (World Bank 1994).

Figure 5.1 suggests that across broadly defined sectors, women earn substantially less than men. In urban areas, the female-to-male earnings ratio is the lowest in manufacturing (30 percent), followed by trade (54 percent) and services (58 percent). In rural areas, the gender earnings ratio is also the lowest in manufacturing (25 percent), followed by trade (30 percent) and services (55 percent). Thus, in terms of relative earnings women fare better in the sectors where they are better represented—such as services and trade—than in productive sectors with a low female participation, such as manufacturing. This actually shows a certain degree of selectivity in terms of the sectors where women are employed; that is, female entrepreneurs tend to concentrate in productive sectors where the gender earnings differential is relatively small.

Given the discussion above, any meaningful analysis of gender earnings differentials should consider the role of both intra- and intersectoral factors in explaining the causes for the male–female disparities in earnings. Understanding the role of inter- and intrasectoral factors has important implications for policymaking in the sense that this type of analysis allows us to assess whether policies should concentrate on gender parity in earnings within each sector, or on redistributing self-employed individuals (or redirecting potentially self-employed individuals) across sectors.

Decomposition Analysis of Gender Differences in Earnings: Methodology

To analyze the role of inter- and intrasectoral factors on gender earnings differentials, the Brown, Moon, and Zoloth (1980a, 1980b) decomposition technique can be employed. Brown, Moon, and Zoloth extended the Oaxaca (1973) earnings decomposition to account for endogenous selection of occupations in the wage-and-salary sector. This methodology has two attractive features that are helpful in identifying the sources of gender earnings differentials. First, the method takes into account that gender differences in sectoral distributions could result from barriers to entry into certain sectors (for example, minimum capital investments or household responsibilities), and it allows for the endogenous determination of the sectoral distribution. Second, the technique takes into account that differences in characteristics vary across economic sectors and, hence, that they play an important role in explaining male–female differences in earnings.

The decomposition involves two steps. First, a multinomial logit model of sectoral choice is estimated for men and then the estimated coefficients are used to predict the sectoral distribution of women. Second, sector-specific log earnings equations are estimated to be able to decompose the earnings gap into inter (across) and intra (within) sectoral factors. Both the multinomial logit model and the log earnings regressions include controls for factors that affect sectoral choice and earnings, namely socioeconomic status, personal characteristics, household demographics, business opportunities in the region, and individual preferences (see Sánchez 1998 for details).

After estimating the econometric models discussed above, the gender earnings gap in urban and rural areas is separated into four components. The first component is the explained or justified intrasectoral gender earnings gap—explained in the sense that it captures gender earnings differentials attributed to male–female differences in both owners' human capital and microenterprise characteristics. The second component is the unexplained or unjustified intrasectoral gender earnings gap—the portion of the gap that can be attributed to differences in male–female compensation for a given set of personal characteristics, and keeping the sectoral distribution constant. The term captures differences in productivity between men and women, unobservable variables, and discrimination. For example, if female-headed microenterprises face greater growth constraints, this component will capture their lower access to markets, networks, technology, and credit. The term also captures gender discrimination in earnings within each sector.

The third and fourth components capture the part of the gender earnings gap that can be attributed to explained and unexplained male–female differences in the sectoral distributions. If male and female entrepreneurs differ only on their sectoral distributions, then the third term captures the effect of differences in the values of characteristics between men and women on their sectoral distributions (explained). The fourth term represents the effect of gender-specific preferences for the economic sector—and barriers to entry and discrimination in access to specific sectors—on the gender earnings gap. See Box 5.3 for a discussion of the results of the analysis of gender differences in earnings.

Box 5.3 Results of Decomposition Analysis of Gender Differences in Earnings

Microdata from the 1994 Survey of Rural Entrepreneurs and Financial Services and the 1992 National Survey of Urban Microenterprises were used to analyze the sources of the gender earnings gap. The explanatory variables used in the analysis can be grouped into three categories:

- *Microenterprise characteristics*: Years in operation, number of hours worked (only for urban areas),[3] number of workers, capital endowments, place of operation, registration with the *Secretaría de Hacienda y Crédito Público*, and involuntary entry into the microenterprise sector (only for urban areas).

- *Personal characteristics of the owner*: Marital status, years of education, ethnicity (only for rural areas), and potential labor market experience (defined as age minus years of education minus six).

- *Market conditions*: Number of inhabitants in the locality of residence (only for rural areas).

The intermediate results from estimating sector-specific earnings equations are not reported here, but suffice it to say that the coefficients of the variables have sensible signs and that the specification employed has a reasonable explanatory power (that is, the regressors explain from 33 to 50 percent of the total variation in earnings in the sector-specific regressions).

The results from these estimations are consistent with other human capital studies: years of formal education have a positive impact on earnings, although substantial differences appear across economic sectors. Owners in manufacturing have the lowest return to schooling in urban areas and they are even negative for males in the rural areas studied. For urban microenterprises, earnings increase with experience but at a decreasing rate; however, for rural microenterprises, experience is statistically insignificant.

Earnings are also positively related to the number of hours worked, especially for female owners in urban areas. Microenterprise owners that have been in business longer have higher earnings, particularly males. This finding might be a result of firm age serving as a proxy for an efficient scale of operations. The number of workers in the firm is positively related to earnings, especially among microenterprises in the trade sector.

Involuntary entry into the microenterprise sector comes at a substantial reduction in earnings among urban microenterprises.[4] The estimated percentage reduction in earnings due to involuntary entry is about 17 percent. Married male owners have an earnings premium across all sectors, especially in urban areas. This premium ranges from 8 percent in manufacturing to 21 percent in services. In rural areas, the marriage premium is only statistically significant for female owners in the service sector (51 percent). Interestingly, among rural microenterprises, market conditions—proxied by the size of the locality—do not seem to be related to earnings.

Tables 5.3 and 5.4 present the results from the earnings decomposition for urban and rural microenterprises. The gender earnings differential is about 0.7012 log-points for the urban sample, and 1.0177 for the rural sample; that is, the average female-to-male earnings ratio is 50 percent for urban areas, and 36 percent for rural areas. The main findings from the decomposition are that intersectoral factors explain a relatively small proportion of the earnings gap: about 3.2 percent and –1.1 percent in urban and rural areas, respectively. This finding indicates that efforts to reallocate female-headed microenterprises would not significantly increase their mean overall earnings. Hence, policies that attempt to increase women's earnings within an economic sector would be far more successful than the reallocation of workers into different sectors.

Most of the gender earnings gap can be explained by intrasectoral factors—about 96.9 percent in urban areas and 101.1 percent in rural areas.[5] Thus, policymakers should consider sector-specific policies to reduce gender disparities in earnings.

Differences in productive and personal characteristics are more important in explaining the male–female earnings gap in rural than in urban areas. Among urban microenterprises, about 35 percent of the earnings gap is explained by differences in personal characteristics, whereas in the rural areas studied, this component explains almost 42 percent of the overall earnings gap.

Male–female differences in returns to factors (explanatory variables) explain 62 percent of the earnings gap in urban areas and 59 percent in rural areas. Among urban microenterprises, this component fluctuates from a low of 60 percent to a high of 68 percent. In the rural areas studied, the service sector has the largest size of this component—about 68 percent. The magnitude of this component illustrates that unobservable factors—such as discrimination, competition, entrepreneurial ability, credit supply con-

(Box 5.3 continues on the following page.)

Box 5.3 (continued)

straints, differential attitudes toward risk, and women's reproductive responsibilities—are responsible for a large share of the gender earnings gap.

It is interesting to note that the magnitude of the unexplained component of the gender earnings gap is lower in Mexican microenterprises than the magnitude found in typical labor studies of male–female differences in earnings in Latin America.[6] However, the results are more in line with those of gender pay studies for industrialized countries (Psacharopoulos and Tzannatos 1992). Parker (1995) found an unexplained gender earnings gap of about 75 percent for the self-employed—which would include most microenterprises—and from 88 to 131 percent for salaried workers in the major urban areas of Mexico during 1986–92. She also finds that this unexplained gap increased from 1986 to 1992 and suggests that this could be due to rising labor market discrimination for women. In another important study, Duval Hernández (1999) argues that lack of access to flexible employment opportunities has forced women to accept full-time employment, optimize their time, and, thus, be very productive in both market and nonmarket activities. This could partially explain why the unexplained component of earnings is somewhat small in Mexico when compared to other Latin American countries.

In all, the empirical results indicate that gender earnings differentials in the microenterprise sector are largely due to the fact that men's microenterprises are bigger than women's in each economic sector, and have differential constraints to profitability. Gender differences in sectoral distribution account for a small share of the gender earnings gap in both rural and urban areas.

Gender Differences in Credit Access

One of the main findings from the earnings decomposition discussed in Box 5.3 is that men and women face differential constraints that affect profitability and earnings. For example, male-headed microenterprises are relatively larger and more profitable than those headed by females.

Lack of access to credit services has been identified as one of the most important impediments to microenterprise growth (Evans and Jovanovic 1989; Rhyne and Holt 1994). The presence of credit constraints affects the ability of microentrepreneurs to smooth consumption over time and undertake profitable investments. As such, the investment behavior of microenterprises—and, therefore, their growth potential—could be restrained by limited access to credit services (Tybout 1983; Nabi 1989).

Table 5.3 Urban Microenterprises: Male–Female Earnings Decomposition (with hours worked)

	All sectors	%	Services	Com-merce	Manu-facturing
Decomposition of male–female earnings differential by economc sector (in log-points)					
Average Earnings					
Male	6.8260		6.8364	6.7567	6.8952
Female	6.1251		6.2869	6.1347	5.7027
Male–female earning differentials	0.7009		0.5495	0.6220	1.1925
Attributed to differences in:					
Explanatory variables (Xs)			0.2163	0.1992	0.4796
Estimated parameters (unexplained)			0.3332	0.4227	0.7129
Decomposition of male-female earnings differential (in log-points)	0.70127				
Intra-sectoral earnings effect	0.6790	96.9			
Attributed to differences in:					
Explanatory variables (explained)	0.2455	35.0	0.0747	0.1018	0.0690
Estimated parameters (unexplained)	0.4336	61.9	0.1150	0.2160	0.1025
Intersectoral earnings effect	0.0222	3.2			
Attributed to differences in:					
Explanatory variables (explained)	0.0026	0.4	–0.1882	–0.0506	0.2414
Estimated paramters (unexplained)	0.0196	2.8	1.2282	–1.4701	0.2615
Actual and predicted sectoral distribution of microenterprises (in percentages)					
Females					
Predicted			52.5%	29.3%	18.2%
Actual			34.5%	51.1%	14.4%
Males					
Actual			49.7%	28.6%	21.7%

Table 5.4 Rural Microenterprises: Male–Female Earnings Decomposition

	All sectors	%	Services	Com- merce	Manu- facturing
Decomposition of male–female earnings differential by economc sector (in log-points)					
Earnings					
Male	6.3886		6.1131	6.6502	6.2927
Female	5.3709		5.5221	5.4611	4.9116
Male–female earning differentials	1.0177		0.5910	1.1892	1.3810
Attributed to differences in:					
Explanatory variables (explained)			0.6013	0.3052	0.4076
Estimated parameters (unexplained)			–0.0103	0.8840	0.9734
Decomposition of male–female earnings differential (in log-points)	1.01767				
Intrasectoral earnings effect	1.0284	101.1			
Attributed to differences in:					
Explanatory variables (explained)	0.4245	41.7	0.2004	0.1421	0.0821
Estimated parameters (unexplained)	0.6039	59.3	–0.0034	0.4115	0.1958
Intersectoral earnings effect	–0.0107	–1.1			
Attributed to differences in:					
Explanatory variables (explained)	0.0152	1.5	–0.2424	0.1506	0.1070
Estimated paramters (unexplained)	–0.0259	–2.5	–0.3811	–0.6905	1.0457
Actual and predicted sectoral distribution of microenterprises (in percentages)					
Females					
Predicted			27.1%	36.2%	36.7%
Actual			33.3%	46.6%	20.1%
Males					
Actual			23.1%	38.4%	38.4%

Tables 5.5 and 5.6 report some basic indicators on the participation of urban and rural microenterprises in credit markets. In analyzing the sources of start-up funding, most microenterprises—especially those located in rural areas—rely mainly on the owner's personal wealth. Potential entrepreneurs might face liquidity constraints and would therefore need to accumulate capital before initiating their entrepreneurial activities (Evans and Jovanovic 1989). Some microenterprise owners—particularly men—use savings from their previous employment to start operations.

A key finding from the surveys is that owners who are able to obtain start-up capital generally do so from informal lenders (moneylenders, friends and relatives, input credit, and other sources). Unlike male owners, female owners are more likely to draw funds from family and

Table 5.5 Urban Microenterprises: Participation in Credit Markets

	All MEs	Female	Male
All MEs (% all MEs)	100	24	76
Have received credit since starting operations from[a]			
Formal lenders	5.0	3.5	5.5
Banks	4.3	2.6	4.9
Cajas de ahorro	0.7	0.8	0.7
Informal lenders	7.4	8.8	6.9
Friends and relatives	3.0	3.3	2.9
Moneylenders	0.8	0.9	0.8
Supplier credit	3.3	4.7	2.8
Other	0.4	0.1	0.4
Have not requested credit because			
Prefer to use own resources	25.7	27.2	25.2
High interest rates	6.9	7.1	6.8
Too many requirements	5.5	3.8	6.0
Do not know how to obtain credit	2.4	1.9	2.5
Do not know that credit exists	0.4	0.2	0.4
Other	1.2	1.5	1.1
Have not needed credit	44.3	45.3	44
Have requested and did not receive it	1.7	1.1	1.9

(Table continues on the following page.)

Table 5.6 (continued)

	All MEs	Female	Male
Have used credit to[a]			
Buy business premises	1.2	0.3	1.5
Repair premises or vehicles	1.5	0.6	1.7
Expand premises	0.4	0.3	0.4
Buy inputs or merchandise	7.3	9.4	6.7
Pay debts	0.5	0.6	0.5
Buy equipment	1.4	1.2	1.5
Buy tools	0.5	0.1	0.6
Consumption	0.4	0.4	0.4
Other	0.3	0.2	0.3
Source of funds to start up[a]			
Formal lenders	2.3	1.8	2.4
Banks	1.7	1.5	1.8
Cajas de ahorro	0.5	0.4	0.6
Informal lenders	22.9	30.6	20.4
Friends and relatives	17.4	23.9	15.3
Moneylenders	1.8	2.1	1.8
Credit from clients	0.7	0.6	0.7
Credit from suppliers	3.4	4.6	3.0
Own resources	57.2	51.7	58.9
Personal savings	50.7	46.9	52.0
Liquidation from			
previous employment	5.4	2.2	6.4
Other	2.3	3.6	1.9
Did not need it	22.8	20.2	23.6

a. Question allows for multiple responses.
Source: Encuesta Nacional de Micronegocios 1992.

Table 5.6 Rural Microenterprises: Participation in Credit Markets
(% of each column heading)

	All MEs	Female	Male
All MEs (% all MEs)	100	39	61
Have received credit during			
the previous two years from[a]			
Formal lenders	6.1	2.2	8.6
Banks	2.7	0.9	3.8
Development banks	0.4		0.6

	All MEs	Female	Male
Cajas de ahorro, UC,			
and SAP	3.3	1.3	4.5
Informal lenders	48.9	44.1	51.9
Moneylenders	5.2	3.9	6.0
Friends and relatives	10.0	7.4	11.7
Trader	0.7	0.9	0.6
Commercial credit	36.2	34.8	37.0
Sales with advances	6.5	4.5	7.8
None	48.3	55.5	43.7
Market for cash loans			
Received	21.2	14.3	25.6
Both sectors	0.6		1.0
Formal sector only	5.6	2.2	7.7
Informal sector only	15.1	12.1	17.0
Rejected	2.1	1.5	2.6
Did not apply because	76.7	84.2	71.8
Would not be approved	7.7	8.4	7.3
Many requirements	9.2	6.6	10.9
Afraid to request	8.2	8.9	7.7
Do not need credit	26.2	29.4	24.2
Too risky	19.3	23.4	16.6
Other	5.9	7.6	4.9
Missing value	0.2		0.3
Source of funds to start up[a]			
Formal lenders	2.9	0.8	4.2
Banks	1.0	0.8	1.1
Cajas de ahorro	1.9		3.1
Informal lenders	18.6	22.3	16.2
Friends and relatives	11.9	16.6	8.9
Moneylenders	0.4		0.6
Credit from clients	0.8	0.5	1.1
Credit from suppliers	5.9	5.7	6.0
Own resources	65.4	56.7	70.9
Personal savings	56.2	50.4	59.9
Liquidation from			
previous employment	4.5	1.3	6.6
Sale of assets	1.3	0.9	1.6
Other	6.5	7.0	6.3
Did not need it	19.9	23.6	17.5

a. Question allows for multiple responses.
Source: Encuesta Regional de Servicios Financieros a Unidades de Producción Rural 1994.

friends. In urban areas, about 24 percent of female and 15 percent of male owners borrowed from friends and relatives to initiate their business. Loans from family and friends—which are at zero nominal interest—are basically granted because of altruistic or mutual insurance motives across households. Thus, it is likely that family and friends support women's entrepreneurial interests because they mostly initiate their activities to supplement household income.

Overall, only 2 to 3 percent of microenterprises borrow from formal lenders (commercial banks and *cajas de ahorro*) to start their operations. Formal lenders usually view lending to start-up microenterprises as a risky activity because it is difficult to assess their viability and the owner's entrepreneurial ability and creditworthiness. Moreover, most microenterprises have a relatively short life span, which significantly contributes to sectoral riskiness.

Tables 5.5 and 5.6 also report the main sources of credit, the reasons why some business owners have not requested credit, and the reasons for and purpose of requesting credit. First, note that microenterprises in both urban and rural areas participate in credit markets only to a limited degree and operate almost in financial autarky, reflecting the poor development of formal and informal financial markets. In urban areas, only 12 percent of male- and female-headed microenterprises have received a loan since starting their activities, and only 13 percent have applied for a loan. Compared to other Latin American countries, microenterprise participation in credit markets is much lower in Mexico. For example, the reported use of credit services in Costa Rica, the Dominican Republic, Guatemala, and Honduras ranges from 20 percent to 68 percent (see Table 5.7).

In urban areas, 7.4 percent of microenterprises borrowed from informal lenders and 5 percent borrowed from formal lenders. Thus, Mexican informal urban credit markets seem rather underdeveloped. Almost the same number of urban microenterprises received loans from formal and informal lenders, in contrast to other developing countries where the number of microenterprises or households receiving loans from informal sources is 2 to 16 times higher than those from formal lenders.

Male-headed microenterprises are more likely to borrow funds from formal lenders than their female counterparts, while female-headed microenterprises participate more actively in informal credit markets than their male counterparts. These male–female differences in the choice of lender might reflect gender-specific differences in the demand and supply of credit. For example, if female-headed microenterprises demand smaller loans than male-headed microenterprises—perhaps as a result of being in small-scale production—then informal lenders might be able to better meet their credit needs than formal lenders.

Table 5.7 Credit Market Participation across Selected Latin American Countries

	% of microenterprises		
	All	Women	Men
Mexico, 1992[a]	12.1	12.0	12.1
Mexico, 1994[a]	13.8		
Mexico, 1996[a]	13.2		
Rural Mexico, 1994[b]	51.8	44.5	56.4
Dominican Republic, 1992[c]	20.7	16.5	21.2
Honduras, 1996	15.0		
Valle Central, Costa Rica, 1993[d]	67.5		

Sources:
a. National Survey of Microenterprises 1992, 1994, 1996.
b. Sánchez (1998).
c. Cabal (1993).
d. Chaves and Sánchez (1995).

There are no substantial male–female differences in reasons for not requesting credit. Almost half of owners in urban areas report that they have not needed credit within the past two years, and about one fourth prefer to use their own resources instead of borrowing. Loan rejection rates are also relatively low (1.1 percent for females and 1.9 percent for males), and most have used credit to buy inputs or merchandise, particularly female-headed microenterprises.

Rejection rates on cash loans are relatively low in the rural areas surveyed—1.5 percent for females and 2.6 percent for males. Interestingly, about 23 percent of females and 16.6 percent of males did not apply for cash loans because they deemed this type of activity too risky. This finding is consistent with the idea that, unlike males, females enter the microenterprise sector to complement family income and, as such, are more interested in having a steady source of income than in undertaking high-risk, high-return activities.

Conclusion

Microenterprises are particularly active in both rural and urban areas of Mexico, and they substantially contribute to household earnings, employment creation, and overall economic growth. There are significant gender differences in earnings in the microenterprise sector, particularly in the rural areas studied. Because women are particularly active in this sector, reducing gender disparities can potentially increase their ability to increase household income.

The results from decomposing the gender earnings gap suggest that the most effective policies are those that attempt to reduce male–female earnings disparities within each economic sector (for example, encouraging diversification into nontraditional activities within each sector of economic activity). Two aspects are important here: first, reducing the unequal gender distribution of productive characteristics, and second, eliminating differential growth constraints that influence returns to productive and personal characteristics. The results also indicate that efforts to reallocate and redirect women into targeted economic sectors are not likely to be effective in reducing the gender earnings gap in both rural and urban areas.

Public policies that are consistent with reducing gender differences in productive characteristics include broad-based education and training programs for women—both formal and informal—since formal education and training systems are the main avenues to prepare successful entrepreneurs through the acquisition of basic business and literacy skills. In addition, access to formal and informal education expands individuals' choices, increases their capacity to respond to market opportunities, and increases their productivity.

The provision of direct enterprise development efforts can also increase and facilitate entrepreneurial activities, although they cannot substitute for adequate macroeconomic conditions, infrastructure, and business environment. Such services should assist microenterprises in managing their business more effectively, increasing their access to information and technology, and managing risk (USAID 1995). However, the development of nonfinancial assistance methodologies remains somewhat unexplored. Some basic principles to design successful strategies to provide nonfinancial services are to charge market prices (recovery costs), be customer oriented, be market driven, work within specific sectors, and deliver services in a timely fashion (USAID 1995).

Because differences in returns to productive individual characteristics explain a substantial portion of the gender earnings gap, strategies dealing with getting at the source of gender differences in the returns to personal characteristics within each economic sector could have a desirable long-term impact in increasing the earnings of female entrepreneurs. The findings point out the need to examine differential firm growth constraints across gender. Excess reliance on informal lending by female-headed urban microenterprises is certainly indicative of gender-specific market constraints in credit access. However, this result does not arise in rural areas. Gender differences in the type of credit needs of microenterprises could also help explain why female-owned enterprises stabilize at a smaller size of operation than male-owned enterprises.

Most constraints to entrepreneurship result from the business environment and macroeconomic conditions in which microenterprises operate. Public policy should promote a business environment in which microenterprises can enforce contracts and have lower costs of accessing professional services, output and input markets, information, training, and technology. De Soto (1989) argues that many firms operating outside formal institutions are willing to pay to become formal, but that excessive transaction costs and bureaucracies keep them outside of the formal economy. By increasing the participation of microenterprises in the institutions of civil society—such as federal and local treasuries, social security, and the legal system—microenterprises can augment their productivity and growth potential as their participation becomes increasingly important in the development process (Levenson and Maloney 1997). The overall impact of these policies is that they increase competition and thereby reduce the potential of gender-based discrimination in access and opportunities in the microenterprise sector.

Gender roles within the family might also be a fundamental source of distinct male–female structural barriers to economic parity which influence women's work, productivity, and earnings (Blau 1998). Although changing gender roles within the household might not be feasible in the short term, it is certainly feasible to explore best practices that raise women's social and intrahousehold status, and which could eventually have a positive impact on profitability and growth. For example, providing community-based childcare reduces structural barriers to male–female economic parity because it leads to more time available for market-based activities.

Microenterprises—both male- and female-owned—need access to a broader range of financial services to manage risk better, finance investment, keep the business afloat when cash flow is tight, exploit profitable opportunities, and smooth household consumption. Hence, financial services are seen as a tool for greater efficiency and productivity, which would have an impact on reducing the gender earnings gap.

Finally, given data limitations, the analysis centered only on disentangling gender disparities in earnings across three broadly defined sectors—manufacturing, trade, and services. As such, the finding that the most effective policies to reduce gender disparities in earnings do not include redistribution across sectors could be due partly to aggregation bias. Nonetheless, the results are a reasonable first approximation of the role that sectoral gender differences have in explaining male–female outcomes in relative earnings.

Notes

1. Unfortunately, hours of operations were not asked in the rural survey.

2. Earnings are measured as the difference between gross earnings and operating costs; that is, they are net earnings.

3. An important limitation of the rural survey is that the number of hours worked is not available. Thus, the decomposition results overestimate the unexplained portions of the intrasectoral and intersectoral components.

4. This variable is not available for the rural survey.

5. The intra- and intersectoral factors must add up to 100 percent; however, each one can be larger than 100 percent if the other is negative.

6. An exception to this result is the study by Valdez Moreno (1997), who finds that the unexplained gender earnings gap is only 30 percent in Monterrey, Mexico.

References

Blau, Francine D. 1998. "Trends in the Well-Being of American Women, 1970–1995." *Journal of Economic Literature* 36(1):112–65.

Brown, Cynthia, José A. Pagán, and Eduardo Rodríguez. 1999. "Occupational Attainment and Gender Earnings Differentials in Mexico." *Industrial and Labor Relations Review* 53(1):123–35.

Brown, Randall S., Marilyn Moon, and Barbara S. Zoloth. 1980a. "Occupational Attainment and Segregation by Sex." *Industrial and Labor Relations Review* 33(4):506–17

_____. 1980b. "Incorporating Occupational Attainment in Studies of Male/Female Earnings Differentials." *Journal of Human Resources* 15(1):3–28.

Cabal, Miguel. 1993. Evolución de las Microempresas y Pequeñas Empresas en la República Dominicana, 1992–93. Santo Domingo: Fondo Micro.

Chaves, Rodrigo A., and Susana M. Sánchez. 1995. "Mexico: Rural Financial Markets." Green Cover Report No. 14599-MX. World Bank, Natural Resources and Rural Poverty Division, Country Department II, Latin America and the Caribbean Region, Washington, D.C.

_____. 2000. "Poverty, Rural Entrepreneurs, and Financial Markets in the Rural Areas of Mexico." In Alberto Valdés and Ramón López, eds., *Rural Poverty in Latin America: Analytics, New Empirical Evidence, and Policy*. New York: St. Martin's Press.

Cohen, Gary L. 1996. "Women Entrepreneurs." *Perspectives on Labour and Income* 8(1):23–8.

De Soto, Hernando. 1989. *The Other Path: The Invisible Revolution in the Third World*. New York: HarperTrade.

Duval Hernández, Robert. 1999. "El trabajo doméstico y los salarios: Un estudio para los hogares mexicanos." Thesis. División de Economía, Centro de Investigación y Docencia Económicas, México, D.F.

Evans, David S., and Boyan Jovanovic. 1989. "An Estimated Model of Entrepreneurial Choice under Liquidity Constraints." *Journal of Political Economy* 97(4):808–26.

Hersch, Joni. 1991. "Male-Female Differences in Hourly Wages: The Role of Human Capital, Working Conditions, and Housework." *Industrial & Labor Relations Review* 44(4):746–59.

Levenson, Alex R., and William F. Maloney. 1997. "The Informal Sector, Firm Dynamics and Institutional Participation." University of Illinois and the Milken Institute, Urbana–Champaign. Processed.

Lucas, R. E., Jr. 1978. "On the Size Distribution of Business Firms." *Bell Journal of Economics* 9(2):508–23.

Maloney, William F., and Wendy V. Cunningham. 1997. "Heterogeneity in Small Scale LDC Enterprises: The Mexican Case." University of Illinois, Urbana–Champaign. Processed.

Nabi, Ijaz. 1989. "Investment in Segmented Capital Markets." *Quarterly Journal of Economics* 104(3):453–62.

Oaxaca, Ronald. 1973. "Male-Female Wage Differentials in Urban Labor Markets." *International Economic Review* 14(3):693–708.

Pagán, José A., and Susana M. Sánchez. 2000. "Gender Differences in Labor Market Decisions: Evidence from Rural Mexico." *Economic Development and Cultural Change*, 48(3) :620–37.

Parker, Susan W. 1995. "Niveles salariales de los hombres y las mujeres asalariados y trabajadores auto-empleados en el México urbano 1986–1992: Un enfoque microeconómico." In José A. Tijerina Guajardo and Jorge Meléndez Barrón, eds., *Capital humano, crecimiento, pobreza: Problemática mexicana (Segundo encuentro internacional)*. Monterrey, NL, México: Centro de Investigaciones Económicas, Facultad de Economía, Universidad Autónoma de Nuevo León.

Psacharopoulos, George, and Zafiris Tzannatos. 1992. *Women's Employment and Pay in Latin America: Overview and Methodology*. Washington, D.C.: World Bank.

Rhyne, Elisabeth, and Sharon Holt. 1994. "Women in Finance and Enterprise Development." ESP Discussion Paper Series No. 40. World Bank, Education and Social Policy Department, Washington, D.C.

Rothstein, Frances A. 1995. "Gender and Multiple Income Strategies in Rural Mexico." In Christine E. Bose and Edna Acosta-Belén, eds., *Women in the Latin American Development Process*. Philadelphia: Temple University Press.

Sánchez, Susana M. 2000. "Dominican Microenterprises and Financial Markets. World Bank, Washington, D.C.

———. 1998. "Gender Earnings Differentials in the Microenterprise Sector: Evidence from Rural and Urban Mexico." World Bank, Washington, D.C.

Tybout, James R. 1983. "Credit Rationing and Investment Behavior in a Developing Country." *Review of Economics and Statistics* 65(4):598–607.

USAID. 1995. "Non-financial Assistance to Microentrepreneurs." Microenterprise Development Brief 5. Washington, D.C.

Valdez Moreno, Francisco. 1997. "Condiciones laborales para hombres y mujeres en el área metropolitana de Monterrey: La discriminación salarial por sexo." In José A. Tijerina Guajardo and Jorge Meléndez Barrón, eds., *Capital humano, crecimiento, pobreza: Problemática mexicana (tercer encuentro internacional)*. Monterrey, NL, México: Centro de Investigaciones Económicas, Facultad de Economía, Universidad Autónoma de Nuevo León.

Wilson, Sandra, and Arvil V. Adams. 1994. "Self-employment for the unemployed. Experience in OECD and transitional economies." World Bank Discussion Paper No. 263. Washington, D.C.

World Bank. 1994. "Enhancing Women's Participation in Economic Development." World Bank Policy Paper. Washington, D.C.

6

Gender Issues in Workforce Participation and Self-Employment in Rural Mexico

José A. Pagán and Susana M. Sánchez

The labor market in Mexico has experienced profound gender-related changes over the last two decades. Most notably, occupational segregation has decreased, the female employment rate increased from 31.4 percent in 1987 to 36.1 percent in 1993, and the female–male gender earnings ratio fell from 0.792 to 0.780 during the same period (Brown, Pagán, and Rodríguez-Oreggia 1999). Gender differences in labor market outcomes have been identified as being the result of male–female differences in domestic responsibilities, and the expectation that men are the primary source of income within the household (see Chapters 1 and 2, this volume). These expectations and differentiated roles within the household have a substantial impact on the acquisition of education and labor market experience, with men accumulating more human capital and having longer employment spells over the life cycle than women (see Introduction, this volume).

As a result of these changes in the labor market, the role of gender in economic development has been of interest to social scientists and policymakers. For example, the Mexican government has started to incorporate gender issues when formulating public policy programs and proposals to foster economic growth (*Poder Ejecutivo Federal* 1995). Most international organizations have also integrated gender issues into their development strategies (Inter-American Development Bank 1995). In addition, researchers have recognized that effective policymaking should take into account gender roles over the life cycle, the fact that gender bias is concentrated in only some sectors, and household structure (Chaves and Sánchez 2000; also see Chapter 1, this volume).

This paper is an extension of the paper written by the authors, entitled "Gender Differences in Labor Market Outcomes: Evidence from Rural Mexico," published in *Economic Development and Cultural Change* 48(3):620–37.

The role of gender-specific factors in male–female differences in Mexico's rural labor market outcomes is particularly policy relevant. The human capital levels of the employed are about equal for men and women; nonetheless, employment rates are much higher for men than for women (Inter-American Development Bank 1995). Furthermore, self-employment rates are about the same for men and women, yet there are substantial differences in human capital and individual responses to self-employment (Parker 1995).

This chapter analyzes the role of gender-specific factors in explaining male–female differences in employment and the incidence of self-employment in rural Mexico. Gender-related labor market outcomes are analyzed using the 1994 Survey of Rural Entrepreneurs and Financial Services.

The empirical analysis begins by studying the differences in employment patterns across gender and marital status to study heterogeneity in household composition. Bivariate probit models of workforce participation and self-employment are then estimated separately for men and women, by marital status. The effects of male–female differences in observable individual, household, and labor market characteristics—including education, experience, fertility, and household demographics—are separated from gender differences that can be attributed to differential responses to employment and self-employment (for example, preferences, available opportunities, labor market discrimination, and other market conditions) using a decomposition analysis based on the Oaxaca (1973) method.

The results indicate that there are substantial gender disparities in individual responses to employment participation and the incidence of self-employment. Gender differences in individual characteristics explain less than one tenth of the observed differences in workforce participation, but male–female differences in employment responses explain most of the gender gap in the workforce participation rate. The incidence of self-employment is higher for married men than for married women, but higher for single women when compared with single men. Hence, policies that focus solely on increasing the productivity-related characteristics of women would have a limited impact on increasing female workforce participation if these are not accompanied by policies addressing differential employment responses—in particular, those affecting the entrance and long-term stay of women in the workforce.

Besides analyzing gender differences in workforce participation and the incidence of self-employment in rural Mexico, this chapter discusses the econometric methodology, presents the data-descriptive statistics and empirical results, discusses the sources of gender differences in workforce participation and self-employment, proposes public policy recommendations designed to reduce gender inequality, and presents some concluding remarks.

Male–Female Differences in Employment: Conceptual Issues

During the early 1990s, Mexico experienced a substantial increase in the labor force participation rate of women (Brown, Pagán, and Rodríguez-Oreggia 1999). Gender differences in workforce participation narrowed in both urban and less urban areas, yet the reduction of gender differences in labor market outcomes has been more noticeable in self-employment, particularly in less urban areas (Table 6.1).

The participation of women in the self-employment sector also rose during the first half of the 1990s, especially in nonagricultural sectors (Parker 1995). From 1991 to 1995, women accounted for 68 percent of the total rise in nonagricultural self-employment; in the less urban areas, female nonagricultural self-employment increased by almost 90 percent during the same period. This phenomenon is not unique to Mexico; recent trends in the United States and Canada show similar female self-employment growth patterns (Devine 1994; Cohen 1996).

Gender differences in workforce participation in Mexico's rural areas are significant (Table 6.1). When it comes to workforce participation, only

Table 6.1 Workforce Participation and Incidence of Self-Employment in Mexico

	All		More urban areas		Less urban areas	
	Men	*Women*	*Men*	*Women*	*Men*	*Women*
Workforce participation						
1991	76.4	30.4	72.1	33.9	80.2	27.2
1993	77.2	32.0	72.4	35.7	81.4	28.7
1995	74.7	32.8	69.7	35.5	78.9	30.3
1994*					86.5	28.5
Self-employment**						
1991	36.0	21.0	21.6	14.4	45.3	27.0
1993	33.9	23.9	20.5	15.9	42.0	30.6
1995	32.4	23.7	22.3	13.8	37.8	29.8
1994*					29.8	28.5

* The 1994 Survey of Rural Entrepreneurs and Financial Services.
** Self-employment as a percentage of total employment.
Source: National Employment Survey (various years).

29 percent of women—compared with 87 percent of men—are employed. In contrast, the self-employment rate of men and women are very similar—about 30 percent of working men are self-employed compared to 29 percent of working women.

Conceptually, the observed gender differences in workforce participation and the incidence of self-employment arise from (a) differences in individual, household, and labor market characteristics, including human capital (for example, women having less schooling and work experience than men, gender differences in other productivity-related characteristics); and (b) differential male–female responses to employment choices (for example, household demographics, gender differences in employment preferences, time constraints, and work opportunities).

On the demand side, differential responses might arise from, for example, labor legislation that raises the costs of employing women relative to men, exclusionary practices by male-dominated trade unions, employer preferences, or discrimination. These demand factors can in turn feed back into labor supply decisions by affecting the intertemporal return of joining the labor force, female perceptions on the value of being employed, and, ultimately, the decision to join the workforce, the sectoral choice, and investments in schooling.

In the case of Mexico, there is evidence that the earnings penalty from combining work and school is higher for women than for men, perhaps as a result of gender differences arising from the occupational distribution of workers at a very young age. Some researchers have found that gender differences in the occupational structure at an early age do not allow women to acquire the skills that are better rewarded in other economic sectors as these individuals become adults (see also Brown, Pagán, and Rodríguez-Oreggia 1999; and Chapters 1 and 2, this volume).

Separating the role of male–female differences in responses to labor market outcomes from gender differences in individual, household, and demographic characteristics has important public policy implications when designing policies attempting to reduce gender inequities in the labor market. The relative importance of each component will indicate whether policy measures should focus on reducing gender-related inequities in individual characteristics (for example, male–female differences in schooling), or on attempting to correct gender-related differences in labor market responses.

Empirical Methodology

Individual workforce and self-employment choices can be conceptually based on a relative comparison between the utility obtained from working and not working, and the same type of net utility comparison can be used to analyze the choice of becoming self-employed or working for a wage or salary. Utility is derived from the pecuniary and nonpecuniary aspects of these choices (Mortensen 1986). For example, if offered wages from salaried work and self-employment are below the minimum wage necessary to entice individuals to work—the reservation wage—then potential workers will choose not to work. Of those choosing to work, some will select self-employment if the expected benefits in this sector are higher than in the wage and salary sector (Pagán and Sánchez 2000).

The determinants of these two choices can be modeled using a bivariate probit approach: first, an analysis of the determinants of the propensity of individuals to enter the workforce is conducted, and second, the determinants of the incidence of self-employment are analyzed. The labor market decisions themselves are modeled as dichotomous dependent variables using a bivariate probit model with selectivity because the sector of employment decision is only observed for those employed (Brown and Pagán 1998). A correlation parameter across errors captures whether those unobserved factors that increase the likelihood of workforce participation are also related to the self-employment choice.

The model is estimated separately by gender and marital status to capture whether rural labor markets are segmented.[1] The empirical model incorporates labor demand and supply factors through personal and household characteristics and local labor market conditions.

An Oaxaca-type (1973) decomposition adapted for the probit case is employed to analyze the sources of the observed gender differences in workforce and sectoral employment outcomes in rural Mexico (Jones and Makepeace 1996; Pagán and Tijerina-Guijardo 2000). As discussed above, there are two possible explanations as to the existence of gender differences in workforce participation and self-employment. First, gender differences could arise as a result of male–female differences in observable individual, household, and labor market characteristics. Alternatively, men and women might respond differently to workforce participation and self-employment, perhaps as a result of gender-related differences in individual preferences for work, or simply labor market discrimination.[2]

Data and Empirical Results

As mentioned, gender differences in workforce participation and self-employment outcomes are analyzed using microdata from the 1994 Survey of Rural Entrepreneurs and Financial Services (*Encuesta Regional de Servicios Financieros a Unidades de Producción Rural*, SREFS). See Box 6.1 for a description of how the survey was conducted and for a discussion on model estimation.

Box 6.1 How the 1994 SREFS Was Conducted and Some Model Details

The SREFS was conducted in the summer of 1994 in rural regions in the states of Guanajuato (Bajío Guanajuatense), Puebla (Sierra Norte de Puebla), and Veracruz (Huasteca Veracruzana).

The survey universe includes rural entrepreneurs residing in localities with a population of 1,000 to 20,000 inhabitants in the three selected areas, with the sampling unit being the household, due to the lack of a framework specifically designed for rural entrepreneurs (see Chaves and Sánchez 2000 for details). The SREFS contains data on the labor market decisions of respondents, household demographic characteristics, and individual-level basic socioeconomic data. The full sample consists of 8,512 individuals, of which 5,189 were 15 years old or more and, thus, considered eligible to work.

The model outlined in the previous section was estimated using explanatory variables that can be grouped into three categories: personal characteristics, household demographics, and current labor market and economic conditions. Table 6.2 reports the variables used in the analysis and the descriptive statistics for the full sample, by gender and marital status.

Personal characteristics include the level of education (specified by a series of dummy variables indicating the different levels of the highest educational attainment), age and its square, a dummy variable for head of household, and whether the individual speaks an indigenous language.[3] Household characteristics include the number of children living in the household (divided into two age groups: 0 to 2 and 3 to 5), total number of rooms in the dwelling unit, total number of working individuals in the household (excluding the respondent), and whether the respondent owns the home. Local labor market and economic conditions are captured by the number of inhabitants in the locality of residence, the percentage of workers employed in the secondary and tertiary sectors in the locality of residence, and an agricultural sector dummy.[4]

Theoretically, these explanatory variables may solely influence labor demand, labor supply, or both. For example, marital status and the total number of young children living at home most likely influence both labor supply and demand since they affect the value of nonmarket activities. Furthermore, if employers discriminate against married women, then marital status also affects labor demand.

Some variables influence only individual labor demand since they capture current labor market conditions (for example, the number of inhabitants in the locality of residence and the percentage of workers in the secondary and tertiary sectors in the locality of residence).

An indigenous background is related to labor supply decisions through, for example, culture and tradition. On the other hand, employers (and consumers) may potentially discriminate on the basis of ethnicity. Similarly, educational levels are also a function of both labor demand and supply responses.[5]

Table 6.2 shows that in the rural areas surveyed single men and women have higher levels of education than married men and women. Single women are relatively older than single men, but married men are older than married women. Indigenous individuals are also more likely to be married than nonindigenous individuals.

Almost 18 percent of single women are household heads compared to 29 percent of single men. Married men, however, have the highest headship rate (83.8 percent) and single women the lowest (2.2 percent). In urban areas, however, gender differences in household headship are less pronounced (see Chapter 3, this volume).

Table 6.3 reports descriptive statistics for the employed. Both single and married employed females have somewhat higher educational levels than single and married employed males. In addition, employed single females are older than employed single males, but employed married males are older than employed married females.

Employment rates are relatively lower for both single and married indigenous women when compared to men. About 84 percent of married men are household heads compared to only 4.1 percent of married women. However, 24 percent of employed single women are heads of households. As one would expect, married individuals who are employed have more young children. About 40.4 percent of married men are employed in the agricultural sector compared to 5 percent of married women. Qualitatively similar gender differences in sectoral employment are observed for singles.

Table 6.4 presents descriptive statistics for the self-employed. Both male and female entrepreneurs have relatively low levels of education, particularly single and married females. Married self-employed men are also older than single male and single and married female entrepreneurs. Interestingly, more than 90 percent of self-employed married men are heads of households, but only 6.7 percent of self-employed married women are heads of households. Married entrepreneurs have more children, particularly married women, and come from larger households. Married men have larger dwelling units, followed by single women, married women, and single men.

About 40.4 percent of married male entrepreneurs are in the agricultural sector, but only 5.2 percent of married women. A similar result ensues for single men and women. Thus, there seems to be substantial sectoral segmentation across genders.

Tables 6.5 and 6.6 report the results from the bivariate probit estimations for single and married men and women. Both models include the same regressors since both decisions are likely to be influenced by per-

(Text continues on page 217.)

Table 6.2 Descriptive Statistics: Full Sample

	Single men		Single women		Married men		Married women	
	Mean	S.D.	Mean	S.D.	Mean	S.D.	Mean	S.D.
Personal characteristics								
Incomplete primary (1 = yes)	0.207	0.406	0.205	0.404	0.319	0.466	0.269	0.444
Completed primary (1 = yes)	0.193	0.395	0.200	0.400	0.201	0.401	0.244	0.430
Some secondary (1 = yes)	0.243	0.429	0.198	0.398	0.149	0.357	0.144	0.351
Some postsecondary (1 = yes)	0.238	0.426	0.165	0.371	0.118	0.323	0.078	0.268
Age	29.423	16.388	34.370	19.210	43.122	15.219	39.051	13.590
Age squared/100	11.341	14.582	15.501	17.861	20.910	14.915	17.095	11.957
Indigenous (1 = yes)	0.160	0.366	0.173	0.378	0.212	0.409	0.187	0.390
Household characteristics								
Household head (1 = yes)	0.290	0.454	0.176	0.381	0.838	0.369	0.022	0.148
Children aged 0–2	0.288	0.571	0.291	0.584	0.385	0.627	0.389	0.630
Children aged 3–5	0.308	0.577	0.310	0.590	0.408	0.608	0.411	0.612
Working individuals in the household	1.447	1.331	1.652	1.281	0.862	1.137	1.588	1.139
Rooms in dwelling	3.220	1.728	3.242	1.652	3.203	1.685	3.257	1.701
Household owns dwelling (1 = yes)	0.741	0.439	0.747	0.435	0.761	0.426	0.760	0.427
Region/labor market conditions								
Guanajuato (1 = yes)	0.292	0.455	0.300	0.458	0.418	0.493	0.423	0.494
Puebla (1 = yes)	0.334	0.472	0.357	0.479	0.273	0.445	0.271	0.444
Inhabitants in locality of residence (000s)	7.890	5.469	8.003	5.419	7.982	5.783	8.044	5.835
Percentage employed in secondary sector	6.103	3.604	5.858	3.489	5.948	3.832	5.953	3.820
Percentage employed in terciary sector	9.919	4.739	10.273	5.009	9.171	4.773	9.183	4.792
N	1,191		1,402		1,266		1,297	

Table 6.3 Descriptive Statistics: Employed

	Single men		Single women		Married men		Married women	
	Mean	S.D.	Mean	S.D.	Mean	S.D.	Mean	S.D.
Personal characteristics								
Incomplete primary								
(1 = yes)	0.232	0.422	0.190	0.393	0.314	0.464	0.205	0.405
Completed primary								
(1 = yes)	0.224	0.417	0.220	0.415	0.206	0.404	0.172	0.378
Some secondary								
(1 = yes)	0.249	0.433	0.218	0.413	0.154	0.361	0.236	0.425
Some postsecondary								
(1 = yes)	0.176	0.381	0.206	0.405	0.123	0.328	0.254	0.436
Age	29.799	15.124	32.274	15.097	41.591	13.741	37.336	10.925
Age squared/								
100	11.164	12.821	12.691	12.733	19.184	12.703	15.129	9.061
Indigenous								
(1 = yes)	0.181	0.386	0.134	0.341	0.218	0.413	0.123	0.329
Household characteristics								
Household head								
(1 = yes)	0.338	0.473	0.240	0.428	0.840	0.367	0.041	0.199
Children aged 0–2	0.323	0.592	0.260	0.591	0.403	0.636	0.302	0.542
Children aged 3–5	0.341	0.601	0.282	0.572	0.420	0.613	0.362	0.580
Working individuals								
in the household	1.380	1.369	1.544	1.323	0.833	1.119	2.257	1.052
Rooms in dwelling	3.058	1.621	3.380	1.697	3.173	1.682	3.657	1.799
Household owns								
dwelling								
(1 = yes)	0.729	0.445	0.752	0.432	0.757	0.429	0.675	0.469
Region/labor market conditions								
Guanajuato								
(1 = yes)	0.288	0.453	0.326	0.469	0.417	0.493	0.287	0.453
Puebla (1=yes)	0.338	0.473	0.364	0.482	0.277	0.448	0.384	0.487
Inhabitants in								
locality of								
residence	7.544	5.223	8.481	5.620	7.842	5.713	8.929	5.810
Percentage employed								
in secondary								
sector	6.010	3.625	6.230	3.478	5.901	3.837	5.977	3.088
Percentage								
employed in								
terciary sector	9.587	4.647	10.908	4.939	9.076	4.757	11.761	5.102
Economic sector								
Agriculture								
(1 = yes)	0.318	0.466	0.082	0.275	0.404	0.491	0.052	0.223
N	943		500		1,182		268	

Table 6.4 Descriptive Statistics: Self-Employed

	Single men		Single women		Married men		Married women	
	Mean	S.D.	Mean	S.D.	Mean	S.D.	Mean	S.D.
Personal characteristics								
Incomplete primary (1 = yes)	0.322	0.469	0.287	0.454	0.362	0.481	0.378	0.488
Completed primary (1 = yes)	0.208	0.407	0.217	0.414	0.216	0.412	0.200	0.402
Some secondary (1 = yes)	0.142	0.350	0.155	0.363	0.109	0.312	0.144	0.354
Some postsecondary (1 = yes)	0.120	0.326	0.070	0.256	0.082	0.275	0.067	0.251
Age	43.765	18.423	44.039	15.846	46.867	13.819	42.622	11.165
Age squared/100	22.529	17.928	21.886	14.967	23.870	13.843	19.399	10.077
Indigenous (1 = yes)	0.262	0.441	0.171	0.378	0.329	0.470	0.178	0.384
Household characteristics								
Household head (1 = yes)	0.732	0.444	0.543	0.500	0.929	0.257	0.067	0.251
Children aged 0–2	0.311	0.589	0.217	0.599	0.329	0.584	0.311	0.574
Children aged 3–5	0.290	0.572	0.178	0.458	0.356	0.561	0.267	0.515
Working individuals in the household	0.874	1.430	1.101	1.172	0.651	1.010	1.333	1.071
Rooms in dwelling	2.880	1.670	3.364	1.828	3.499	1.872	3.389	1.733
Household owns dwelling (1 = yes)	0.699	0.460	0.760	0.429	0.813	0.390	0.667	0.474
Region/labor market conditions								
Guanajuato (1 = yes)	0.137	0.344	0.225	0.419	0.293	0.456	0.400	0.493
Puebla (1=yes)	0.421	0.492	0.442	0.499	0.342	0.475	0.311	0.466
Inhabitants in locality of residence	7.047	4.562	7.864	5.405	7.212	5.364	9.231	6.002
Percentage employed in secondary sector	5.044	3.173	5.497	2.683	5.003	3.337	6.091	3.281
Percentage employed in terciary sector	9.486	4.821	11.111	4.854	8.570	4.612	10.584	4.754
Economic sector								
Agriculture (1 = yes)	0.318	0.466	0.082	0.275	0.404	0.491	0.052	0.223
N	183		129		450		90	

Table 6.5 Employment and Sector Bivariate Probit: Single Males and Females

| | Employment vs. unemp./OLF | | | |
| | Males | | Females | |
	Coeff.	S.E.	Coeff.	S.E.
Constant	−1.107	0.416***	−2.181	0.284***
Personal characteristics				
Incomplete primary (1 = yes)	0.450	0.186**	0.089	0.124**
Completed primary (1 = yes)	0.757	0.201***	0.327	0.125***
Some secondary (1 = yes)	0.378	0.204*	0.375	0.137***
Some postsecondary (1 = yes)	−0.261	0.206	0.494	0.148***
Age	0.112	0.016***	0.065	0.011***
Age squared/100	−0.133	0.016***	−0.086	0.011***
Indigenous (1 = yes)	0.324	0.178*	0.096	0.128
Household characteristics				
Household head (1 = yes)	0.588	0.187***	0.694	0.121***
Children aged 0–2	0.213	0.100**	−0.070	0.066
Children aged 3–5	0.062	0.106	−0.009	0.065
Working individuals in the household	−0.025	0.045	−0.073	0.031**
Rooms in dwelling	−0.060	0.029**	0.022	0.023
Household owns dwelling (1 = yes)	0.102	0.122	0.077	0.092
Region/labor market conditions				
Guanajuato (1 = yes)	0.086	0.147	0.292	0.108***
Puebla (1 = yes)	0.095	0.127	0.146	0.092
Inhabitants in locality of residence	−0.008	0.011	−0.004	0.009
Percentage employed in secondary sector	0.006	0.017	0.026	0.014*
Percentage employed in terciary sector	−0.010	0.015	0.022	0.011***

| | Self-employment vs. salaried sector | | | |
| | Males | | Females | |
	Coeff.	S.E.	Coeff.	S.E.
Constant	−3.242	0.622***	−1.179	4.345
Personal characteristics				
Incomplete primary (1 = yes)	0.464	0.202**	0.198	0.312
Completed primary (1 = yes)	0.602	0.228***	−0.207	0.341
Some secondary (1 = yes)	0.460	0.243*	−0.016	0.482
Some postsecondary (1 = yes)	0.313	0.255	−0.617	0.353*
Age	0.065	0.026**	0.049	0.108
Age squared/100	−0.040	0.032	−0.024	0.118

| | Self-employment vs. salaried sector | | | |
| | Males | | Females | |
	Coeff.	S.E.	Coeff.	S.E.
Indigenous (1 = yes)	–0.226	0.193	–0.270	0.255
Household characteristics				
Household head (1 = yes)	0.727	0.160***	0.341	0.886
Children aged 0–2	0.011	0.105	0.017	0.140
Children aged 3–5	–0.167	0.122	–0.160	0.174
Working individuals in the household	0.053	0.042	0.010	0.107
Rooms in dwelling	0.048	0.042	0.017	0.053
Household owns dwelling (1 = yes)	–0.029	0.140	0.240	0.282
Region/labor market conditions				
Guanajuato (1 = yes)	–0.668	0.214***	–0.437	0.230*
Puebla (1 = yes)	0.003	0.146	–0.073	0.204
Inhabitants in locality of residence	0.024	0.016	0.004	0.017
Percentage employed in secondary sector	–0.026	0.024	–0.038	0.035
Percentage employed in terciary sector	–0.021	0.018	–0.015	0.024
Economic sector				
Agriculture (1 = yes)	0.500	0.141***	–0.053	0.312
ρ	0.464	0.560	–0.488	1.265
χ^2	507.473		311.880	
Pseudo-R^2	0.279		0.129	
N	1,191		1,402	

*/**/*** Significant at the 90, 95, and 99 percent confidence intervals, respectively.

Table 6.6 Employment and Sector Bivariate Probit: Married Males and Females

| | Employment vs. unemp./OLF | | | |
| | Males | | Females | |
	Coeff.	S.E.	Coeff.	S.E.
Constant	1.199	0.797	–2.952	0.507***
Personal characteristics				
Incomplete primary (1 = yes)	–0.044	0.226	0.184	0.143
Completed primary (1 = yes)	–0.169	0.259	0.077	0.165

(Table continues on the following page.)

Table 6.6 (continued)

| | Employment vs. unemp./OLF | | | |
| | Males | | Females | |
	Coeff.	S.E.	Coeff.	S.E.
Some secondary (1 = yes)	0.037	0.325	0.670	0.174***
Some postsecondary (1 = yes)	−0.074	0.406	1.404	0.212***
Age	0.052	0.031*	0.083	0.020***
Age squared/100	−0.100	0.027***	−0.094	0.023***
Indigenous (1 = yes)	0.457	0.260*	−0.141	0.165
Household characteristics				
Household head (1 = yes)	0.853	0.307***	0.586	0.315*
Children aged 0–2	0.320	0.164*	−0.067	0.082
Children aged 3–5	−0.017	0.155	−0.060	0.083
Working individuals in the household	−0.106	0.065*	−0.202	0.040***
Rooms in dwelling	−0.037	0.054	0.030	0.030
Household owns dwelling (1 = yes)	0.077	0.228	−0.231	0.111**
Region/labor market conditions				
Guanajuato (1 = yes)	0.332	0.261	0.040	0.134
Puebla (1 = yes)	0.136	0.265	0.235	0.128*
Inhabitants in locality of residence	−0.042	0.019**	0.005	0.011
Percentage employed in secondary sector	0.007	0.034	−0.011	0.017
Percentage employed in terciary sector	0.006	0.030	0.053	0.014***

| | Self-employment vs. salaried sector | | | |
| | Males | | Females | |
	Coeff.	S.E.	Coeff.	S.E.
Constant	−2.149	0.619***	0.807	3.859
Personal characteristics				
Incomplete primary (1 = yes)	0.299	0.124**	0.120	0.371
Completed primary (1 = yes)	0.558	0.150***	0.059	0.268
Some secondary (1 = yes)	0.215	0.171	−0.718	0.271***
Some postsecondary (1 = yes)	0.026	0.184	−1.468	0.320***
Age	0.005	0.027	0.006	0.123
Age squared/100	0.018	0.032	0.017	0.119
Indigenous (1 = yes)	0.242	0.132*	0.439	0.390
Household characteristics				
Household head (1 = yes)	0.565	0.164***	−0.076	0.697
Children aged 0–2	−0.023	0.084	0.248	0.201
Children aged 3–5	0.086	0.077	−0.008	0.145
Working individuals in the household	−0.138	0.042***	0.175	0.091*

| | Self-employment vs. salaried sector | | | |
| | Males | | Females | |
	Coeff.	S.E.	Coeff.	S.E.
Rooms in dwelling	0.153	0.028***	−0.049	0.045
Household owns dwelling (1 = yes)	0.149	0.107	−0.012	0.317
Region/labor market conditions				
Guanajuato (1 = yes)	−0.519	0.128***	0.262	0.361
Puebla (1 = yes)	−0.020	0.113	−0.186	0.217
Inhabitants in locality of residence	0.025	0.010**	−0.002	0.018
Percentage employed in secondary sector	−0.019	0.015	−0.002	0.035
Percentage employed in terciary sector	−0.017	0.014	−0.031	0.036
Economic sector				
Agriculture (1 = yes)	0.642	0.106***	−0.303	0.389
ρ	−0.181	0.654	−0.869	0.543*
χ^2	541.24		345.98	
Pseudo-R^2	0.248		0.208	
N	1,266		1,297	

*/**/*** Significant at the 90, 95, and 99 percent confidence intervals, respectively.

sonal characteristics, household demographics, and current labor market and economic conditions. In addition, the self-employment equations include a dummy variable capturing whether individuals work in the agricultural sector. This is important because self-employed females are largely found in nonagricultural sectors (Tables 6.3 and 6.4).

The models have a reasonable fit, as suggested by the χ^2 and pseudo-R^2 measures reported in the tables. Table 6.5 clearly shows that there is great heterogeneity across gender when it comes to workforce participation and the incidence of self-employment.

Education, age, and household headship are all positively related to employment. However, the presence of very small children in the household reduces the workforce participation of single females but not males. There is also great heterogeneity in employment probabilities in the location of residence for women but not for men, suggesting that employment opportunities differ greatly across communities for women but not for men. The size of the labor market, provided by the number of inhabitants in the locality of residence, plays no role in either the employment or sectoral choices of single men.

When it comes to the self-employment choice, schooling, age, household headship, the size of the locality of residence, and employment in the agricultural sector, all are positively related to single males being self-employed. However, the only statistically significant predictors of single female self-employment are some postsecondary education and residence in Guanajuato, as compared to all other regions—both of which reduce the self-employment propensity of single women.

Table 6.6 reports the regression results for married men and women. Once again, substantial heterogenity across gender exists in the employment and entrepreneurship choices. When it comes to workforce participation, only age, an indigenous background, and being a household head are positively related to married male employment. For married women, education, age, household headship, household size—which measures wealth—and residence in Puebla—are all positively related to workforce participation. However, the number of working individuals in the household and dwelling ownership are negatively related to the likelihood of employment.

The size of the labor market—as reflected by the number of inhabitants in the locality of residence—influences gender differences in workforce participation either because a greater range of job opportunities exists for women in larger localities, or simply because women perceive having more opportunities in larger communities and, thus, are more likely to seek and find employment in these localities. In contrast, men in larger localities are less likely to be working than in smaller localities. This may be a result of men searching more intensively for a job before accepting one in larger communities, or perhaps a result of men facing more competition from female labor in more populated areas.

Gender differences in workforce participation across regions can be attributed to regional differences in labor market opportunities and regional differences in productivity. Moreover, the composition of the local economy may also be an important determinant of employment. The results show that this is true only for females; that is, the female employment propensity is larger when the tertiary sector in the community of residence is large. Thus, the availability of employment opportunities in the service-related tertiary sector seems to significantly increase employment opportunities for married women.

Gender differences in the impact of small children on employment are most likely related to male–female differences in the household allocation of time to market and nonmarket activities, and specialization within the household (Blau and Ferber 1992). In particular, the presence of young children could make current working opportunities less attractive for married women. In addition, it is interesting to note that schooling plays a role in increasing the likelihood of employment for married women, but not for men.

The bottom half of Table 6.6 also reports the results for the self-employment choice of married men and women. Low levels of education, being indigenous, having a large dwelling unit, residing in Guanajuato and in a large locality, and working in the agricultural sector are all positively related to self-employment. However, having a large household reduces the likelihood of being self-employed. In particular, wealthier men—proxied by dwelling size—might select self-employment because they are less likely to experience liquidity constraints for starting a business or for staying in business (Evans and Jovanovic 1989; Evans and Leighton 1989).

For married women, secondary and postsecondary education increases the chances that they are in the salaried sector when compared to self-employment. This is consistent with the hypothesis that education is positively related to the propensity of being in a salaried occupation, perhaps as a result of the existence of less labor market discrimination for more experienced, more educated Mexican women (see Pagán and Ullibarri 2000 for empirical evidence).

Decomposing Gender Differences in Labor Market Outcomes

Table 6.7 reports the results from the decomposition analysis of gender differences in workforce and self-employment rates discussed above. Only about 35.66 percent of single women are employed compared to 79.18 percent of single men. If the bivariate probit model estimates for single males are used to predict the employment rate of single females, the employment rate of women would increase to 75.76 percent.

Table 6.7 also shows the decomposition of the 43.51 percent employment rate differential between single men and women. Most of this differential—99.03 percent—is explained by gender differences in individual responses to employment and only 0.97 percent is explained by male–female differences in personal characteristics. Thus, the results suggest that the rural labor market in Mexico is heavily segmented by gender, and that women's workforce participation rates would more than double if they had the same workforce responses as men.

The gender gap between married men and women is much larger; 93.36 percent of married men are employed but only 20.66 percent of married women are employed. The predicted employment rate for married women is 88.6 percent, which suggests that when compared to their male counterparts, married women face more barriers to employment than single women.

Table 6.7 Decomposition Analysis of Gender Differences in Workforce Participation and Self-Employment

	Workforce participation	Percentage	Self-Employment	Percentage
Single men				
Observed	79.18		19.41	
Single women				
Observed	35.66		25.80	
Predicted	75.76		15.44	
Observed gender difference	43.51	100.00	–6.39	100.00
Due to individual characteristics	0.42	0.97	3.96	61.97
Due to differential responses	43.09	99.03	–10.35	–161.97
Married men				
Observed	93.36		38.07	
Married women				
Observed	20.66		33.58	
Predicted	88.06		15.82	
Observed gender difference	72.70	100.00	4.49	100.00
Due to individual characteristics	5.30	7.29	22.26	510.02
Due to differential responses	67.40	92.71	–17.77	–362.65

This finding is partly a result of specialization of labor and tasks within the household. However, it is also consistent with the idea that the accumulation of skills differs by gender from an early age within the life cycle, and the male–female differences in acquired experience obtained at a young age reduces the propensity of employment of married women (see Chapter 2, this volume).

When it comes to the incidence of self-employment, the decomposition analysis of gender differences shows that gender-related differential responses work in an opposite direction from the male–female differences in productive characteristics. Self-employment rates are 19.41 percent for single males and 25.80 percent for females; yet, if the bivariate probit estimates were used to predict the incidence of female self-employment, this would decrease to 15.44 percent.

This result is consistent with the idea that women might be relatively concentrated in self-employment due to barriers to entry into salaried jobs and to household structure. This idea is further reinforced by the findings in the decomposition analysis that single male–female differential responses to self-employment explain most of the overrepresentation of single women in entrepreneurial activities.

Married women have a lower incidence of self-employment than married men (38.07 versus 33.58 percent). Nonetheless, the predicted self-employment rate of married women is 15.82 percent, which implies that married women are relatively overrepresented in this sector. An interesting result here is that most of the male–female self-employment gap is explained by differences in individual characteristics and not differential responses to self-employment. In other words, the productive characteristics of married women are substantially different from those of married men, a result consistent with the idea that marked specialization of labor and tasks is prevalent within rural households in Mexico.

Gender-specific preferences for type of employment, culture, child-care options, and labor market discrimination in the wage/salary sector might explain how differential responses could potentially induce women into self-employment (Duval Hernández 1999; and Psacharopoulos and Tzannatos 1992). According to the results, self-employment might be a relatively more attractive choice for women for various reasons: it might offer easy entry into the labor force and a flexible work schedule, and it might also allow women to work from a home-based setting. Nonetheless, the empirical results are also consistent with the conjecture that women are disproportionately represented in self-employment as a result of relatively lower barriers to entry into this sector, perhaps as a result of labor market discrimination in the wage and salary sector.

Conclusion

The labor force participation of women has been steadily increasing over the last three decades (Brown, Pagán, and Rodríguez-Oreggia 1999; Parker 1995). Thus, continuing growth is contingent upon the implementation of public policy measures that are consistent with increasing labor force participation. The results of this study have important implications for labor market public policy in rural Mexico. The national development plan, Plan Nacional de Desarrollo, 1995–2000, considers gender equity an important component of the country's overall economic development strategy through "the promotion of a set of programs and actions that guarantee women equal opportunity in education, training and employment." In particular, the national development plan calls for government programs that seek to correct male–female inequities in employment outcomes, and it recognizes gender as a legitimate criterion in the development and implementation of these programs (Poder Ejecutivo Federal 1995).

The main message of this chapter is that policies focusing solely on, for example, increasing the relative human capital levels of women have a limited impact on reducing gender inequality if they are not accompanied by policy measures addressing the sources of gender differences in responses to workforce participation and self-employment. Although some of the gender differences in responses are certainly due to individual choice, and despite the fact that women perform valuable nonmarket work that is not captured by the standard labor measures, male–female differences in labor market access and discrimination might also explain the observed gender differences in responses.

Given the results of this study, public policy measures can be implemented to reduce gender disparities in workforce participation in rural Mexico. For example, policies that attempt to reduce the gap between offered and reservation wages end up increasing the workforce participation of women. As suggested by Nakamura, Nakamura, and Cullen (1979), public policies designed to increase the offered wage rate of women might be more effective than programs decreasing the reservation wage. Examples of these policies are the stimulation of female-dominated industries and occupations instead of implementing equal pay legislation or gender-based job quotas.

In addition, the negative impact of the presence of young children on the employment rates of married women suggests that community-based childcare services might be an effective way to meet the needs for safe, affordable childcare while at the same time providing employment opportunities for women who run the programs. Husbands also need incentives to contribute to home-based work. The results point out that the need to balance family and market responsibilities is a major source of male–female differences in responses to employment (Blau 1998).

The findings also illustrate the strong and positive effect of education on the workforce participation of single and married women. Policy measures that provide better access to formal and informal education expand employment choices, increase the capacity of women to respond to market opportunities, and lead to increasing productivity and earnings (see Chapter 1, this volume).

Gender-specific differences in workforce and self-employment responses mostly explain the male–female differences in labor market outcomes. As such, strategies attempting to diminish these differential responses would have a desirable long-term impact on reducing gender disparities in the labor market. For example, the finding that the presence of young children has a different impact across gender in the work and self-employment choices suggests the existence of within-family gender barriers.

Finally, labor market discrimination is evident in the findings of an unexplained gender gap in workforce participation, together with an overrepresentation of women in the self-employment sector compared to the wage and salary sector. In a rural setting, this is more difficult to eradicate if the bias is rooted in employer preferences and, particularly, if rural labor and production markets are not integrated into the formal economy. Thus, policies promoting rural development and more competition in the rural wage and salary sector and in production markets might be effective in reducing employer bias.

The study has some limitations, which are related mostly to the survey data employed. For example, the survey is representative of only the rural areas of the states of Guanajuato, Puebla, and Veracruz. There is also a lack of alternative measures of human capital that might be relevant in a rural setting (for example, measures of physical strength and endurance), and there are limitations in our proxy for tenure and actual labor market experience. Nonetheless, the study can be helpful in assessing the expected impact of different labor market policies, and also provides a benchmark for other studies dealing with gender disparities in employment outcomes in rural settings.

Notes

1. Likelihood ratio tests suggest that individual responses to workforce participation and self-employment differ by gender and marital status.

2. The probit decomposition employed here is thoroughly discussed by Brown and Pagán (1998) and Pagán and Sánchez (2000).

3. Age is used primarily to proxy labor market experience, although admittedly it also captures changes in employment outcomes over the life cycle (Dávila and Pagán 1999; Psacharopoulos and Tzannatos 1992).

4. The secondary sector includes mineral extraction, manufacturing, and construction. The tertiary sector includes trade, transportation, and all the service-related sectors.

5. The specification of educational levels employed in this study is fairly standard in the literature, although it is subject to the usual criticism that it does not

incorporate quality of education, time spent in school, and informal schooling and training, which are particularly important when analyzing rural labor market outcomes.

References

Blau, Francine D. 1998. "Trends in the Well-Being of American Women, 1970–1995." *Journal of Economic Literature* 36(1):112–65.

Blau, Francine D., and Marianne A. Ferber. 1992. *The Economics of Women, Men, and Work*. Englewood Cliffs, N.J.: Prentice-Hall.

Brown, Cynthia, and José A. Pagán. 1998. "Changes in Employment Status across Demographic Groups during the 1990–91 Recession." *Applied Economics* 30:1571–83.

Brown, Cynthia, José A. Pagán, and Eduardo Rodríguez-Oreggia. 1999. "Occupational Attainment and Gender Earnings Differentials in Mexico." *Industrial and Labor Relations Review* 53(1):123–35.

Chaves, Rodrigo A., and Susana M. Sánchez. 2000. "Poverty, Rural Entrepreneurs, and Financial Markets in the Rural Areas of Mexico." In Alberto Valdés and Ramón López, eds., *Rural Poverty in Latin America: Analytics, New Empirical Evidence, and Policy*. New York: St. Martin's Press.

Cohen, Gary L. 1996. "Women Entrepreneurs." *Perspectives on Labour and Income* 8(1):23–28.

Dávila, Alberto, and José A. Pagán. 1999. "Gender Pay and Occupational-Attainment Gaps in Costa Rica and El Salvador: A Relative Comparison of the Late 1980s." *Review of Development Economics* 3(2):215–30.

Devine, Theresa J. 1994. "Changes in Wage-and-Salary Returns to Skill and the Recent Rise in Female Self-Employment." *American Economic Review Papers and Proceedings* 84(2):108–13.

Duval Hernández, Robert. 1999. "El trabajo doméstico y los salarios: Un estudio para los hogares mexicanos." Thesis. División de Economía, Centro de Investigación y Docencia Económicas, México, D.F.

Evans, David S., and Boyan Jovanovic. 1989. "An Estimated Model of Entrepreneurial Choice under Liquidity Constraints." *Journal of Political Economy* 97(4):808–26.

Evans, David S., and Linda S. Leighton. 1989. "Some Empirical Aspects of Entrepreneurship." *American Economic Review* 79(3):519–35.

INEGI (*Instituto Nacional de Estadística Geografía e Informática*). 1997. *Mujeres y Hombres en Mexico.* Aguascalientes, México: Instituto Nacional de Estadística, Geografía e Informática.

Inter-American Development Bank. 1995. *Women in the Americas: Bridging the Gender Gap.* Washington, D.C.: The John Hopkins University Press.

Jones, David R., and Gerald H. Makepeace. 1996. "Equal Worth, Equal Opportunities: Pay and Promotion in an Internal Labor Market." *The Economic Journal* 106:401–09.

Mortensen, Dale T. 1986. "Models of Search in the Labor Market." In Orley Ashenfelter and Richard Layard, eds., *Handbook of Labor Economics.* Amsterdam: North-Holland.

Nakamura, Masao, Alice Nakamura, and Dallas Cullen. 1979. "Job Opportunities, the Offered Wage, and the Labor Supply of Married Women." *American Economic Review* 69(5):787–805.

Oaxaca, Ronald. 1973. "Male-Female Wage Differentials in Urban Labor Markets." *International Economic Review* 14(3):693–708.

Pagán, José A., and Susana M. Sánchez. 2000. "Gender Differences in Labor Market Outcomes: Evidence from Rural Mexico." *Economic Development and Cultural Change* 48(3):620–37.

Pagán, José A., and José A. Tijerina-Guajardo. 2000. "Increasing Wage Dispersion and the Changes in Relative Employment and Wages in Mexico's Urban Informal Sector: 1987–1993." *Applied Economics* 32:335–47.

Pagán, José A., and Miren Ullibarri. "Group Heterogeneity and the Gender Earnings Gap in Mexico." *Economía Mexicana*, 9(1):23–40.

Parker, Susan W. 1995. "Niveles salariales de los hombres y las mujeres asalariados y trabajadores auto-empleados en el México urbano 1986–1992: Un enfoque microeconómico." In José A. Tijerina Guajardo and Jorge Meléndez Barrón, eds., *Capital humano, crecimiento, pobreza: Problemática mexicana.* Monterrey, NL: Universidad Autónoma de Nuevo León.

Poder Ejecutivo Federal. 1995. *Plan Nacional de Desarrollo: 1995–2000. Secretaría de Hacienda y Crédito Público*, México, D.F.

Psacharopoulos, George, and Zafaris Tzannatos. 1992. *Women's Employment and Pay in Latin America: Overview and Methodology.* Washington, D.C.: World Bank Regional and Sectoral Studies.

7

Gender, Generation, and Off-Farm Employment on the Mexican *Ejido*

Elizabeth Katz

Since the 1930s, most rural Mexicans have had access to their most important productive resource—land—mediated by membership in the *ejido*, a semicollective form of tenure which makes up over half of Mexico's farmland and incorporates 75 percent of agricultural producers (World Bank 1998). Traditionally, *ejidatarios* have combined the cultivation of basic grain crops with small-scale commercial agriculture and seasonal migration to generate their income. Beginning in 1992, with the reform of Article 27 of the Mexican Constitution and the launching of the national *Ejido* Titling Program (PROCEDE), the *ejido* sector has been undergoing a process of privatization, in which parcels that were previously held in individual usufruct, and some common property resources, are being converted into privately held land. Simultaneously, the agricultural sector as a whole has been significantly affected by the lifting of price and credit subsidies, and by the passage of NAFTA, which has threatened small-scale basic grains producers by allowing for the importation of cheap grains from the United States and Canada. Taken together, these changes have prompted *ejidatarios* to make necessary adjustments in their livelihood strategies, including the expansion of off-farm employment.[1]

As discussed in several other chapters in this volume, the past several decades have also witnessed an important increase in female education and labor force participation. While the rural areas lag significantly in both of these trends, young women in the *ejido* sector have much higher levels of educational attainment and are much more likely to hold wage or salaried employment than the older generation of rural women (Katz 1998).[2] This chapter examines the intersection of the transformation of the *ejido* sector and shifts in the gender composition of the Mexican workforce. It analyzes the determinants of off-farm employment for *ejido* residents and assesses the degree to which these determinants differ by gender and generation. The findings support the broad hypothesis that intrahousehold labor allocation—in particular, the deployment of household members to off-farm employment—is differentially responsive to individual and household characteristics, depending on members' gender and generation. Perhaps most important, the analysis reveals the ways in which gender-specific sources of farm-based income—which are themselves part of the adjustment patterns of households—have distinct impacts on the off-farm labor supply behavior of different household members.

The chapter offers a descriptive picture of off-farm employment in the *ejido* sector, drawing on both secondary literature and primary data analysis; estimates the determinants of off-farm employment for two generations of men and women in a national sample of Mexican *ejidos* and interprets the results; and concludes with a discussion of the policy implications of the analysis.

Off-Farm Employment in the *Ejido* Sector

The increasing importance of nonfarm (and in some cases nonagricultural) employment and earnings to *ejido* households has been documented by many observers of the Mexican rural economy.[3] Davis (1998) calculates that almost 25 percent of total *ejidatario* household income is generated by wage employment, and another 12 percent by off-farm self-employment.[4] Lanjouw (1998) estimates both individual- and household-level determinants of off-farm earnings among the *ejido* population. He finds that educational level, household size, dependence on corn cultivation, and paved-road access to an urban center are all positively associated with off-farm incomes, while women and people residing in households with more dependents and U.S. migrants, and on farms with more irrigation, earn significantly less. Lanjouw also finds that households with more members employed in the off-farm sector are significantly less likely to have total incomes below the poverty line (1998).

To more closely examine off-farm employment patterns by gender and household role, we must confine our attention to wage and salaried work, since the data set used here (the *Encuesta a Ejidatarios y Comuneros 1997*, carried out by the *Instituto Nacional de Desarrollo Agrario*, the World Bank, and the University of California at Berkeley) disaggregates only this type of income by individual.[5] Farm income and income from self-employment and unearned sources is registered at the household level.[6] Limiting ourselves to wage and salaried employment, then, Table 7.1 shows the breakdown of labor force participation rates by geographic region, employment sector, gender, and household role.[7] All data are weighted to correct for sample stratification. Several patterns are indicated.

Table 7.1. Off-Farm Employment by Region, Sector, Gender, and Household Role

		Men			Women		
	All	All men[1]	Male household heads	Sons	All women[2]	Wives	Daughters
Weighted N	6,367	3,270	1,537	1,478	3,096	1,396	1,160
Region/sector							
All Mexico							
All sectors[3]	18.9	28.3	26.8	29.6	9.1	2.7	18.2
Agriculture	33.3	40.5	40.7	38.7	9.5	13.2	9.0
Industry[4]	23.1	27.1	27.0	27.6	9.9	8.1	9.4
Commerce	6.7	3.8	0.7	5.9	16.5	8.1	18.4
Other[5]	36.9	28.7	31.3	27.7	64.0	71.1	63.5
North[6]							
All sectors	28.5	42.4	35.2	48.9	13.6	6.7	25.3
Agriculture	27.7	34.1	36.0	32.3	7.3	16.7	5.1
Industry	19.0	19.0	14.7	24.5	14.8	15.4	2.8
Commerce	3.3	2.2	2.7	1.1	7.4	8.3	7.7
Other	50.6	44.9	45.3	43.0	70.4	66.7	72.5
Pacific North[7]							
All sectors	13.0	18.0	12.7	23.1	7.3	1.7	15.6
Agriculture	34.7	41.5	44.4	34.6	15.8	50.0	13.3
Industry	15.3	18.9	16.7	23.1	5.0	0.0	6.3
Commerce	9.7	5.7	0.0	3.7	21.1	0.0	13.3
Other	40.8	34.0	38.9	38.5	60.0	50.0	66.7
Center[8]							
All sectors	21.5	32.2	30.4	33.3	10.6	1.7	21.6
Agriculture	28.3	34.0	30.7	34.2	10.6	10.0	11.4
Industry	30.4	36.1	37.4	35.6	12.8	11.1	11.5
Commerce	7.5	3.9	0.6	6.8	18.3	11.1	19.5
Other	33.9	25.8	31.3	23.3	58.5	66.7	57.5
Gulf[9]							
All sectors	16.3	24.9	27.8	22.6	6.9	2.9	14.1
Agriculture	50.5	62.6	66.7	54.8	2.5	0.0	3.4
Industry	11.2	14.1	16.0	12.9	0.0	0.0	0.0
Commerce	9.7	7.1	0.0	16.1	20.0	0.0	27.6
Other	28.7	16.7	17.3	17.5	75.0	100.0	66.7

(Table continues on the following page.)

Table 7.1. (continued)

		Men			Women		
	All	All men[1]	Male household heads	Sons	All women[2]	Wives	Daughters
South[10]							
All sectors	11.6	17.6	19.6	15.9	4.9	2.2	7.7
Agriculture	38.8	45.7	41.0	57.9	13.8	20.0	6.7
Industry	22.6	26.9	29.5	15.4	3.6	0.0	0.0
Commerce	3.8	0.0	0.0	0.0	17.2	16.7	21.4
Other	35.3	26.9	28.5	25.6	65.5	66.7	73.3

1. Includes men who are neither household heads nor sons.
2. Includes women who are neither wives nor daughters.
3. The figures in the "All Sectors" rows refer to labor force participation rates, while the sector-specific numbers are for employed individuals only.
4. Includes construction.
5. Includes services.
6. Includes the states of Chihuahua, Coahuila, Durango, Nuevo León, Tamaulipas, and Comarca Lagunera.
7. Includes the states of Baja California Norte, Baja California Sur, Colima, Nayarit, Sinaloa, and Sonora.
8. Includes the states of Aguascalientes, Guanajuato, Hidalgo, Jalisco, México, Michoacán, Morelos, Puebla, Querétaro, San Luis Potosí, Tlaxcala, and Zacatecas.
9. Includes the states of Campeche, Quintana Roo, Tabasco, and Veracruz.
10. Includes the states of Chiapas, Guerrero, and Oaxaca.

National Trends

At the national level, 18.9 percent of all working-age *ejido* residents have off-farm wage or salaried employment (Table 7.1). About one third of such employment is in the agricultural sector, another quarter in industry (including construction), and the remainder in services and commerce. Men are three times as likely to participate in the labor force as women (28.3 percent versus 9.1 percent). The generation gap, while not significant for men either in terms of overall employment rates or sectoral distribution, is striking for women: daughters still living at home (regardless of marital status) are almost seven times more likely to work off-farm compared to their mothers (18.2 percent versus 2.7 percent). They are also less likely to be employed in agriculture, and more likely to work in the industrial or commercial sectors than the older generation of employed women. What is unclear, without the benefit of long-term panel data or retrospective information on individuals' work histories, is whether the female generation gap in off-farm employment rates is a life cycle or cohort phenomenon; in other words, whether women who are now "daughters" will maintain their labor force participation rates once they form their own separate households.[8]

Regional Variation

Off-farm employment rates of *ejidatarios* and their families vary significantly by region, with exceptionally high rates of over 28 percent in the Northern states, extremely low rates of less than 12 percent in the South, and between 13 and 21.5 percent in the states of the Center, Gulf, and Pacific North regions. The share of agricultural employment is highest in the Gulf and Southern regions, with two thirds of male household heads who work off-farm employed in this sector in the Gulf states of Campeche, Quintana Roo, Tabasco, and Veracruz. Gender disparities in off-farm employment rates are relatively high in the Gulf and Southern states—where agricultural sector jobs predominate—and relatively low in the regions where there is more industrial employment.

Sectoral Differences

Sectoral distribution is highly differentiated by gender: while over 40 percent of men working off of their own farms have salaried employment in agriculture, women (especially younger women) are more likely to be found in commerce, industry, or other (most likely service sector) wage jobs. Looking at the regional figures, it appears that sons are more concentrated in industrial jobs compared to their fathers only in the Northern and Northwestern states. In the South, there is a surprising intergenerational trend in male sectoral employment patterns, where sons are better represented in agriculture and are less likely to hold industrial jobs than their fathers.

Generational Differences

As mentioned above, at the national level the relationship of younger women to the off-farm labor market is changing more dramatically (with respect to the older generation of women) than for men. This also implies that the gender gap in off-farm employment is narrowing for the younger generation: while male household heads are almost 10 times as likely to be employed off-farm as their wives, the labor force participation rates of sons are less than twice those of daughters. Regional variation in generational differences is apparent, too: while both sons and daughters are more likely than their parents to work off-farm in the Northern and

Pacific Northern states, this trend is true only for women in the other regions, and the labor force participation rate of sons is actually lower than their fathers' in the Center, Gulf, and Southern regions.[9] A striking finding for the Pacific Northern states of Baja California Norte, Baja California Sur, Nayarit, Sinaloa, and Sonora is that off-farm employment rates for the younger generation of women actually exceed those of male household heads (15.6 percent versus 12.7 percent).

Overall, then, the 19 percent rate of off-farm employment for *ejido* residents masks significant variation by gender, generation, and region. In the Northern states, labor force participation rates are especially high for the younger generation of men and women, who are less likely to work in agriculture and more likely to work in the industrial sector than their parents. In the Southern and Gulf states, where agricultural employment is still dominant, even the labor force participation of younger women remains below 12 percent. These differences are attributable in part to labor market conditions, in part to the profitability of the *ejido* sector, and in part to the labor supply characteristics of individuals and households. The following section examines the determinants of off-farm employment in a multivariate context in order to analyze the differential factors influencing the labor force participation status of men and women.

Determinants of Off-Farm Employment

Tables 7.2 and 7.3 present the relevant descriptive statistics and the results of a binomial probit model of off-farm employment among the *ejido* population. The data are drawn from the *Encuesta a Ejidatarios y Comuneros 1997*.[10] The probit model estimates the impact of a series of individual, household, and regional characteristics on the off-farm labor force participation of *ejido* residents. Specifically, off-farm employment is hypothesized to be a function of:

- **Individual Demographic Characteristics.** As is common in labor supply models, the age, sex, and marital status of individuals are expected to influence their employment patterns. We have already seen that men are significantly more likely to hold off-farm jobs than women. Labor force participation is allowed to be quadratic in age, with employment increasing and then decreasing as a person gets older. Being married is hypothesized to have a positive effect on male employment but a negative effect on female employment because of socially defined roles regarding income generation and domestic labor.

Table 7.2. Descriptive Statistics

| | All | | | Men | | | | | | | Women | | | | | |
| | | | | All Men | | Male household heads | | Sons | | All women | | Wives | | Daughters | |
Variable	Mean	Median	S.D.	Mean	S.D.	Mean	S.D.	Mean	S.D.	Mean	S.D.	Mean	S.D.	Mean	S.D.
Individual characteristics															
Weeks worked off-farm (including zeros)	5.1	0.0	13.3	6.8	14.4	5.4	12.3	7.9	15.5	3.3	11.7	1.0	6.8	6.4	15.7
Weeks worked off-farm (employed only)	26.9	24.5	18.6	24.2	17.7	20.1	16.5	26.5	17.8	36.1	18.3	36.6	20.0	35.0	18.6
Age	35.3	32.0	17.4	36.2	18.2	51.1	12.8	21.0	6.4	34.4	16.6	45.7	12.4	20.9	7.1
% married	55.0		50.0	53.0	49.9	89.6	30.6	16.6	37.2	56.6	50.0	97.7	15.0	7.7	26.7
Years of education	5.0	6.0	3.6	5.2	3.6	3.3	2.9	7.2	3.1	4.9	3.5	3.1	2.9	7.3	2.9
% indigenous	13.0		33.7	13.4	33.7	15.8	36.5	12.0	32.5	12.6	33.2	14.8	35.5	10.5	30.6
Household characteristics															
Number of household members[1]	6.9	7.0	3.0												
Dependency ratio[2]	0.28	0.3	0.2												

(Table continues on the following page.)

Table 7.2. (continued)

Variable	All Mean	All Median	All S.D.	Men All Men Mean	Men All Men S.D.	Men Male household heads Mean	Men Male household heads S.D.	Men Sons Mean	Men Sons S.D.	Women All women Mean	Women All women S.D.	Women Wives Mean	Women Wives S.D.	Women Daughters Mean	Women Daughters S.D.
Number of rooms in house	3.5	3.0	1.5												
% houses with indoor plumbing	47.9		50.0												
Farm size 1994 (NRE hectares)	8.0	4.7	10.7												
Number cattle owned by household 1994	5.7	0.0	12.8												
PROCAMPO payments (1997 pesos)	2,000	1,400	2,400												
Ejido *characteristics*															
Number of households resident in the *ejido*[3]	223.4	161.0	202.1												
Travel time to nearest urban center[4]	47.1	30.0	48.4												

1. Resident members only.
2. Defined as the ratio of children under age 15 to total household members.
3. Includes *ejidatarios, posesionarios,* and *avecindados.*
4. Defined as towns with populations over 2,500; travel time is in minutes, by public transportation.

Table 7.3. Binomial Probit Model of Off-Farm Employment among *Ejido* Residents

| | All | | Men | | | | | | Women | | | | | |
| | | | All men | | Male household heads | | Sons | | All women | | Wives | | Daughters | |
Variable	∂Y/∂X	P(|Z|>z)	∂Y/∂X	P(|Z|>z)	∂Y/∂X	P(|Z|>z)	∂Y/∂X	P(|Z|>z)	∂Y/∂X	P(|Z|>z)	∂Y/∂X	P(|Z|>z)	∂Y/∂X	P(|Z|>z)
Intercept	-.57	.00	-.54	.00	-.15	.43	-1.1	.00	-.31	.00	-.07	.04	-1.2	.00
Individual characteristics														
Sex/generation	.20[1]	.00	.09[2]	.01					.05[3]	.00				
Female head of household									.05	.09				
Age	.02	.00	.02	.00	-.001	.87	.07	.00	.01	.00	.001	.18	.08	.08
Age squared	-.0002	.00	-.0003	.00	-.0001	.38	-.001	.00	-.0002	.00	-.00002	.15	-.001	.00
Married	-.04	.01	.05	.07	.06	.21	.02	.67	-.02	.13	.002	.05	-.02	.65
Education	.01	.00	-.01	.12	-.01	.03	-.005	.34	.01	.00	.001	.78	.01	.06
Indigenous	.02	.37	.001	.98	-.05	.23	.04	.37	.02	.20	.001	.78	.04	.37
Household characteristics														
Household size	.01	.01	.002	.51	-.01	.03	.02	.01	.002	.08	-.0001	.93	.01	.18
Dependency ratio	-.03	.28	-.04	.50	.17	.03	-.10	.32	-.01	.46	.01	.40	-.004	.97
Rooms in house	-.01	.25	-.02	.01	-.02	.09	-.02	.15	.003	.26	.003	.04	-.01	.46
Indoor plumbing	.03	.02	.10	.00	.07	.01	.12	.00	-.01	.20	-.004	.18	-.01	.81
Farm size	-.001	.08	-.002	.08	.001	.68	-.01	.01	.0001	.81	.0001	.38	-.002	.37
Cattle	-.01	.00	-.01	.00	-.01	.00	-.01	.00	-.001	.01	-.0003	.16	-.01	.00
PROCAMPO (thousands)	-.01	.02	-.02	.00	-.03	.00	-.01	.34	-.001	.57	-.0003	.57	.004	.47

(Table continues on the following page.)

Table 7.3. (conintuned)

Variable	All		Men				Women					
			All men		Male household heads		Sons		All women		Wives		Daughters

Variable	All		All men		Male household heads		Sons		All women		Wives		Daughters	
Ejido characteristics														
No. *ejido* HHs (hundreds)	.01	.00	.02	.00	.03	.00	.01	.31	.003	.07	.001	.48	.008	.16
Travel time to urban center (hours)	.012	.22	.024	.08	.012	.51	.06	.03	-.001	.91	.002	.26	.001	.99
Regional effects														
Southeast Gulf	-.05	.00	-.06	.02	-.04	.31	-.10	.02	-.02	.02	-.001	.82	-.08	.02
North Pacific	-.09	.00	-.16	.00	-.19	.00	-.12	.07	-.02	.29	.001	.93	-.04	.40
North	1.0	.00	.16	.00	.15	.00	.17	.00	.03	.00	.01	.05	.06	.07
South	-.12	.00	-.21	.00	-.17	.00	-.22	.00	-.03	.04	.003	.45	-.18	.00
Model statistics														
Log likelihood function	-1,825.9		-1,196.5		-534.3		-537.6		-518.8		-76.1		-347.3	
% Correct predictions	81.1		72.5		75.1		73.2		90.0		97.1		81.4	

1. Coefficient refers to the effect of being male.
2. Coefficient refers to the effect of being a son.
3. Coefficient refers to the effect of being a daughter.

- **Education and Ethnicity.** Human capital in the form of educational attainment is expected to increase labor force participation, while the relationship between ethnicity (defined as the ability to speak an indigenous language) and off-farm employment is a priori indeterminate. On one hand, insofar as indigenous people have fewer productive assets than their nonindigenous counterparts, they might be more compelled to seek off-farm work.[11] On the other hand, indigenous populations are concentrated in areas with fewer labor market opportunities and may suffer from hiring discrimination (Psacharopoulos and Patrinos 1994).

- **Household Demographics.** The impact of two variables measuring household size and dependency ratio on off-farm employment is hypothesized to vary by both gender and generation. Larger families represent higher levels of both consumer demand and income-generating potential, so the effect of household size on off-farm employment is difficult to predict. Higher dependency ratios (as measured by the percentage of household members under age 15), on the other hand, represent a pure demand effect. For men, this is likely to increase the likelihood of off-farm labor force participation, while for women, who are generally responsible for childcare, greater numbers of children will most likely reduce their wage and salaried employment rates.

- **Housing Characteristics.** As proxy measures of wealth, the number of rooms in people's houses, and whether they have internal plumbing, are expected to be negatively correlated with off-farm employment.

- **Farm-Level Productive Resources.** Two measures of productive assets are used: farm size and the number of cattle in the household's livestock herd.[12] Because of potential endogeneity with current labor supply (wages may be used to purchase land and livestock), 1994 values of these assets are used.[13] Insofar as these variables represent the viability of own-farm production and income generation, they are expected to reduce the probability that a given household member will seek off-farm employment.

- **Unearned Income.** Since 1993, many *ejidatario* households have become eligible for an income support program (PROCAMPO) intended to compensate traditional basic grains producers for the elimination of price guarantees.[14] The level of the payment is based on the amount of land which a household registered as having been historically planted in one of nine basic grains prior to the initiation of the program. PROCAMPO income can therefore be considered exogenous to current labor allocation decisions, and is expected to reduce the probability of off-farm employment.

- *Ejido* **Characteristics.** Since almost 80 percent of off-farm employment is obtained on or near the *ejido*, it is appropriate to include variables which measure aspects of potential local labor market demand. These include the total number of households residing in the *ejido* (including *ejidatarios, posesionarios,* and *avencindados*)[15] and the travel time (using public transportation) to the nearest population center (defined as a town with more than 2,500 inhabitants).

- **Region.** As is clear from Table 7.1 and the discussion in the previous section, off-farm employment rates vary significantly by region. In the model, dummy variables capture the marginal effects of living in regions other than Central Mexico. Consistent with the descriptive statistical analysis, it is expected that *ejidatarios* in the North are more likely to work off-farm, while people from the Southern states are less likely to engage in off-farm employment, with some variation by gender and generation.

As detailed in Table 7.3, the model testing for the determinants of off-farm employment was run for the full sample of individuals, and for men only, women only, male household heads, wives, sons, and daughters. This disaggregation allows for the examination of differences in the signs and magnitudes of the estimated coefficients among the subgroups of interest, to see whether and to what extent the forces driving off-farm employment are distinct for *ejido* residents of different genders and belonging to different generations.

Looking first at the full sample regression, which allows only the intercept term to shift by gender, we see that many, but not all, of the hypothesized relationships are confirmed in the population as a whole. Controlling for all the other supply-side characteristics, and for *ejido*- and regional-level demand factors, men are 20 percent more likely to work off-farm than women. Employment has the expected quadratic relationship to age, with the likelihood of working off-farm increasing to age 36.8 and then decreasing. Marriage deters employment, although this coefficient is picking up the "wife" rather than the "husband" effect—in other words, the off-farm labor market participation of married women but not married men is lower than their single counterparts. Educational level is weakly positively associated with off-farm work, with each additional year of schooling increasing the probability of employment by only 1 percent. For the population as a whole, ethnicity is not statistically correlated with off-farm employment rates. Family size increases employment rates, and dependency ratios have no statistically significant effect for the pooled sample. The only wealth variable with a statistically significant coefficient is the presence of indoor plumbing, which has the surprising effect of increasing labor market participation by 3 percent.

As expected, greater farm assets (land and cattle) reduce off-farm employment probabilities. The level of unearned PROCAMPO income also significantly reduces the probability that an *ejido* resident will seek wage work. People from larger *ejidos*, where there is presumably more internal demand for hired labor, are more likely to work off-farm, but distance to the nearest urban center does not appear to be a statistically significant determinant of labor force participation. In terms of regional effects, as expected, labor demand factors in the North significantly increase off-farm probabilities (by 10 percent compared to the Central states), while Southern, Gulf state, and Northern Pacific *ejidatarios* with similar individual and household-level characteristics are between 5 and 12 percent less likely to work off-farm than their counterparts in Central Mexico. The full sample model correctly predicts 81 percent of the off-farm employment outcomes.[16]

Disaggregating the sample by gender and generation sheds additional light on the influence of individual-, household-, and *ejido*-level factors on off-farm employment patterns. First, with regard to individual characteristics, male employment rates peak at a later age (37.6) than for women (whose participation increases until age 33 and then drops off). Further, as mentioned above, married men are 5 percent more likely to work off-farm compared to single men, while being married has a downward effect on women's labor force participation.[17] Education appears to be more important for women's than for men's employment; more years of schooling even correlates negatively with off-farm work for male heads of households (the group most likely to have a job in the agricultural sector). Together, these results suggest that the role of married men as "breadwinners" on the *ejidos* includes off-farm employment requiring low levels of formal education, while women—especially unmarried daughters—are more likely to acquire a skilled or semiskilled job requiring some human capital.

Turning to the household-level variables, the lack of statistical significance of the family size and dependency ratio measures for the male subsample masks a more complicated picture, which is revealed when the data are further disaggregated by generation. Interestingly, male household heads with large families are less likely to work off-farm; but if a large percentage of those household members are children, employment rates increase significantly. For sons, on the other hand, the signs on the two household composition variables are just the opposite—labor force participation increases with family size and falls with dependency ratios.[18] One interpretation of this result is that sons "replace" (substitute for) their fathers' off-farm earnings in more mature households, while male heads have greater responsibility for materially providing for the young children in families that are closer to the beginning of their life cycles. For women as a group, off-farm employment increases with family size, but is surprisingly insensitive to dependency ratios.

For men as a group, and for male household heads, house size has the expected negative correlation with off-farm employment; however, labor force participation rates are higher for those same groups if their home has indoor plumbing. Wealthier wives (as measured by house size) are more likely to work off-farm. One interpretation of these findings is that wealthier households are characterized by male agriculturalists and wives who can use the family capital base to launch their own off-farm enterprises.

The interaction between farm assets, government agricultural payments, and off-farm employment reveals some of the starkest gender and generational differences in the analysis. For men as a group, farm size, number of livestock, and level of PROCAMPO payments all reduce the chances of working off-farm. Upon disaggregation by generation, it appears that livestock and PROCAMPO income—but not farm size—act as deterrents to labor force participation of male heads, while the employment of sons is affected by farm size and livestock but not PROCAMPO payments. The probability of labor force participation of male household heads decreases by 10 percent for every additional 10 cattle owned, and by 3 percent for every additional thousand pesos received in PROCAMPO payments. The likelihood of sons' employment falls by 5 percent with every additional 10 hectares, and by 7 percent for every additional 10 head of cattle owned by the household. Among women, only the off-farm labor market activities of daughters are negatively associated with larger livestock holdings, with the magnitude of the effect very close to that for sons.

How can we interpret these results? One possibility is to consider land, cattle, and government payments as resources over which different household members exercise some discretionary power. In other words, the fact that assets and unearned income have markedly different effects on the labor supply behavior of subgroups of household members may imply the existence of "separate spheres" of resource control within these families.[19] Specifically, it would seem that male household heads, who as the official *ejidatarios* receive PROCAMPO payments in their name, use this income (over which they have at least initial control) to reduce their off-farm employment.[20] Sons, on the other hand, for whom farm size significantly reduces labor market participation probabilities, may be influenced by the fact that they are the likely inheritors of their fathers' land; the larger the farm, the more the labor of sons is needed, and the greater incentive sons have to learn agricultural skills and demonstrate a commitment to the *ejido*. Livestock appears to be the only farm asset that reduces off-farm employment odds for all categories of household members (except wives).

The coefficients on the *ejido*-level labor demand and transportation cost variables suggest that the different demographic groups in the sample are dependent on distinct local labor markets for their off-farm employment opportunities. Male household heads are the only group whose off-farm employment is higher on larger *ejidos*, where there is potentially greater internal demand for hired labor. Sons are more likely to work if they live in a relatively remote *ejido* (as measured by travel time to the nearest urban center), also implying that the source of their employment is local. Women's off-farm employment patterns appear to be insensitive to these *ejido*-level characteristics. Finally, the regional demand effects, while consistent in sign, do vary in magnitude and statistical significance by gender and generation. Northern men, for example, are 15 percent more likely to work off-farm relative to their counterparts in the Central states, while the effect for women is only 3 percent.

In addition to the question of whether an individual works off-farm at all, it may be of interest to know how much of their time is occupied by such employment, and how this varies by gender and generation. A simple comparison of the number of weeks devoted to wage or salaried work by each demographic group suggests a wide range of degree of attachment to the labor market (see Table 7.2)—and the pattern is not necessarily what might be expected. Employed *ejido* women actually worked more weeks during 1997 (an average of 36.1) than men did (24.2), and male household heads, who have the highest overall labor force participation rates, devote the fewest number of weeks per year to these activities (20.1). This suggests that once women—especially daughters—take up paid employment, they are more likely to hold these jobs over long periods of time. Men, on the other hand, may be more inclined to combine shorter-term wage work with seasonally fluctuating farm management responsibilities. The results of a series of estimations of the factors influencing the number of weeks devoted to wage or salaried employment corroborate the off-farm employment patterns reported in Table 7.3, including the gender- and generation-specific impacts of farm assets and PROCAMPO income on employment duration.[21,22]

Conclusion

Our exploration of off-farm employment patterns among *ejido* residents and our analysis of the variation in such patterns among men and women of different generations in the context of institutional and macroeconomic reform have led to the following findings.

First, it is clear that the opportunities to earn wage income, and the availability of jobs in sectors other than agriculture, are quite unevenly distributed among the major rural regions of Mexico. This has implications for the gender composition of employment insofar as labor market competition and sectoral allocation (which may comprise both discrimination by employers and sectoral preferences by potential workers) differentially affect the ability of men and women to obtain off-farm jobs.[23] Judging by the estimated coefficients on the education variable, it appears that women are more likely to obtain skilled or semiskilled jobs, while men are filling unskilled positions. Second, while women's overall labor force participation rates remain low in *ejido* communities, the younger generation is beginning to catch up with their male counterparts—actually significantly exceeding their duration of off-farm employment in a given year. However, since the majority of these women are still single, it is unclear whether they will continue to work once they marry and form households of their own—in other words, whether the high off-farm employment rates of daughters represent a truly generational or a short-term life cycle phenomenon.

A third major finding concerns the relationship between farm-based assets and income and the decision to participate in the wage labor market. All household members are less likely to work off-farm—and to work for longer time periods—if they have relatively large livestock holdings. However, this inverse relationship is especially strong for male household heads, which is also the only group whose off-farm employment patterns are altered by the receipt of PROCAMPO payments. Together, these findings suggest the existence of some degree of private appropriation of farm-based income and assets among the *ejido* population, which in turn influences the labor supply decisions of daughters.

The policy implications of the analysis lie principally in three areas: investment in gender-neutral, off-farm employment opportunities; raising the skill level of all *ejido* residents; and increasing access of all household members to government land tenure and income support programs. First, it has been clear for some time that *ejidatarios* and their families need to supplement their agricultural incomes with wage-based earnings—and as often as not, those wages are earned in the United States. As long as the profitability of small-scale agriculture remains low, it is in everyone's interest that the local labor market develop to provide *ejido* residents with an alternative to international migration—an alternative that will allow them to continue working their farms as well. In some regions, namely the North and Center, the off-farm rural economy is relatively well developed, but incentives and investment are needed in the Southern, Gulf, and Northern Pacific states to promote viable off-farm sources of employment within commuting distance from the *ejidos*. In planning such investments, it is important that the resulting sectoral and occupational distribution be able to provide jobs for both men and women.[24]

A second possible area for public investment is in the education and training of young *ejido* residents, to better prepare them for skilled and semiskilled off-farm employment. Girls, in particular, seem to be highly responsive to formal education in terms of their propensity to work off-farm, and the length of their labor market attachment. Since fewer than half of the *ejidos* in the sample have their own secondary school, there appears to be ample room for investing in educational infrastructure in these areas. Programs like PROGRESA, which provide educational grants to families, could also raise the level of human capital among *ejido* residents.

Finally, there is the issue of leveling the relationship between farm assets and off-farm employment among household members. Here, public policy could improve the distribution of such assets among family members simply by modifying the allocational mechanisms of the two most important programs in the *ejido* sector: PROCEDE and PROCAMPO. With regard to PROCEDE, it has been argued elsewhere that joint titling in the name of both husband and wife would help alleviate problems associated with a lack of property rights for women, including dispossesion and capital market access (Katz 1998). In the context of off-farm employment, the argument extends to enhancing the ability of women to draw on land assets as an alternative or complement to wage work. The findings in this chapter also suggest that along with PROCEDE titles, PROCAMPO payments should be distributed more equitably among family members. This would mitigate the prospect of the monopolization of this unearned income source by male heads, with implications not only for off-farm employment rates, but also possibly for household expenditure and consumption patterns.

Notes

1. Davis (1998) identifies four principal "adjustment paths": (a) expansion of corn production and land accumulation; (b) diversification into off-farm activities, including migration to the United States; (c) cattle accumulation (often financed by migration remittances); and (d) selling off livestock to finance household consumption.

2. Among married women, another important phenomenon is the emergence of de facto female household headship—and, therefore, female farm management—in the context of widespread male migration. Unfortunately, the data set

used here does not allow for the identification of these types of households, which may pursue land use and livelihood strategies significantly different from (resident) male-headed *ejido* households.

3. See, for example, the publications of the Ejido Reform Research Project of the Center for U.S.–Mexican Studies at the University of California, San Diego, including Cornelius and Myhre (1998).

4. As would be expected, this share varies inversely with farm size. While landless and land-poor households (those cultivating less than 2 hectares) earn one third of their income from wages and one quarter from self-employment, larger farmers with more than 10 hectares of land derive only 10 to 15 percent of their income from wages and another 10 percent from self-employment (Davis 1998).

5. The survey is part of a longitudinal data-gathering effort which began in 1990 and was repeated, with significant alterations, in 1994 and 1997. The 1997 data cover 1,665 households from 286 *ejidos*. Detailed household-level information is available on demographics (including migration), land use and transactions, common property access, agricultural technology and farm production, livestock, credit and insurance, off-farm income, and participation in community organizations and government programs. In addition, a survey conducted at the level of the *ejido* collected data on collective land use and distribution, governance, and social services. For the purposes of the off-farm employment analysis conducted here, 6,135 individuals between the ages of 14 and 75 were included in the data set.

6. This is unfortunate because one third of households earn income from self-employment. However, there is no reliable way of attributing these activities or earnings to individuals within the household.

7. "Sons" and "daughters" are children of the household head still residing with their natal families, regardless of their own marital status. Off-farm employment for all household members between ages 14 and 75 was recorded.

8. Conversely, we do not know whether women who are now "wives" were more active labor force participants before they formed their own households.

9. It should be recalled that the analysis excludes the large number of adult sons who were migrating (and most likely engaging in wage labor) at the time of the survey.

10. As with Table 7.1, all data are weighted to correct for sample stratification.

11. Indigenous households have less land (median 5 hectares, compared to 8 hectares for nonindigenous households), significantly less irrigation (only 3 percent of their land is under irrigation, compared to 21 percent for nonindigenous households), and smaller livestock herds (mean value of 4 cows, compared to 7 cows for nonindigenous households). Wodon and Molnar (1999) find for rural Mexico that, controlling for other observed household characteristics, indigenous households have levels of per capita income 11 percent lower than nonindigenous households.

12. Following De Janvry, Gordillo, and Sadoulet (1997), farm size is converted into National Rainfed Equivalent (NRE) units. This corrects for differences in land quality by weighting plots according to agroecological region (humid tropical, subhumid tropical, humid temperate, subhumid temperate, and arid/semiarid); use of irrigation; and whether the land is in pasture or forest. For a discussion of the precise methodology and weights used, see De Janvry, Gordillo, and Sadoulet (1997).

13. Ideally, 1994 housing wealth would also have been used, but unfortunately these variables were collected only in 1997. Using the panel data reduces the total number of observations to 4,411.

14. For more detailed information on PROCAMPO, see World Bank (1998, Volume II), especially Chapter 7, "Government Programs."

15. *Ejidatarios* possess full membership rights in the governing bodies of the *ejido*; *posesionarios* have formally approved access to *ejido* lands, but cannot vote; *avecindado*s live on the *ejido* without any formal property rights and may be children of *ejidatarios* who have started their own family, or households that have relocated to the *ejido* from elsewhere.

16. The model is much better at predicting negative than positive outcomes: while 82.1 percent of predicted nonparticipation in off-farm employment is correct, only 53.5 percent of predicted off-farm employment is correct.

17. Note that adult sons living with their parents are twice as likely to be married as daughters; this patrilocal pattern is due in part to inheritance practices that favor sons (Katz 1998).

18. Only the family size coefficient is statistically significant at < 2 percent.

19. The idea that income and wealth are individually appropriated within families, with important effects on a range of household behavior and welfare outcomes (including expenditures, consumption, and investment in human capital) is

one that is gaining increasing acceptance in the literature on the microeconomics of resource allocation. Some recent empirical examples include Doss (1996); Katz (1995); Lundberg, Pollak, and Wales (1997); Schultz (1990); and Thomas (1990). Theoretical work on the implications of "separate spheres" for intrahousehold resource allocation has been done by Carter and Katz (1997); Chiappori (1997); and Lundberg and Pollak (1993). A particularly relevant application of an intrahousehold perspective to labor supply decisions can be found in Ott (1992).

20. This finding is consistent with case studies that have observed exclusive male participation in the PROCAMPO program, often to the detriment of wives who are left in charge of farm management (but who do not hold title to their land) while their husbands are migrating (Katz 1998).

21. For all groups except wives, a Tobit specification was used in order to account for the large number of zero observations of the dependent variable. In the case of wives, it was decided not to estimate a "weeks worked" equation, since the small number of positive observations (n = 39) would yield biased results. (Results available from author.)

22. For male household heads, each additional 10 head of cattle reduces off-farm employment by three weeks, while every thousand-peso increase in PROCAMPO is associated with a 0.6-week reduction in off-farm labor supply. For sons, the marginal impact of a hectare of land is a loss of 0.2 week's work. Both sons and daughters reduce their labor supply by approximately 0.2 weeks for every 10 additional cattle owned by the household.

23. As discussed, gender disparities in employment rates are highest in regions with large agricultural sectors and lowest in regions with more diversified off-farm employment opportunities.

24. The expansion of the *maquiladora* sector into nonborder regions is a positive development in this regard (see Chapter 4).

References

Carter, Michael R., and Elizabeth G. Katz. 1997. "Separate Spheres and the Conjugal Contract: Understanding the Impact of Gender-Biased Development." In Lawrence Haddad, John Hoddinott, and Harold Alderman, eds., *Intrahousehold Resource Allocation in Developing Countries: Methods, Models and Policies*. Baltimore: The Johns Hopkins University Press.

Chiappori, Pierre-André. 1997. "'Collective' Models of Household Behavior: The Sharing Rule Approach." In Lawrence Haddad, John Hoddinott, and Harold Alderman, eds., *Intrahousehold Resource Allocation in Developing Countries: Methods, Models and Policies.* Baltimore: The Johns Hopkins University Press.

Cornelius, Wayne A., and David Myhre, eds. 1998. *The Transformation of Rural Mexico: Reforming the Ejido Sector.* La Jolla: Center for U.S.–Mexican Studies, University of California, San Diego.

Davis, Benjamin. 1998. "Adjustment in the Ejido Sector." Background paper prepared for *Economic Adjustment and Institutional Reform: Mexico's Ejido Sector Responds.* Washington, D.C.: World Bank.

De Janvry, Alain, Gustavo Gordillo, and Elisabeth Sadoulet. 1997. *Mexico's Second Agrarian Reform: Household and Community Responses, 1990–1994.* La Jolla: Center for U.S.–Mexican Studies, University of California, San Diego.

Doss, Cheryl. 1996. "Women's Bargaining Power in Household Economic Decisions: Evidence from Ghana." Department of Applied Economics, University of Minnesota Staff Paper No. P96–11.

Katz, Elizabeth G. 1995. "Gender and Trade within the Household: Observations from Rural Guatemala." *World Development* 23(2):327–42.

———. 1998. "Gender and Ejido Reform." Background paper prepared for *Economic Adjustment and Institutional Reform: Mexico's Ejido Sector Responds.* Washington, D.C.: World Bank.

Lanjouw, Peter. 1998. "Poverty and the Non-Farm Economy in Mexico's Ejidos: 1994–1997." Background paper prepared for *Economic Adjustment and Institutional Reform: Mexico's Ejido Sector Responds.* Washington, D.C.: World Bank.

Lundberg, Shelly J., and Robert A. Pollak. 1993. "Separate Spheres Bargaining and the Marriage Market." *Journal of Political Economy* 101(6):988–1010.

Lundberg, Shelly J., Robert A. Pollak, and Terence J. Wales. 1997. "Do Husbands and Wives Pool Their Resources? Evidence from the United Kingdom Child Benefit." *Journal of Human Resources* 32(3):463–81.

Ott, Notburga. 1992. *Intrafamily Bargaining and Household Decisions.* Berlin: Springer-Verlag.

Psacharopoulos, George, and Harry Anthony Patrinos, eds. 1994. *Indigenous People and Poverty in Latin America : An Empirical Analysis.* Washington, D.C.: World Bank.

Schultz, T. Paul. 1990. "Testing the Neoclassical Model of Family Labor Supply and Fertility." *Journal of Human Resources* 25(4):599–634.

Thomas, Duncan. 1990. "Intra-household Resource Allocation: An Inferential Approach." *Journal of Human Resources* 25(4):635–664.

Wodon, Quentin, and Augusta Molnar. 1999. "Poverty and Indigenous Attitudes towards Government Programs in Mexico." Background Paper No. 6 for *Mexico: Poverty and Public Policy.* Washington, D.C.: World Bank.

World Bank. 1998. *Economic Adjustment and Institutional Reform: Mexico's Ejido Sector Responds.* Vol. I and II. Washington, D.C.: World Bank.

8
Welfare of Male and Female Elderly in Mexico: A Comparison

Susan W. Parker and Rebeca Wong

As a result of the demographic and epidemiological transitions in the last two decades, the age structure of the population in Mexico has undergone important transformations. The population aged 65 and older represented 4.5 percent of the total population in 1997, but its annual growth rate is increasing—from 2 percent in 1970 to 3.7 percent in 1990 to 3.9 percent in 1998 (Tuirán 1998). Although the elderly population is already large—at about 4.3 million—the speed at which this segment is growing may represent future increasing demands on social services. Therefore, it is essential for researchers and policymakers to understand the consequences of the rhythm and pace of the aging of the population, and the nature of the economic and social processes that may accompany it. Some of the most significant consequences of aging involve the social sector needs of the population, including the financial resources to meet general consumption needs, in addition to healthcare, housing, and social services (Ham Chande 1999; Tuirán 1999).

This chapter focuses on differences in welfare between the male and female elderly populations in Mexico. While the welfare of the elderly has numerous dimensions, we take a limited approach. We examine three main aspects of well-being of the elderly: (a) poverty, (b) availability of healthcare, and (c) pension income. While the entire population may be vulnerable at old age, for a variety of reasons female elderly may be at a particular disadvantage in terms of well-being. First, since women live longer than men, on average, more elderly women than men are widowed at old age, and the resources available to elderly women must last a greater number of years than those of men (Partida Bush 1999; Gomes da Conceicao 1997). Thus elderly women may be more likely to live in poverty than elderly men. Second, many social security benefits such as access to healthcare are associated with employment in Mexico. Since women historically have participated less in the labor market than men (Pedrero Nieto 1999), we hypothesize that women are less likely to receive the benefit of healthcare in old age. Third, because women tend to participate less in the formal labor market throughout their lives (Pedrero Nieto 1999; Salas Páez 1999), and because their careers tend to be interrupted and their jobs have fewer social benefits than men's, we hypothesize that women are less likely to have a pension in old age. Fourth, as a result of these lifetime patterns, we expect that women have sources of economic support that differ from those of men in old age, relying more on informal family support (Ham Chande 1999; Leñero Otero 1999; Montes de Oca Zavala 1999), while men tend to count more on the institutional support provided by pensions.

We test these hypotheses and examine whether empirical data for Mexico support the overall hypothesis that, on average, women experience worse living conditions and receive less institutional support in old age than men, placing women in a disadvantaged and relatively more vulnerable position regarding old age security. This chapter describes the data sets used for the analyses (see Box 8.1), examines well-being using consumption information at the household level to classify households and individuals living in poverty, analyzes the availability of healthcare benefits and the availability of pensions among the elderly, examines the contribution of elderly pension income toward total income in the household, and examines the association between receiving pension income and the likelihood of the elderly to live in poverty. While our main focus is on the differences by gender, we also consider the well-being of the elderly compared with younger age groups. Finally, the chapter presents conclusions and policy implications of our findings.

Socioeconomic Characteristics of the Elderly Population in Mexico

Table 8.1 presents descriptive statistics of four age groups of the Mexican population aged 12 and older by sex. Roughly the same proportion of men and women are married or in consensual union at ages 16 to 39 (about 50 to 55 percent). Due to the higher survival rate of women compared to men, and the fact that men tend to marry women younger than themselves, at ages 40 and older, the proportion of women who are widowed is much higher than that of men. Ten percent of women and 2 percent of men are widowed at ages 40 to 59, whereas 47 percent of women and 14 percent of men aged 60 and older are widowed.

Men and women of young and peak working ages report similar living arrangements. More women than men are reported to live in extended rather than nuclear households as the proportion of widowed women increases; that is, among ages 40 and older. Thirty-two percent of women and 24 percent of men aged 40 to 59 live in extended households, where-

Box 8.1 Data Sources

The paper uses primary data analysis from two sources. For the poverty analysis and sources of income, we use the 1996 Mexican National Household Survey of Income and Expenditures (ENIGH), carried out by INEGI (*Instituto Nacional de Estadística, Geografía e Informática*). This is a nationally representative, repeated, cross-sectional data set including detailed information on income and expenditures for approximately 14,000 households, and socioeconomic and demographic characteristics of the individual members. The ENIGH is by far the most appropriate data source for the study of poverty levels and is the data set used to generate official poverty statistics in Mexico. One drawback, however, is that all pension incomes are aggregated in one source, which makes it impossible to separate different types of pensions, such as retirement pensions from widowhood pensions.[1] We define an elderly person as an individual aged 60 or older. The total sample of ENIGH households with elderly persons is 3,360, which corresponds to a total of 4,565 elderly individuals.

For the analysis on healthcare benefits and pensions at old age, we use data from the National Employment Survey 1996 (ENE–96), also carried out by INEGI. This is an annual survey with national representation, which includes detailed questions on employment, wages, hours of employment, and sociodemographic characteristics of each household member (INEGI 1998). The 1996 survey includes a module on social security, applied to a representative sample of 12,100 households, to gather information on individuals of all ages. For our purposes we use this subsample, which is designed to ensure national representation. The analysis sample includes 55,242 individuals aged 12 and older. Of these, 4,154 are individuals aged 60 or older. In addition to the socioeconomic and demographic information asked in the ENE, our analysis sample includes the following information about each individual: whether the person has access to medical coverage; the reason for receiving coverage; whether each person contributes to social security in any job; whether the individual receives any pension; the institution providing the pension; the type of pension received (retirement, severance, work disability, survivor); how long the pension has been received; and the monthly amount.

as among those aged 60 and older, 45 percent of women and 36 percent of men live in extended households. The prevalence of individuals living alone is very low among those under age 59 (about 2 percent of ages 40 to 59), but 11 percent of women and 9 percent of men live alone among those aged 60 and older.

In peak working ages, between 16 and 39 and 40 and 59, about the same proportion of men and women live in less-urban as in more-urban

Table 8.1. Percent Distribution of the Population by Age Group and Gender According to Main Characteristics (Mexico)

Main characteristics	Age group (years) by gender							
	Women				Men			
	12–15	16–39	40–59	60+	12–15	16–39	40–59	60+
Marital status								
Married/ consensual union	1.4	55.4	72.3	42.6	0.1	50.5	88.1	78.4
Widowed	0.0	1.1	10.1	46.7	0.0	0.1	1.7	13.8
Single/ divorced	98.6	43.5	17.6	10.7	99.9	49.4	10.2	7.8
Household structure								
Nuclear	75.3	66.5	59.6	35.3	74.5	67.4	67.8	50.2
Extended	18.1	23.7	31.7	44.6	19.9	22.2	23.7	35.9
One person	0.0	0.6	1.7	11.1	0.0	1.4	2.3	8.9
Area of residence								
Less urban	57.9	50.8	51.1	54.5	62.6	50.7	52.7	62.0
More urban	42.1	49.2	48.9	45.5	37.4	49.3	47.3	38.0
Children (for women)								
% women with children	0.8	59.8	93.1	92.6	—	—	—	—
Mean (S.D.), if women	1.0	2.7	5.1	6.7				
Have at least 1 child	(0.2)	(1.7)	(3.0)	(3.7)				
Disability								
Yes, temporary	0.9	1.5	2.1	4.1	0.6	1.0	3.2	6.9
Yes, permanent	1.6	2.5	6.7	15.3	1.9	2.9	8.6	19.1
No	97.2	94.8	91.0	79.8	97.0	94.6	87.2	73.5
Years of education								
0	1.9	5.4	18.5	42.9	2.0	4.1	13.5	37.6
1–6	52.5	35.1	53.1	45.2	55.5	31.2	53.1	51.1
7+	45.6	59.5	28.4	11.8	42.4	64.6	33.4	11.2
Dwelling conditions								
Electricity, water, sewerage	70.6	76.3	77.6	74.4	69.4	74.7	76.7	69.0
Telephone connection	27.0	32.1	39.5	36.4	22.3	29.2	37.5	27.9

— Not observed.

( ) indicate standard deviations.

Source: National Employment Survey (ENE) Module on Social Security, 1996, INEGI, Mexico; authors' calculations.

areas.[2] At ages 60 or above a larger proportion of men (62 percent) than women (55 percent) live in less-urban areas. This pattern could be explained because overall there are more extended households in urban than in rural areas. Alternatively, because there are more widowed women at old ages than men, upon widowhood, older women may move to more-urban areas to share residence with their adult children's families.

Men report a higher prevalence of disabilities[3] compared to women. At age 60 and above, 4 percent of women and 7 percent of men report a temporary disability, and 15 percent of women and 19 percent of men report a permanent disability. A similar pattern exists for permanent disability at younger ages; for example, between ages 40 and 59, 7 percent of women and 9 percent of men report a permanent disability. These gender differences can be explained because disabilities, as they are reported in the ENE–96, are likely to be associated with work,[4] and men have a higher rate of labor force participation throughout their lives than women. About 18 percent of women and 56 percent of men of all ages are currently employed.

There is little gender difference in years of education at young ages, with a slight female advantage: 46 percent of women and 42 percent of men aged 12 to 15 report seven or more years of education. Starting with the age group 16 to 39 and through age 59, men report slightly more years of education than women. For the population aged 60 and older, there is no gender difference in the percentage of the population with seven or more years of education. The percentage of women aged 60 and older, however, who report no education is higher than that of men (43 percent and 38 percent, respectively).[5]

On average, women report better dwelling conditions than men at all ages, and the gap appears to widen with old age: 74 percent of women aged 60 and older live in dwellings with electricity, water, and sewerage, compared with 69 percent of men of comparable ages. Of the same ages, 36 percent of women and 28 percent of men report having a telephone in the dwelling. These differences are likely due to the fact that at old ages, a larger proportion of women than men live in more-urban areas and in extended households, as previously mentioned.

Living Standards and Poverty Levels of the Elderly

This section considers the overall well-being of the elderly and uses measures of adult equivalent consumption to construct simple indicators of poverty based on the Foster, Greer, and Thorbecke (FGT) poverty indexes.[6] We compare the poverty rates of the elderly and nonelderly populations and we analyze whether poverty tends to be more severe for the "older" elderly (over age 70) than the "younger" elderly (aged 60 to 70). We also consider differences by urban–rural residence and by type of living arrangements of the elderly.

We have adopted a poverty line equivalent to the 30th percentile of adult equivalence consumption, that is, the threshold below which the poorest 30 percent of the households fall. This poverty line corresponds to approximately US$35 to US$40 monthly per capita consumption, and falls between the range of extreme and moderate poverty lines traditionally used in Mexico. (See Lustig and Szekely 1997 for a summary of poverty lines). For our measure of living standard we use total (monetary and nonmonetary) household expenditures in both urban and rural areas, adjusted for adult equivalence from the ENIGH 1996. As is common in the poverty and development literature, we use expenditure rather than income measures of well-being. Consumption is thought to be a preferred measure of permanent income to capture well-being because it is less subject to seasonal variation than income (Deaton 1997).

Adult Equivalence Scales and Economies of Scale

The use of adult equivalence scales for consumption is generally justified by the idea that children should be weighed to a lesser degree than adults, and in some cases, additional adults less than the first adult because of economies of scale. It is well known that the weights of adult equivalence scales can drastically alter the conclusions reached on poverty and inequality within a population. This is likely to be even more so in the present case, where the interest is to evaluate the well-being of the elderly, and as we shall see later, the elderly tend to live in types of households different from the rest of the population. Nevertheless, the obvious problem arises of which weights are appropriate to use. Per capita measures are problematic; they tend to overstate the poverty of large families with small children because they weigh the needs of children equally with those of adults. If the elderly tend to live in families without small children, then the poverty of the elderly may be understated.

The appropriate adult equivalence weights are likely country specific, and unfortunately, there are no studies in Mexico that could orient us. In the absence of such studies we experiment with several different adult equivalence scales.[7] For our poverty measures in the main text tables we use the Organisation for Economic Co-operation and Development (OECD) countries adult equivalence assumption, while the additional equivalence measures are included in Appendix Tables 8.A.1 through 8.A.6.[8]

Poverty of Households with and without Elderly Members

Table 8.2 shows the distribution of households with an elderly member (defined as age 60 or over), reflecting that about 23 percent of all households in Mexico have an elderly member. A larger percentage of households have elderly females than males, which is expected given the higher life expectancy of women in Mexico.

Table 8.3 begins the analysis of poverty levels and shows that households with elderly members have higher poverty levels than households with no elderly members. According to the headcount measure of the proportion below the poverty line, about 27 percent of households with no elderly members are poor, versus 42 percent of households with two or more elderly members. The higher order FGT indexes show even larger differences between the poverty level of households with and without elderly members. For example, according to $\alpha = 2$, or the poverty severity index, the poverty level of households with elderly members is more than twice the level of households with no elderly members. Nevertheless, the difference between households with and without elderly members is much larger in urban areas than in rural areas for all of the poverty indicators used.

In summary, the analysis thus far indicates that *households* with elderly members tend to have a higher likelihood of being poor than other households, and this gap is larger in urban than in rural areas. This, however, is not equivalent to demonstrating that the elderly are always poorer than other groups of the population.

Table 8.2. Distribution of Households with Elderly Members Age 60 and Above
(Mexico, percent)

Type of household	% distribution
With no elderly members	76.07
With one elderly female	8.18
With one elderly male	7.58
With one elderly male and one elderly female	7.36
Other	0.81
Total	100.0

Source: National Income and Expenditures Survey (ENIGH), Mexico, 1996.

Table 8.3. Indicators of Poverty by Number of Elderly Members in the Household (Mexico, poverty line = 30th percentile)

Residence & number of elderly members in household	Adult equivalence Measures of consumption levels (%) (OECD)		
	$\alpha = 0$ Headcount[a]	$\alpha = 1$ Poverty gap	$\alpha = 2$ Poverty severity
National level			
No elderly	27.2	9.9	5.1
1 elderly	36.9	15.3	8.9
2 or more elderly	42.4	17.7	10.2
Urban residence			
No elderly	16.0	4.7	2.0
1 elderly	25.3	9.1	4.9
2 or more elderly	28.4	10.4	5.7
Rural residence			
No elderly	51.3	21.2	11.9
1 elderly	57.3	26.4	16.1
2 or more elderly	61.9	27.9	16.4

a. Foster, Greer, and Thorbecke (FGT) indicators. See Note 6 for an explanation of each indicator.

Source: National Income and Expenditures Survey (ENIGH), Mexico, 1996.

Elderly versus Nonelderly Poverty

Overall, the poverty rates of male and female elderly members are similar (Table 8.4). The results show that both male and female elderly individuals tend to be much poorer than working-age adults, and their poverty rate is slightly higher than that of children, particularly when poverty is measured using the poverty gap or severity of poverty index. Between rural and urban areas, nevertheless, there are some variations. In urban areas, both male and female elderly exhibit higher poverty rates than either children or working-age adults. In rural areas, however, the poverty rates between children and the elderly appear to be quite similar. This analysis suggests that the elderly and children tend to be disproportionally concentrated in poor households.

Poverty According to the Age of the Elderly

In Table 8.5 we consider the extent to which the standard of living varies among the elderly according to age. We divide the elderly into two groups, aged 60 to 70 and above age 70, and compare poverty levels.

Table 8.4. Indicators of Poverty by Age Group and Gender (Mexico, poverty level = 30th percentile)

Residence by age group and gender	Adult equivalence measures of consumption levels (%) (OECD)		
	$\alpha = 0$ Headcount[a]	$\alpha = 1$ Poverty gap	$\alpha = 2$ Poverty severity
National level			
Children 0–17	40.0	15.3	8.1
Adults 18–59	29.4	10.6	5.4
Elderly (60 and above)			
Male	40.2	16.3	9.2
Female	39.0	16.7	9.8
Urban residence			
Children 0–17	24.3	7.2	3.0
Adults 18–59	17.4	4.9	2.1
Elderly (60 and above)			
Male	26.5	9.2	4.9
Female	27.0	10.2	5.6
Rural residence			
Children 0–17	63.1	27.4	15.7
Adults 18–59	54.0	22.2	12.3
Elderly (60 and above)			
Male	59.0	26.2	15.2
Female	60.6	28.3	17.3

a. Foster, Greer, and Thorbecke (FGT) indicators. See Note 6 for an explanation of each indicator.
Source: National Income and Expenditures Survey (ENIGH), Mexico, 1996.

The results show that the oldest elderly are more likely to be poor than the younger elderly. For example, according to the headcount measure, 44 percent of men over age 70 are poor versus 38 percent of those aged 60 to 70. In reference to the analysis of Table 8.4, where we compared the poverty of the elderly to that of children and working-age adults, the older elderly show poverty rates that are higher than any other group, even for children in rural areas. These results thus provide evidence that the oldest old are among the poorest individuals in Mexico. Furthermore, as aging of the population continues, the group of the oldest old are likely to become predominantly female, given the higher life expectancy of females than males. If this pattern remains as the demographic transition continues in Mexico, a type of "feminization" of elderly poverty is likely to emerge.

Table 8.5. Indicators of Elderly Poverty by Age Group and Gender (Mexico, poverty level = 30th percentile)

Residence by age group and gender	Adult equivalence measures of consumption levels (%) (OECD)		
	$\alpha = 0$ Headcount[a]	$\alpha = 1$ Poverty gap	$\alpha = 2$ Poverty severity
National level			
Male elderly			
Ages 60–70	37.9	14.7	7.9
Ages above 70	44.0	19.0	11.4
Female elderly			
Ages 60–70	36.7	14.7	8.1
Ages above 70	42.8	19.9	12.6
Urban residence			
Male elderly			
Ages 60–70	25.7	8.0	3.9
Ages above 70	30.0	11.1	6.3
Female elderly			
Ages 60–70	25.7	9.3	4.8
Ages above 70	29.0	11.7	6.9
Rural residence			
Male elderly			
Ages 60–70	56.1	23.7	13.2
Ages above 70	63.9	30.3	18.5
Female elderly			
Ages 60–70	56.6	24.6	14.0
Ages above 70	66.8	34.1	22.4

Note: See Note 6 for an explanation of each indicator.
a. Foster, Greer, and Thorbecke (FGT) indicators.
Source: National Income and Expenditures Survey (ENIGH), Mexico, 1996.

Summary

In summary, while overall poverty levels in rural areas are much higher than in urban areas in Mexico, the elderly living in urban areas tend to have higher levels of poverty and worse standards of living relative to all other age groups in urban areas. In rural areas, however, while the elderly continue to have higher poverty levels than other working-age adults, their standard of living and likelihood of living in poverty appear to be similar to those of children, if not slightly better.

Poverty levels of elderly women in rural areas are slightly higher than those of elderly men, although both groups have very high rates of poverty. Our results indicate that the "oldest old" (those above age 70) have higher poverty levels than the "younger old" (age 60 to 70), which implies that the "oldest old" both in urban and rural areas are likely the worst-off population group in Mexico. Given the longer life expectancy of women, the oldest elderly are likely to be predominantly female, which implies that the group of the worst-off elderly is likely to be increasingly female.

Healthcare Coverage for the Population Aged 12 and Older (by age and gender)

In this section, we turn to another dimension of well-being in old age: access to healthcare. We begin with a brief description of the healthcare system in Mexico.

Among social security institutions in Mexico, the *Instituto Mexicano del Seguro Social* (IMSS) represents the largest social security provider covering the formal private sector workers, retirees, and their dependents, a population of about 40 million. The *Instituto de Seguridad Social al Servicio de los Trabajadores del Estado* (ISSSTE) is the second largest social security institute covering federal, state, and municipal public sector employees, retirees, and their dependents, amounting to approximately 9 million beneficiaries, and is similar to IMSS both in terms of services offered and the organization of healthcare delivery.[9] It is important to note that according to all social security systems, men may cover their wives who are not already covered by social security benefits through current or previous employment.[10]

The Ministry of Health (SSA) is the major provider of healthcare services for the uninsured population. Public services are supplied in exchange for a small user charge, which seeks to take into account the economic conditions of the patient. Although in principle all Mexicans are eligible to receive SSA services, in practice those without physical access to SSA facilities (the rural poor) and those with private insurance or social security coverage do not make use of the services. IMSS *Solidaridad* is a recently established program run by IMSS but funded with federal tax revenues. The program is free of charge at the point of service and is targeted to the rural poor that do not have access to alternative public providers. Finally, the private sector relies mostly on out-of-pocket payments and insurance premiums.

For our analysis, we use the ENE–96 report from the family respondent to the household survey, regarding healthcare of each household member. We use information on whether each person has the right to receive services or benefits from either IMSS, ISSSTE, medical service from PEMEX,[11] private medical services either self-paid or provided through employment, or other public institutions.

Table 8.6 presents the proportion of the population that is covered by an institution by gender and age. Overall, coverage is similar for men and women, although the absolute level of coverage is low, particularly at young ages. Almost two thirds of the population aged 12 to 15 receive no health benefits, compared with 54 to 59 percent of those aged 16 through 59, and 50 percent of those aged 60 or older. The institution with greatest coverage is IMSS, and its coverage increases with age: 24 percent of girls aged 12 to 15 receive IMSS benefits compared with 39 percent of women aged 60 or older. The second-most-important institution providing coverage is ISSSTE: roughly 7 to 9 percent of women in all age groups receive ISSSTE benefits, compared to about 5 to 8 percent of men. In comparison, coverage by other institutions (PEMEX, private, and other public) is negligible.

The low prevalence of healthcare benefits received by the Mexican population does not necessarily imply that only employed individuals have healthcare coverage. Table 8.6 shows that among the employed population, approximately 50 percent of women aged 16 through 59 have no coverage, compared with 60 percent of working men of the same age group. For young workers aged 12 to 15, the lack of healthcare coverage is even more generalized: 80 percent of women and 83 percent of men receive no health benefits. This latter finding can be explained because most young workers are active in the informal sector or in unpaid family business jobs without benefits. The table also shows the reasons for receiving institutional benefits—that is, whether benefits are received due to employment, indirectly through coverage of a family member, or through some other arrangement. Among men, the majority of those aged 16 to 59 (about 70 percent) receive benefits because they are the employee. For women, however, the proportion receiving benefits as employees is comparatively lower than the proportion receiving benefits as spouses of employees (25 percent of those aged 40 to 59 and 39 percent of those aged to 16 to 39 receive benefits as employees, compared to 50 percent and 42 percent, respectively, as spouses).

In summary, men and women at old age have similar levels of health insurance coverage. Comparisons by age show that the elderly are the most protected and children the least protected by health insurance coverage.

A Multivariate Model of Healthcare Coverage

We now turn toward a more formal analysis of the determinants of health care coverage through a probit regression that includes age, education, dwelling conditions, area of residence, disability status, and marital status as explanatory variables. Table 8.7 presents the probit results in the form of marginal effects. The entries in the table represent the estimated change in the probability of receiving benefits from a one-unit change in each explanatory variable, holding all other variables constant at the mean value. In all subsamples, men and women with more years

Table 8.6. Employment and Healthcare Benefits Received by Gender and Age Group (Mexico, weighted data)

| | Age group (years) by gender | | | | | | | |
| | Women | | | | Men | | | |
Group	12–15	16–39	40–59	60+	12–15	16–39	40–59	60+
Employment status								
Currently employed	12.9	39.8	40.5	17.8	28.7	82.3	90.3	56.3
Ever employed	16.6	69.5	71.7	59.0	33.6	88.9	98.0	99.4
Among all population (working & nonworking)								
Receiving benefits by institution [a, b]								
No	64.4	57.6	54.1	50.7	64.5	58.8	58.9	50.1
IMSS	24.1	30.5	34.0	38.9	26.0	31.3	29.6	39.9
ISSSTE	8.9	7.1	9.1	8.9	6.8	5.1	7.7	7.1
PEMEX	0.5	0.8	1.0	1.0	0.6	0.7	0.7	1.5
Private	0.9	2.2	1.8	0.6	0.9	1.6	1.6	1.9
Among those receiving benefits, reasons								
Employee	1.5	39.2	25.3	4.4	3.8	72.4	69.3	16.7
Self-pay	0.0	1.0	1.0	2.0	0.0	2.8	7.0	3.7
Retired	0.1	0.2	3.6	13.5	0.0	0.3	7.6	52.4
Spouse	0.1	42.1	50.3	42.0	0.0	1.8	3.0	0.4
Parent	0.0	0.3	17.9	35.8	0.0	0.1	9.4	25.0
Child	93.3	11.9	0.1	0.4	92.0	15.7	1.1	0.1
Among working population								
Receiving benefits by institution								
No	80.2	49.8	51.8	62.4	83.1	60.0	60.4	65.9
IMSS	17.5	34.6	33.9	27.1	15.2	32.5	28.8	28.5
ISSSTE	0.9	11.4	12.9	9.5	1.2	4.4	8.0	4.2
PEMEX	0.0	0.5	0.6	0.5	0.1	0.6	0.5	0.9
Private	1.6	3.9	1.8	0.6	0.1	1.6	1.7	1.9
Contributing to IMSS	2.7	26.8	17.6	6.8	3.8	30.2	24.1	12.3

a. Percentages may not add up to 100 because other institutions (small proportion of cases) offer coverage as well.

b. IMSS = Social Security Institute, ISSSTE = Federal Workers Social Security Institute, PEMEX = Oil Workers Institute.

Source: National Employment Survey (ENE) Module on Social Security, 1996, INEGI, Mexico; authors' calculations.

of education, better socioeconomic conditions as measured by the condition of their dwelling, and residing in urban areas are more likely to receive healthcare coverage. In addition, having children is positively associated with coverage for women of all age groups.

The marginal effects also indicate that the effect of marriage is greater for men than for women in all age groups. Being married (compared to being single or divorced) is associated with a 0.10 higher probability of coverage for women aged 16 to 39, compared to 0.16 for men of comparable ages. This is probably related to the fact that employed individuals are more likely to have social security health benefits, and married men are more likely to be employed than married women. For those over age 60, widowhood increases the likelihood of coverage only for men. This result can be interpreted to imply that, whereas women exhibit a healthcare benefits advantage due to marriage, there is no disadvantage (compared to single women) due to widowhood.

The marginal effect of having children increases as age increases. Having children is associated with a higher probability of coverage by 0.03 for women aged 16 to 39, compared to 0.13 for women aged 40 to 59 and 0.19 for women aged 60 and older. This result could indicate that as individuals age, their adult children are increasingly likely to enlist their mothers as recipients of healthcare benefits; thus, all else remaining constant, women with older children are more likely to receive benefits.

To isolate the effect of education for the three age cohorts and separately for men and women, we use the results of the multivariate regression presented in Table 8.7 to calculate the estimated probability of receiving healthcare coverage according to the individual's years of education. These results are provided in Table 8.8. In general, regardless of age and education, women are slightly more likely to receive healthcare benefits than men, the likelihood of coverage is higher for older ages, and the probability of being covered increases with more education. Holding all other variables constant, women aged 16 to 39 with 6 years of education have a similar probability (0.31) of being covered compared to men of comparable age and education level (0.29). At older ages, the gender gap is maintained or widens slightly in favor of women. Women aged 60 or older with 6 years of education have a 0.62 likelihood of being covered compared with 0.57 for men. Women with 12 years of education have a probability 0.63 of being covered, compared to 0.56 for men. These results could indicate that more educated women are more likely to (a) be employed, (b) be married to someone who is employed with healthcare benefits, or (c) have children who are employed with healthcare benefits.

In summary, the overall levels of healthcare coverage in Mexico are low. Individuals aged 60 or older, however, have higher coverage compared with other age groups, particularly the young (aged 12 to 15). Women tend to have coverage similar to men, and married individuals of both genders are more likely to be protected than single individuals. Our multivariate models allow us to conclude that holding all else constant,

Table 8.7. Marginal Effects of Explanatory Variables on the Probability of Receiving Healthcare Coverage by Age Group and Gender (Mexico)

	Age group (years) by gender											
	16–39				40–59				60 and older			
	Women		Men		Women		Men		Women		Men	
Explanatory variables	Marginal effects[a]	P value	Marginal effects	P value	Marginal effects	P value	Marginal effects	P value	Marginal effects	P value	Marginal effects	P value
Individual characteristics												
Age	-0.0138	**0.051**	-0.0195	**0.006**	-0.0196	0.464	-0.0520	**0.047**	0.0308	0.123	0.0620	**0.003**
Age squared	0.0004	**0.006**	0.0004	**0.004**	0.0003	0.253	0.0006	**0.029**	-0.0002	0.110	-0.0004	**0.005**
Married	0.0094	**0.000**	0.1614	**0.000**	0.0709	**0.004**	0.1331	**0.000**	0.0932	**0.035**	0.2025	**0.000**
Widowed	0.1113	**0.040**	0.1688	0.235	0.0679	**0.062**	0.0714	0.326	0.0117	0.797	0.1428	**0.010**
Number of children[b]	0.0349	**0.040**	—	—	0.1315	**0.000**	—	—	0.1867	**0.000**	—	—
Slope education 1–6	0.0343	**0.000**	0.0320	**0.000**	0.0431	**0.000**	0.0390	**0.000**	0.0507	**0.000**	0.0420	**0.000**
Slope education 7–9	0.0603	**0.000**	0.0555	**0.000**	0.0131	0.285	0.0386	**0.001**	-0.0618	**0.046**	-0.0260	0.383
Slope education 10+	0.0283	**0.000**	0.0136	**0.000**	0.0303	**0.001**	0.0027	0.680	0.0673	**0.054**	0.0205	0.273
Permanent disability	0.1047	**0.003**	0.0104	0.751	0.0209	0.537	0.1276	**0.000**	0.0054	0.869	0.0612	**0.046**
Household/community characteristics												
Services in dwelling	0.1292	**0.000**	0.1266	**0.000**	0.1914	**0.000**	0.1614	**0.000**	0.2309	**0.000**	0.1912	**0.000**
Telephone in dwelling	0.0522	**0.001**	0.0288	**0.065**	0.0863	**0.000**	0.0962	**0.000**	0.1002	**0.002**	0.0937	**0.005**
More urban	0.1095	**0.000**	0.1414	**0.000**	0.0905	**0.000**	0.0364	**0.090**	0.1876	**0.000**	0.1831	**0.000**
Proportion (YES)	0.3987		0.3774		0.4323		0.3897		0.4406		0.4305	
Predicted P (YES)	0.3843		0.3601		0.4215		0.3737		0.4321		0.4240	
N	11,012		10,065		4,314		4,077		2,122		2,030	
Pseudo R²	0.1270		0.1180		0.1410		0.1280		0.1630		0.1340	

— Not applicable.

Note: Values in bold are p-values of 0.10 or less.

a. The effect of a one-unit change in the explanatory variable on the probability of receiving healthcare benefits. The effect is estimated at the mean values of the other explanatory variables.

b. Only for women.

Source: National Employment Survey (ENE) Module on Social Security, 1996, INEGI, Mexico.

Table 8.8. Probability of Receiving Healthcare Coverage by Gender and Age Group; Observed, and Simulated According to Education Level (Mexico)

Observed and simulated results	Age group (years) by gender					
	16–39		40–59		60 or older	
	Women	Men	Women	Men	Women	Men
Observed proportion	0.399	0.377	0.432	0.390	0.441	0.430
Prob (X-mean)[a]	0.384	0.360	0.422	0.374	0.432	0.424
Prob (X-mean, educ = 6)[b]	0.307	0.288	0.501	0.420	0.619	0.570
Prob (X-Mean, educ = 9)[b]	0.478	0.446	0.539	0.535	0.451	0.498
Prob (X-Mean, educ = 12)[b]	0.562	0.487	0.623	0.543	0.633	0.555

Note: Probabilities simulated using the probit regression model in Table 8.7.
a. Assumes all explanatory variables are held constant at the mean values for each group.
b. Assumes all other explanatory variables are held constant at the mean values for each group, except for education.
Source: National Employment Survey (ENE) Module on Social Security, 1996, INEGI, Mexico.

women are slightly more likely than men to receive healthcare benefits, particularly during old age. The main differentiating factor of health coverage seems to be the level of education of individuals. We have also concluded that, at least in part, the relatively higher healthcare protection of older women may be due to their being married and receiving the extended benefits of their spouses, or having adult children who extend coverage to their mothers.

Pension Coverage of Individuals Aged 60 and Older

We now turn to the analysis of pension coverage in old age using data from ENE–96, and limiting this analysis to individuals aged 60 and older. The main sources of pensions are the various social security institutions (IMSS, ISSSTE, and PEMEX) and the private sector. In general, a minimum number of years contributing is required to be eligible to receive a pension, and the retirement age is 65, or 60 if old age unemployment is claimed. One feature of Mexico's pension system is that years contributed are not transferable among social security systems. For example, an individual contributing 10 years in IMSS and then switching to a government job with ISSSTE benefits would effectively begin from zero in terms of years contributing to the ISSSTE social security system.

The rules for contribution and receipt of own old age and disability pensions are identical for men and women. Nevertheless, only women can receive widowhood pensions, so that if a woman with her own pension dies, her surviving husband will no longer continue to receive the pension.[12] It is worth pointing out that whereas rules for own pensions do not vary by gender, clearly women will be less likely to receive a pension for own work, given their generally fewer years worked than men in Mexico.

Table 8.9 presents the distribution of pension coverage according to three measures: (a) whether the individual has his or her own pension, (b) whether the individual or his or her spouse receives a pension, and (c) whether the individual or anybody in his or her household receives a pension. We then combine these three measures to capture the extent to which a person aged 60 or older receives the benefit of a pension directly through his or her own pension, or indirectly through a spouse or someone else in the household of residence. The results show that the unadjusted likelihood of receiving a pension is low in absolute terms for all individuals aged 60 and older. Women are much less likely to receive their own pension (14.8 percent) than men (30.5 percent). This gender gap closes, however, if we consider the measure of own or spouse's pension: about 27 percent of women and 31 percent of men receive a pension. Similarly, if the measure for own or someone in the household is considered, almost 30 percent of women and 32 percent of men receive the benefit of a pension.

The type of own pension varies considerably between men and women, as would be expected given the difference in work histories between them, and the likelihood of women outliving their husbands. Among people receiving their own pension, 74 percent of men have a retirement pension, compared to 32 percent of women. More men than women receive severance and disability pensions (about 13 percent compared to 2 percent), and the majority of women (63 percent) receive a survivor (widowhood or parenthood) pension, compared to 0.1 percent of men.

Table 8.10 shows the distribution of own pension coverage according to the area of residence of recipients. For both men and women, pensions are more common among those living in more-urban areas, which conforms to the expectation that those working in urban areas would be more likely to have jobs providing the benefit of a pension at old age. Among men, 39 percent of those living in more-urban areas receive retirement pensions, compared to 12 percent of those living in less-urban areas. Urban women are four times more likely to receive own pensions than rural women. Sixteen percent of women living in more-urban areas receive widowhood pensions compared to only 4 percent of those living

Table 8.9. Percent Distribution of Pension Coverage for Age 60 and Older, by Gender, Source of Pension Recipient, Type of Own Pension, and Institution Providing Own Pension (Mexico, weighted data)

| Pension | Distribution by gender | |
recipients	Women	Men
Source of pension recipient		
Own	14.8	30.5
Own/spouse's	26.7	30.9
Own/household	29.5	31.9
Among those with own pension		
Type of own pension received		
Retirement	31.8	74.0
Severance	2.4	13.2
Disability	2.3	12.7
Widow/parenthood	63.6	0.1
Don't know	0.2	0.0
Institution[a] providing own pension		
IMSS	75.1	76.2
ISSSTE	16.2	11.1
PEMEX	0.7	3.2
Private	0.1	4.7
Other public	2.7	4.4
Don't Know	5.2	0.4

a. IMSS = Social Security Institute, ISSSTE = Federal Workers Social Security Institute, PEMEX = Oil Workers Institute.
Source: National Employment Survey (ENE) Module on Social Security, 1996, INEGI, Mexico.

in less-urban areas. The largest gender difference is exhibited among those receiving severance and disability own pensions. Urban men are 23 times more likely than urban women to receive disability pensions.

A Multivariate Model of Pension Coverage

Table 8.11 shows the results of a probit regression model of the likelihood of receiving a pension among individuals aged 60 or older, separately for the three measures of pension availability, and for women and men. The results, presented as marginal effects of the explanatory variables on the probability of receiving pension coverage, reveal that holding all other variables constant, the likelihood of receiving a pension significantly

Table 8.10. Gender Ratios and Area of Residence Ratios of the Percent Distribution of Own Pension Coverage for Age 60 and Older, by Type of Own Pension Received (Mexico, weighted data)

| | Area of residence | | | | Ratio of men/women | | Ratio of more-urban/ less-urban | |
| | More-urban | | Less-urban | | | | | |
Own pension	Women	Men	Women	Men	More-urban	Less-urban	Women	Men
Own pension Coverage	25.0	53.4	6.3	16.4	2.1	2.6	4.0	3.3
Type of own pension received								
Retirement	8.4	39.1	1.6	12.4	4.6	7.8	5.3	3.2
Severance	0.4	7.2	0.3	2.0	18.0	6.7	1.3	3.6
Disability	0.3	7.1	0.3	1.9	23.7	6.3	1.0	3.7
Widow/parenthood	15.8	0.0	4.1	0.1	0.0	0.03	3.9	0.0

Source: National Employment Survey (ENE) Module on Social Security, 1996, INEGI, Mexico.

increases with age. In addition, individuals with more years of education, residing in more-urban areas, and with better dwelling conditions, are more likely to receive a pension, and this holds for all measures of pension receipt. Being disabled increases the likelihood of receiving a pension for men, but not for women.[13]

Controlling for all other factors, having ever been employed does not significantly affect the likelihood of receiving a pension for all types of pensions and for both men and women. This surprising result could be explained because the measure of having ever been employed fails to capture two attributes that are closely associated with receiving a pension: the type of job held (for example, salaried versus self-employed) and the length of labor force participation. Marital status also affects the likelihood of receiving a pension, although some variation in effects occurs by type of pension. Married men are more likely to receive pensions than their single or divorced counterparts. Married women, however, are less likely to receive own pensions than single or divorced women, but are more likely to receive a pension when we use own/spouse or own/household measurements of pension coverage. Holding all other variables constant, the number of children a woman has

Table 8.11. Marginal Effects on Probability of Receiving Pension for Ages 60 or Older (Mexico)

	Pension recipient by gender											
	Own pension				Own/spouse's pension				Own/household pension			
	Women		Men		Women		Men		Women		Men	
Explanatory variables	Marginal effects[a]	P value	Marginal effects	P value	Marginal effects	P value	Marginal effects	P value	Marginal effects	P value	Marginal effects	P value
Individual characteristics												
Age	0.016	**0.034**	0.076	**0.000**	0.035	**0.019**	0.083	**0.000**	0.028	**0.060**	0.074	**0.000**
Age squared	-0.000	**0.035**	-0.000	**0.000**	-0.000	**0.018**	-0.000	**0.000**	-0.000	**0.064**	-0.000	**0.000**
Married (omit: single)	0.000	**0.000**	0.096	**0.004**	0.173	**0.000**	0.105	**0.002**	0.148	**0.000**	0.048	0.176
Widowed	0.033	**0.029**	0.079	**0.094**	0.086	**0.014**	0.088	**0.073**	0.087	**0.015**	0.027	0.545
Number of children[b]	0.001	0.620	—	—	0.001	0.611	—	—	0.002	0.333	—	—
Education 1–3 (omit: 0)	0.031	**0.024**	0.058	**0.013**	-0.064	**0.005**	0.065	**0.007**	-0.063	**0.006**	0.058	**0.016**
Education 4–6	0.062	**0.000**	0.123	**0.000**	0.129	**0.000**	0.135	**0.000**	0.124	**0.000**	0.121	**0.000**
Education 6 +	0.242	**0.000**	0.252	**0.000**	0.363	**0.000**	0.281	**0.000**	0.334	**0.000**	0.234	**0.000**
Ever employed	0.013	0.181	0.158	0.102	0.017	0.324	0.154	0.135	0.030	**0.091**	0.112	0.310
Permanent disability	-0.016	0.182	0.085	**0.001**	-0.021	0.398	0.077	**0.003**	-0.034	**0.002**	0.080	**0.002**
Household/community characteristics												
Services in dwelling	-0.021	**0.072**	0.114	**0.000**	0.086	**0.000**	0.120	**0.000**	0.090	**0.000**	0.130	**0.000**
Telephone in dwelling	0.011	0.335	0.056	**0.026**	0.032	0.152	0.048	**0.062**	0.041	**0.089**	0.057	**0.032**
More urban	0.025	**0.032**	0.153	**0.000**	-0.096	**0.000**	0.151	**0.000**	-0.107	**0.000**	0.157	**0.000**
Proportion (yes)	0.0938		0.2269		0.2007		0.2327		0.2139		0.2416	
Predicted P (yes)	0.0531		0.1982		0.1737		0.2028		0.1904		0.2154	
Pseudo R²	0.1951		0.1289		0.1215		0.1328		0.1085		0.1207	
N	2,122		2,032		2,063		1,947		2,122		2,032	

Note: Values in bold are p-values of 0.10 or less.

a. The effect of a one-unit change in the explanatory variable on the probability of receiving a pension. The marginal effects are evaluated at the mean value of each of the other explanatory variables.

b. Women only.

Source: National Employment Survey (ENE) Module on Social Security, 1996, INEGI, Mexico.

268

does not affect the likelihood that she will receive any type of pension. A possible explanation for this result is that once we control for marital status and education of the individual, the number of children per se does not affect the likelihood of receiving a pension.

Since pursuing an education or working may affect marriage decisions, and vice versa, we simulate the simultaneous effect of these variables on the probability of receiving a pension, holding all else constant. We use the results of the probit regression to estimate the probability of receiving a pension by marital status, education, and rural or urban residence separately. We present the simulated probabilities for men and women, and for own pension and for own or spouse's pension; we omit from further analyses the measure of own/household pensions because the results for this measure are similar to those obtained for own/spouse's pension.

The upper panel of Table 8.12 shows that regardless of years of education and marital status, men are more likely than women to receive own pensions. The size of the gender gap varies according to marital status and level of education, however. The findings are consistent with the fact that married women have lifetime labor force participation patterns that are incompatible with receiving own pension at old age, and this is more so among women with low education levels. Married men have the highest probability of receiving a pension, followed by widowed and then by single or divorced men. Among women, however, widowed women show the highest likelihood of receiving own pensions, followed by single or divorced and then married women. Thus, the gender gap in own pension is largest for married individuals. For people with seven or more years of education, married men have four times the estimated likelihood of receiving own pensions than married women. The gender gap widens further for women with lower education: it is ninefold for those with four to six years of education, and elevenfold for those with one to three years of education. For single, divorced, or widowed people the difference between men and women in the likelihood of receiving a pension virtually disappears if we assume seven or more years of education. For education levels lower than seven years, however, the gender gap persists for single, divorced, and widowed people, and it appears to grow with lower education within each marital status.

The lower panel of Table 8.12 shows the simulated probabilities of receiving own or spouse's pension. The differences between men and women are smaller across all groups compared to the results we obtained for own pension, but the probability is still higher for men than for women, with one important exception. The one instance in which the gender gap closes is again for those married and with 7 or more years of education. The probability of getting a pension is actually higher for

Table 8.12. Predicted Probabilities of Currently Receiving a Pension for Age 60 and Older by Gender, Education, Pension Recipient, and Marital Status (Mexico)

Marital status by pension recipient	Education years by gender					
	1–3		4–6		7 +	
	Women	Men	Women	Men	Women	Men
Own pension						
Married/partnered	0.0378	0.4348	0.0575	0.5147	0.1835	0.6457
Single/divorced	0.1702	0.2931	0.2256	0.3657	0.4685	0.4975
Widow(er)	0.2543	0.3897	0.3223	0.4684	0.5844	0.6017
Own/spouse's pension						
Married/partnered	0.4089	0.4391	0.4932	0.5227	0.7233	0.6682
Single/divorced	0.1864	0.2854	0.2490	0.3607	0.4728	0.5086
Widow(er)	0.2866	0.3903	0.3632	0.4727	0.6025	0.6216

Note: Predicted probability using the probit regression model, assuming that all other variables are held constant as follows: age (65); water, electricity, and sewerage in the dwelling (yes); phone in dwelling (yes); urban residence (yes); permanent disability (no); ever employed (yes); number of children for women (6).

Source: National Employment Survey (ENE) Module on Social Security, 1996, INEGI, Mexico.

women (0.72 compared to 0.67 for men). Thus, if we consider the indirect protection of a pension (that is, own or spouse's pension), it seems that married women are relatively protected. This result can be interpreted as though for many women in the elderly age cohorts, on average, the long-term investment strategy of marriage may pay off as protection at old age. This could be said of women at all education levels, but is increasingly true for those with more years of education.

Table 8.13 presents the estimated probabilities of receiving pensions according to area of residence and marital status, including the area of residence ratios and gender ratios of the estimated probabilities. Comparison of the last two columns of the table shows that the more-urban/less-urban difference in receiving a pension is larger for men than for women. As previously mentioned, this gap can be due to the higher likelihood of obtaining employment with benefits among residents of more-urban areas compared to those in less-urban areas, and this seems to apply more to men than to women. Table 8.13 also shows that the area-of-residence differences are relatively larger than the gender differences, with one notable exception. The only case for which the gender gap is larger than the area-of-residence gap is for the case of own pension among married individuals: regardless of area of residence, and holding

Table 8.13. Predicted Probabilities of Currently Receiving a Pension for Ages 60 and Older, Sex Ratios and Area of Residence Ratios, by Pension Receipt and Marital Status (Mexico)

| Marital status by pension recipient | Predicted probabilities of currently receiving a pension for ages 60 or older by area of residence and gender | | | | Ratio of men/women | | Ratio of more-urban/ less-urban | |
| | More-urban areas | | Less-urban areas | | More-Urban | Less-Urban | | |
	Women	Men	Women	Men	More-Urban	Less-Urban	Women	Men
Own pension								
Married/partnered	0.0808	0.5180	0.0525	0.3332	6.5	6.3	1.5	1.6
Single/divorced	0.2837	0.3711	0.2138	0.2104	1.3	1.0	1.3	1.8
Widow(er)	0.3856	0.4748	0.3042	0.2948	1.2	1.0	1.3	1.6
Own/spouses's pension								
Married/partnered	0.5482	0.5316	0.4073	0.3482	1.0	0.8	1.3	1.5
Single/divorced	0.3000	0.3721	0.1892	0.2130	1.2	1.1	1.6	1.8
Widow(er)	0.4164	0.4837	0.2855	0.3048	1.2	1.1	1.5	1.6

Note: Predicted probabilities using the probit regression model, assuming that all other variables are held constant as follows: age (65); years of education (6); ever employed (yes); water, electricity, and sewerage in the dwelling (yes); phone in the dwelling (yes); permanent disability (no); number of children for women (6).

Source: National Employment Survey (ENE) Module on Social Security, 1996, INEGI. Mexico.

all else constant, men are about six times more likely to receive own pension than women.

In summary, very few of the elderly receive the benefit of a pension. Women are less likely than men to receive a pension if we consider only own pensions, and this gap narrows when we consider own or spouse's pensions. Receiving an own pension is associated with more education and living in urban areas. We find from the multivariate models of own-pension receipt that a large gender gap exists, but urban–rural differences are generally larger than the gender differences. The gender gap in own-pension benefits closes only at high levels of education and among non-married individuals; the largest gender gap is found among married people. On the other hand, the gender gap in receiving own or spouse's pension closes among married individuals with more education. We conclude that elderly women cohorts with little previous attachment to the labor force relative to men are not necessarily worse off because they are likely to be covered by either their husband's pension or pensions based on widowhood.

Pensions and Other Income Sources of the Elderly

We now analyze in further detail the income sources of the elderly both at the individual and household level based on ENIGH–96 data. We consider the role that pensions and other sources of income, such as transfers, play in the overall income levels and poverty of households with elderly members.

Table 8.14 shows the percentage and level of different income sources of the elderly by gender, for the national level and for urban and rural areas, respectively. The table shows that elderly men are more likely than elderly women to have an income source. Over 60 percent of elderly men report positive income associated with self-employment or salaried work, compared to about 17 percent of elderly women. Men are also more likely to have income from pensions, with 19 percent having pension income versus only 9 percent of elderly women.[14] The only category where women are more likely to receive income is from transfers (17 percent versus 15 percent), suggesting that elderly women are slightly more likely than elderly men to be supported by other family members or friends.

The overall result of this analysis is that a much higher percentage of elderly men than women have some individual own source of income, mostly as a result of their current or previous earnings. About 80 percent of elderly men have individual income sources, whereas only about 36 percent of elderly women report having an own income source.

These results differ somewhat by urban and rural areas. Table 8.14 indicates that in urban areas approximately 15 percent of all elderly women receive income from working, compared to about 50 percent of all men. There are striking differences in the receipt of pension income, with men being more than twice as likely to receive pension income as women (28 percent versus 12 percent). Family transfers, on the other hand, are more likely to be received by women than by men (18 percent and 13 percent for men, respectively), perhaps suggesting some degree of compensation by family members for the fact that women are less likely to have pension or labor income.

In rural areas, men and women are more likely to have income from working than in urban areas, with over 21 percent of elderly women and over 75 percent of elderly men reporting income from work. These apparently higher rural labor force participation rates of the elderly are likely related to the very low coverage of the pension system in rural areas, suggesting that pension receipt in rural areas plays a small role in reducing

Table 8.14. Individual Income Sources by Gender of Elderly and Area of Residence (Mexico)

| | Distribution of elderly income by gender | | | | |
| | Elderly women | | | Elderly men | |
Income sources	% with income source	Average amount (of those with income source)		% with income source	Average amount (of those with income source)
National level					
Salaried work	3.3	715	(1,149)	21.3	1,027	(1,600)
Self-employment	13.6	412	(656)	40.1	1,045	(2,186)
Interest and property rental	2.4	1,258	(2,371)	4.0	1,286	(2,164)
Pensions	9.0	847	(622)	19.4	1,045	(1,160)
Family transfers	17.5	625	(822)	15.0	766	(1,125)
PROCAMPO[a]	0.7	1,648	(1,654)	0.4	1,747	(1,646)
Other income[b]	0.3	3,138	(4,629)	0.3	804	(981)
Total income	36.9	852	(1,208)	79.5	1,369	(2,180)
Sample size	2,363			2,202	
Urban residence					
Salaried work	3.9	880	(1,283)	20.7	1,440	(2,016)
Self-employment	11.1	485	(727)	29.1	1,562	(3,028)
Interest and property rental	2.8	1,380	(2,553)	4.9	1,565	(2,457)
Pensions	12.1	864	(642)	27.6	1,093	(1,246)
Family transfers	18.2	679	(839)	13.2	876	(1,289)
PROCAMPO[a]	0.2	3,666	(2,274)*	1.3	1,363	(1,047)
Other income[b]	0.2	778	(1,022)*	0.1	100*	
Total income	38.7	942	(1,211)	77.9	1,632	(2,600)
Sample size	1,516			1,273	
Rural residence					
Salaried work	2.4	227	(256)	22.1	495	(356)
Self-employment	19.2	332	(560)	55.1	672	(1,135)
Interest and property rental	1.5	852	(1,646)	2.6	554	(682)
Pensions	3.3	735	(467)	9.3	827	(559)
Family transfers	16.1	515	(778)	17.5	653	(916)
PROCAMPO[a]	1.7	1,215	(1,197)	8.6	1,829	(1,742)
Other income[b]	0.5	4,318	(5,458)*	0.5	945	(1,026)*
Total income	33.9	668	(1,182)	81.8	1,026	(1,390)
Sample size	847			929	

( ) indicate standard deviation.

* based on less than 10 cases.

a. Public Agricultural Subsidy Program.

b. Other income includes sale of vehicle, secondhand objects, other monetary income not included in the above categories.

Source: National Income and Expenditures Survey (ENIGH), Mexico, 1996.

poverty levels. Family transfers are similar for both genders (17 percent for men and 16 percent for women).

Table 8.15 considers the impact of elderly income contributions on the overall household living standard in extended families, by comparing the adult-equivalent income in the households when the elderly member is included versus excluded from the calculations. This table reinforces the point that the income of elderly men still contributes to raising overall (adult-equivalent) income. Elderly women have the opposite effect; that is, they do not contribute enough, on average, to offset their "cost" to the household. Particularly in rural areas, it is evident that elderly male income (the majority of which is likely from work) is an important source of well-being for extended families; without elderly males, household income would be reduced by over 30 percent. Elderly women tend to reduce household income; without elderly women (and their income) in the household, overall household income levels would be on average 33 percent higher. These calculations, nevertheless, ignore the value of the nonmonetary contributions that elderly women make to their domestic units through household work and caregiving. Pedrero Nieto (1999) shows that, regardless of their participation in economic activity, the number of hours spent by Mexican elderly women in domestic activities is substantially higher than those spent by men.[15] The implication of elderly men being more likely to have individual income sources than elderly women is that elderly women are more dependent on the income sources of other household members. We now turn to a discussion of the importance of pension income in households with an elderly member.

The Importance of Pension Income in the Living Standard of Households with an Elderly Member

For our analysis we take households with an elderly member and separate those that receive income pension from those that do not. We find that even though we established that very few elderly *individuals* receive a pension, this is a relatively important source of income for the *households* in which the elderly reside. The left panel of Table 8.16 shows that among households with an elderly member and that receive pension income, almost 50 percent of the household income comes from pensions and 30 percent from salaried work. The shares of income are very similar by gender of the individual elderly. The right panel of the table shows that among households that do not receive pension income, salaried work has the largest share on average (around 42 percent), followed in importance by self-employment income and transfers income with, respectively, a 30 percent and 21 percent share each.

Table 8.15. Impact of Individual Income on Household Adult-Equivalent Income in Extended Families with Elderly Members (Mexico)

	Elderly males			Elderly females		
	Household adult-equivalent income			Household adult-equivalent income		
Area of residence	With elderly male	Without elderly male	% difference	With elderly female	Without elderly female	% difference
National	786	679	−13.6	828	1,100	32.9
	(950)	(899)		(988)	(1,586)	
Urban	970	889	−8.4	979	1,321	34.9
	(1,127)	(1,050)		(1,099)	(1,793)	
Rural	521	378	−27.4	527	663	25.8
	(513)	(486)		(622)	(918)	

( ) indicate standard deviation.
Note: The figures are calculated by taking all extended families with an elderly male (female) member, and calculating the adult-equivalent income including and excluding the elderly male (female) member.
Source: National Income and Expenditures Survey (ENIGH), Mexico, 1996.

We next consider the extent to which the receipt of different income sources may be associated with poverty at the individual level. Table 8.17 carries out a multivariate regression analysis of the probability of being poor for elderly men and elderly women, as a function of the type of income sources received by the elderly individual and other household members. Being poor at the individual level is defined as living in a household with income below the 30th percentile. We control for characteristics of the individual elderly: age, and whether the individual receives income from each of five different sources (pensions, private transfers, labor, interests and rents, and government programs). We also include controls for the household composition (number of adult males, adult females, and children), urban and rural residence, education of the head of household, and whether other household members received income from each of the five income sources.

For both elderly men and women, and holding all else constant, pension income has by far the largest impact on reducing the probability of poverty. Having an own pension reduces the probability of poverty in old age by more than 25 points for men and by 24 points for women. The next income source in importance is the receipt of interest and rents income.

Table 8.16. Contribution of Income Sources to Total Household Income in Families with Elderly, by Receipt of a Pension of Men and Women (Mexico, mean percent)

	Share of household total income (%)			
	With pension income		Without pension income	
Income sources	Elderly women	Elderly men	Elderly women	Elderly men
Salaried work	29.2	30.8	42.6	41.8
Self-employment	9.2	9.9	29.7	35.6
Interest and property rent	2.5	1.9	2.4	2.2
Pensions	49.6	48.7	—	—
Family transfers	8.1	7.1	21.1	15.7
PROCAMPO[a]	0.7	1.1	3.2	3.9
Other income[b]	0.4	0.1	0.4	0.3
Total income	100.0%	100.0%	100.0%	100.0%
Sample size	489	456	1,841	1,727

— Not applicable.
a. Public Agricultural Subsidy Program.
b. Other income includes sale of vehicle, secondhand objects, other monetary income not included in the above categories.
Source: National Income and Expenditures Survey (ENIGH), Mexico, 1996.

Having income from this source is associated with a reduction of 17 points in the probability of being poor in old age for men, and 21 points for women. Comparatively, other income sources have much less impact on reducing the probability of being poor. While the regressions are meant to be illustrative only, they point out the association of pensions with poverty, controlling for other factors that are also closely associated with living in poverty.[16]

Thus, we find that the pension system currently has a limited coverage, in particular in rural areas, but represents a large portion of household income for those who receive a pension. This suggests that for most elderly, the pension system does not play a large role in improving living standards. Our analysis implies, nevertheless, that pension income has an independent role in differentiating those among the elderly who are likely to be living out of poverty. If pension coverage were to be expanded, it could have a large impact on reducing the poverty of the elderly, both for elderly men and women.

These findings are reinforced by those of the previous section on living standards, suggesting that the elderly, particularly the oldest old, tend to have lower living standards than other individuals. With the aging of the

Table 8.17. Marginal Effects of Income Sources on the Probability of Elderly Poverty (probit regression, Mexico)

Explanatory variable	Elderly men: 60 and over		Elderly women: 60 and over	
	Marginal effects[a]	P values	Marginal effects	P Values
Demographic and household composition				
Elderly age	0.005	**0.001**	0.007	**0.000**
Urban residence	−0.224	**0.000**	−0.214	**0.000**
No. children	0.066	**0.000**	0.042	**0.000**
No. adult males	−0.016	0.193	−0.005	0.656
No. adult females	−0.015	0.195	−0.026	**0.028**
Education of HH head (omitted: high school or above)				
No schooling	0.148	**0.000**	0.116	**0.000**
Incomplete primary	0.212	**0.000**	0.309	**0.000**
Complete primary	0.181	**0.001**	0.270	**0.000**
Secondary	0.066	0.443	0.137	**0.043**
Individual income sources (=1 if positive)				
Labor income	−0.037	0.164	0.000	0.996
Pension income	−0.257	**0.000**	−0.241	**0.000**
Transfer income	−0.040	0.212	−0.045	0.138
Govt. program income	0.057	0.283	−0.051	0.636
Interest/rental income	−0.167	**0.004**	−0.209	**0.002**
Other household members income (=1 if positive)				
Labor income	−0.084	**0.002**	−0.147	**0.000**
Pension income	−0.145	**0.090**	−0.208	**0.000**
Transfer income	−0.124	**0.000**	−0.086	**0.003**
Govt. program income	0.062	0.349	0.121	**0.014**
Interest/rental income	−0.112	0.262	−0.185	**0.004**
N; LLR[b] chi(19)	2,202; 551		2,363; 616	

Note: Values in bold are p-values of 0.10 or less.

a. The effect of a one-unit change in the explanatory variable on the probability that the adult-equivalent consumption of the household in which the elderly resides is below the poverty line. The marginal effects are evaluated at the mean value of each of the explanatory variables.

b. Log likelihood ratio.

Source: National Income and Expenditures Survey (ENIGH), Mexico, 1996.

population, these trends are likely to become even more pronounced, and the elderly will represent a growing portion of the poor population in Mexico. The finding that the elderly with higher overall standards of living are those who tend to have pension income suggests the potential usefulness of an expansion in pension coverage in reducing poverty in Mexico.

Conclusion

This chapter examines the status of the elderly in Mexico compared to younger populations, and of women compared to men, testing several hypotheses on gender differences among the elderly with respect to living standards and healthcare and pension coverage. The overarching hypothesis is that women are in a relatively more vulnerable position regarding old age security than men.

We find evidence that, as in other countries, elderly women are more likely to be widowed and live in extended arrangements than men (U.S. Census Bureau 1992). We find no support for our hypothesis on higher poverty rates among women; elderly women exhibit living standards similar to elderly men, both in urban and rural areas. Compared to other age groups, the elderly show poverty rates similar to children, but lower than working-age adults. Both elderly men and women exhibit heterogeneity as a group; those over age 70 appear to be the poorest group overall.

In Mexico, having access to modern healthcare is largely associated with benefits received through formal employment. Women have had low rates of participation in the labor market throughout their lives, in particular those who are currently aged 60 and older, and given the tendency of women to outlive their husbands and spend the last years of their lives in widowhood, we hypothesized that in old age, women would be particularly at risk of living without the benefits of modern healthcare. The findings on healthcare coverage indicate, however, that women seem to be as protected as men at all ages. The age group with the least protection is the youngest, and the most protected is the elderly. This paradox of healthcare among women is largely due to the profamily orientation of the institutions in Mexico that provide employer-driven healthcare benefits to employees and have historically extended the benefits to the dependents of the employee. Women are largely covered through their status as spouses or as mothers of adult children. Thus the Mexican healthcare system, which tends to protect workers and their families, seems to be protecting elderly women and men equally, although coverage is far from universal.

Regarding pension at old age, we hypothesized a lower coverage of pensions among women than men in old age. Indeed, we find that only a small minority of men aged 60 and older, and even fewer women, receive any kind of pension. Of these, the majority of the men's pensions are due to retirement, while only one third of the women's pensions is of the retirement type, and two thirds receive widowhood pensions. When we consider the pension coverage that women enjoy through their current spouse, we find that men and women are about equally covered by a pension. Thus it seems again that, to the very limited extent that the system of pensions is covering women, this is largely because of their status as spouses or widows.

Although we find no evidence that elderly females are worse off than elderly males regarding living standards, we find support for our hypothesis that women in old age are more dependent than men on the informal income support of others. This is due to a variety of reasons, including the fact that elderly women tend to have worked less in formal labor markets, and therefore are less likely to have contributed to a pension system. Families with female elderly tend to receive more income transfers from individuals outside the household, which in some sense helps compensate for the lower income that elderly females contribute to the household. While high dependence on the income sources of others may not necessarily be disadvantageous for elderly women, these transfers may be unstable sources of income and therefore may increase the likelihood of suffering income fluctuations. This may in turn pose high risks of living in poverty for elderly women in the future.

The evidence supports the hypothesis that an old age pension is a benefit received by relatively few, mostly males, and thus pensions do not seem to play an important role in meeting consumption needs of the elderly in general. Nevertheless, the elderly who receive pensions are less likely to live in poverty than those who lack pensions, indicating that expansion in pension coverage could lead to an important reduction in elderly poverty. The potential importance of own or spouse's pensions in decreasing poverty should not be underestimated, particularly for the oldest members of the population, who are among the poorest in Mexico.

Two limitations of our analyses should be emphasized. The various data sources we used correspond to 1996, a year after the Mexican economic crisis. To the extent that the distribution of income, health insurance coverage, and pension coverage could be affected by the crisis, it would be important to replicate the analyses for different years. In addition, all our analyses of the household living standards exclude the nonquantifiable contributions that various household members make to the economy of the domestic unit in which they reside, most notably in the form of creation and maintenance of human capital of all the unit members. This omitted contribution may be noteworthy for the elderly in general, and for women in particular.

The combined results on living standards, healthcare coverage, and pension coverage seem to indicate that marriage may have been an effective long-term strategy toward old age security for Mexican women in the current elderly cohorts. In exchange for the care and services provided by women to the members of their domestic units throughout their life, our results seem to indicate that women seem to be receiving protection equal to their male counterparts in old age.

In conclusion, the status of the elderly in Mexico seems to be mixed. On one hand, the elderly are clearly poorer than younger working-age generations. The pension system is currently limited in its coverage, but we find that pensions can potentially play a large role in increasing the living standard of the elderly men and women in Mexico. On the other hand, we find that the elderly seem to enjoy relatively good healthcare coverage, and we find no support for marked gender differences among the elderly. These results could be largely due to two factors: (a) the social security and health systems that extend protection to the dependents of workers and widows of former beneficiaries of the systems, and (b) the informal familial support toward the elderly. These two factors are consistent with a scheme in which women receive protection in old age as remuneration for the social contributions they have made toward the survival and productivity of the domestic units over their lifetimes. All members have benefited from these contributions, and it seems that the unwritten social contract to care for Mexican women at least as well as men in old age is being upheld.

It is difficult, based on these results, to predict the situation of the future elderly in Mexico. The future elderly will have fewer children than the current elderly, and thus potentially reduced kinship networks from which elderly women could draw for informal support. The future elderly, however, will be better educated, and women will have participated more in formal labor markets than the current elderly, placing them in an better position to receive old-age formal or institutional support. The overall effect on the old age security of women compared to men is highly unpredictable. To the extent that the Mexican social security and healthcare systems reforms are consistent with the long-term practice of protecting the dependents and the direct beneficiaries, and the family system continues to support the elderly, the well-being of women in old age is likely to continue to be relatively as protected as that of men. If, however, the familial support system in Mexico were to break down before the benefits of more education and increased labor force participation of women materialize, or reforms to the systems were made to, for example, exclude dependents of the workers, then elderly women might be disproportionately placed in a vulnerable position.

Appendix Tables

Poverty Indicators Using Alternative Adult Equivalence Scales

Table 8.A.1. Foster, Greer, and Thorbecke (FGT) Indicators of Poverty by Number of Elderly Members in Household (Mexico weighted data, poverty line = 30th percentile)

Residence & number of elderly members in household	Adult equivalence measures of consumption levels (%) (Deaton)		
	$\alpha = 0$ Headcount	$\alpha = 1$ Poverty gap	$\alpha = 2$ Poverty severity
National level			
No elderly	26.0	8.9	4.3
1 elderly	40.1	12.7	6.2
2 or more elderly	48.1	18.0	9.4
Urban residence			
No elderly	15.4	4.5	1.9
1 elderly	28.8	7.7	3.2
2 or more elderly	35.1	11.4	5.4
Rural residence			
No elderly	48.6	18.4	9.6
1 elderly	60.1	21.3	11.4
2 or more elderly	66.3	27.2	15.0

Source: National Income and Expenditures Survey (ENIGH), Mexico, 1996.

Table 8.A.2. Foster, Greer, and Thorbecke (FGT) Indicators of Poverty by Number of Elderly Members in Household (Mexico weighted data, poverty line = 30th percentile)

Residence & number of elderly members in household	Adult equivalence measures of consumption levels (%) (Wagstaff)		
	$\alpha = 0$ Headcount	$\alpha = 1$ Poverty gap	$\alpha = 2$ Poverty severity
National level			
No elderly	27.6	9.9	5.1
1 elderly	36.4	14.8	8.6
2 or more elderly	40.4	17.0	10.0
Urban residence			
No elderly	16.0	4.6	2.0
1 elderly	24.3	8.7	4.7
2 or more elderly	26.6	10.0	5.5
Rural residence			
No elderly	52.1	21.3	11.8
1 elderly	57.8	25.7	15.5
2 or more elderly	59.8	26.9	16.0

Source: National Income and Expenditures Survey (ENIGH), Mexico, 1996.

Table 8.A.3. Foster, Greer, and Thorbecke (FGT) Indicators of Poverty by Age Group and Gender (Mexico weighted data, poverty line = 30th percentile)

Residence by age group and gender	Adult equivalence measures of consumption levels (%) (Deaton)		
	$\alpha = 0$ Headcount	$\alpha = 1$ Poverty gap	$\alpha = 2$ Poverty severity
National level			
Children 0–17	37.9	14.1	7.1
Adults 18–59	31.2	11.1	5.5
Elderly (60 and above)			
Male	45.1	16.0	8.1
Female	43.3	15.0	7.7
Urban residence			
Children 0–17	23.2	7.0	2.9
Adults 18–59	19.7	5.9	2.5
Elderly (60 and above)			
Male	31.7	9.6	4.4
Female	32.0	9.4	4.3

Table 8.A.3. (continued)

Residence by age group and gender	Adult equivalence measures of consumption levels (%) (Deaton)		
	$\alpha = 0$ Headcount	$\alpha = 1$ Poverty gap	$\alpha = 2$ Poverty severity
Rural residence			
Children 0–17	59.5	24.7	13.5
Adults 18–59	54.9	21.9	11.7
Elderly (60 and above)			
Male	63.6	24.6	13.3
Female	63.5	24.7	13.7

Source: National Income and Expenditures Survey (ENIGH), Mexico, 1996.

Table 8.A.4. Foster, Greer, and Thorbecke (FGT) Indicators of Poverty by Age Group and Gender (Mexico weighted data, poverty line = 30th percentile)

Residence by age group and gender	Adult equivalence measures of consumption levels (%) (Wagstaff)		
	$\alpha = 0$ Headcount	$\alpha = 1$ Poverty gap	$\alpha = 2$ Poverty severity
National level			
Children 0–17	39.8	15.2	8.0
Adults 18–59	28.6	10.0	5.1
Elderly (60 and above)			
Male	38.9	15.8	8.9
Female	37.9	16.0	9.4
Urban residence			
Children 0–17	23.9	7.1	3.0
Adults 18–59	16.6	4.6	1.9
Elderly (60 and above)			
Male	24.7	8.7	4.6
Female	25.9	9.7	5.4
Rural residence			
Children 0–17	63.6	27.2	15.4
Adults 18–59	53.5	21.6	11.9
Elderly (60 and above)			
Male	58.3	25.4	14.9
Female	59.3	27.3	16.7

Source: National Income and Expenditures Survey (ENIGH), Mexico, 1996.

Table 8.A.5. Foster, Greer, and Thorbecke (FGT) Indicators of Elderly Poverty by Age Group and Gender (Mexico weighted data; poverty line = 30th percentile)

Residence of elderly by age group and gender	Adult equivalence measures of consumption levels (%) (Deaton)		
	$\alpha = 0$ Headcount	$\alpha = 1$ Poverty gap	$\alpha = 2$ Poverty severity
National level			
Male elderly			
Ages 60–70	43.1	15.4	7.7
Ages above 70	48.4	16.9	8.7
Female elderly			
Ages 60–70	40.8	14.5	7.5
Ages above 70	47.4	15.5	7.9
Urban residence			
Male elderly			
Ages 60–70	29.7	9.3	4.2
Ages above 70	34.8	10.2	4.7
Female elderly			
Ages 60–70	30.6	9.3	4.3
Ages above 70	34.5	9.8	4.4
Rural residence			
Male elderly			
Ages 60–70	61.1	23.6	12.5
Ages above 70	67.9	26.4	14.5
Female elderly			
Ages 60–70	59.5	24.3	13.4
Ages above 70	69.8	25.3	14.0

Source: National Income and Expenditures Survey (ENIGH), Mexico, 1996.

Table 8.A.6. Foster, Greer, and Thorbecke (FGT) Indicators of Elderly Poverty by Age Group and Gender (Mexico weighted data; poverty line = 30th percentile)

Residence of elderly by age group and gender	Adult equivalence measures of consumption levels (%) (Wagstaff)		
	$\alpha = 0$ Headcount	$\alpha = 1$ Poverty gap	$\alpha = 2$ Poverty severity
National level			
Male elderly			
Ages 60–70	36.4	13.6	7.3
Ages above 70	43.0	19.2	11.6
Female elderly			
Ages 60–70	35.0	13.8	7.6
Ages above 70	42.5	19.6	12.4
Urban residence			
Male elderly			
Ages 60–70	24.4	7.2	3.5
Ages above 70	28.5	11.1	6.3
Female elderly			
Ages 60–70	24.4	8.5	4.4
Ages above 70	28.5	11.6	6.9
Rural residence			
Male elderly			
Ages 60–70	55.2	22.2	12.4
Ages above 70	63.6	30.7	19.0
Female elderly			
Ages 60–70	54.5	23.3	13.3
Ages above 70	66.8	33.5	21.9

Source: National Income and Expenditures Survey (ENIGH), Mexico, 1996.

Notes

1. The 1996 ENIGH is the most recent available, but it should be noted that income and poverty levels reported in 1996 were severely affected by the 1995 economic crisis. Real GDP fell by 7 percent, and real wages were reported to have fallen by as much as 50 percent for some groups during that year. While the central interest here is comparative levels of poverty between the elderly and other groups, rather than absolute levels, it may be that the 1995 crisis affected the well-being of the elderly more than of other groups.

2. More-urban areas in the ENE correspond to metropolitan areas with populations greater than 100,000. The rest of the country is considered to be the less-urban areas.

3. Defined in the survey as physical impediments of the following types: visual, hearing, language, muscular, mental, or other which affects work.

4. The higher prevalence of disabilities among men can be due to the way the questions were asked in the ENE–96 in relation to work. The questions on disabilities were: "[Do you]…have a physical disability, temporary or permanent?" "What type is it?" "Was this disability due to an accident or illness related to your work?" Other studies have found a higher prevalence of disabilities among older women than older men (Parker 1999), particularly among the oldest old.

5. See Chapter 1, this volume, for an additional description of gender differences in education.

6. The FGT indicators are defined as follows:

$$P_\alpha = \frac{1}{N} \sum_{i=1}^{N} \frac{(z - x_i)^a}{z} I_i$$

where z is the poverty line, x_i is adjusted income, N is the number of households in the sample, and I_i is a dummy variable equal to 1 if $x_i < z$. The poverty index when $\alpha = 0$ measures the level of poverty according to the "headcount," that is, the number of households who have an income level below the poverty line. The poverty index when $\alpha = 1$ is called the poverty gap. This index reflects the average distance in income of the poor from the poverty line as a proportion of the poverty line. The poverty index when $\alpha \geq 2$, in addition to reflecting the poverty gap, reflects the distribution of income within the poor population and places greater weight on the income of the "poorest" poor. We refer to this last index as the severity of poverty.

7. The first is the OECD modified scale (Hagenarrs, de Vos, and Zaidi 1998), which weighs the first adult at 1, additional adults at 0.5, and children under age 14 at 0.3. The second is based on Deaton and Muellbauer (1986), where adults are weighted at 1, children aged 0 to 7 at 0.2, children aged 7 to 13 at 0.3, and children aged 14 to 17 at 0.5. A third set are those used by Wagstaff and van Doorslaer (1998):

$$e_h = (A_h + \Phi K_h)^\theta$$

where e_h is the equivalence factor for household h, A_h is the number of adults in household h, and K_h is the number of children. We have set the two parameters Φ and θ equal to 0.75 and defined children as those under age 14.

8. None of the measures make an adjustment for the distribution of consumption within each household. That is, the results assume that consumption is equitably distributed through the household according to the weights used.

9. Two other public sector institutions form part of the social security system. Both the national oil corporation (PEMEX) and the armed forces (ISSFAM) operate as integrated financiers and providers of healthcare and other social security benefits. PEMEX covers a total population of 600,000 oil industry workers, retirees, and their families, and the ISSFAM covers a total of 800,000 beneficiaries.

10. The reverse is not necessarily the case, however, because women must generally show their husband is economically dependent on them (usually defined as unemployed) to be able to cover him as part of her health plan.

11. The IMSS is the Mexican Institute of Social Security, the ISSSTE is the Institute for Security and Social Services (for government workers), and PEMEX is the Oil Workers Institute. These institutions all offer healthcare and social services to their employees and their families. In addition, the IMSS offers services to individuals contributing fees, either through an employment association or as voluntary affiliates.

12. The new Social Security Law (IMSS), in effect since 1997, made a change to this disposition. Female workers, in general, are now eligible to extend benefits to their male dependents or survivors.

13. These findings are also likely related to the requirements for receiving a pension, which (prior to the reform in the pension system of 1997) while requiring only 10 years of contribution, required individuals to be contributing at retirement age. Individuals working in jobs without benefits at retirement age would thus have been ineligible to receive a pension.

14. Note that these percentages of men and women receiving income from pensions are lower than the percentages obtained from the ENE–96 data. According to ENIGH reports, 9 percent of elderly women and 19.4 percent of elderly men report income from pensions. In the ENE–96 data, 14 percent of women and 30 percent of men received pensions. The difference in results may be due to the emphasis made and the form of asking the survey questions. In ENIGH, pensions are one of many sources of income and respondents may tend to underreport pensions. In the ENE, the pension question was a special, individual question with more detailed categories of pensions.

15. Using data from 1995, Pedrero Nieto shows that in more-urban areas, elderly women who are not in the labor force spend on average 33.8 hours per week in domestic activities, compared to 11.1 hours among elderly men who are not in the labor force. The contrast between men and women is even larger in less-urban areas.

16. We performed the regression analysis separately for residents of urban and rural areas (results not included). The results indicate that receiving own income from pensions is associated with a much lower likelihood of living in poverty in rural areas than in urban areas (marginal effects of –0.40 and –0.17, respectively).

References

Deaton, Angus. 1997. *The Analysis of Household Surveys: A Microeconometric Approach to Development Policy*. Baltimore: The Johns Hopkins University Press.

Deaton, Angus, and John Muellbauer. 1986. "On Measuring Child Costs: With Applications to Poor Countries." *Journal of Political Economy* 94(4):720–44.

Gomes da Conceicao, Maria Cristina. 1997. "Envejecimiento y formas de residencia en México." *Papeles de Población* 3(4):171–94. Centro de Investigación y Estudios Avanzados de la Población de la Universidad Autónoma del Estado de México.

Hagenarrs, Aldi, Klaas de Vos, and Asghar Zaidi. 1998. "Patterns of Poverty in Europe." In Stephen Jenkins, Arie Kapteyn, and Bernard van Praag, eds., *The Distribution of Welfare and Household Production: International Perspectives*. Cambridge: Cambridge University Press.

Ham Chande, Roberto. 1999. "El envejecimiento en México: De los conceptos a las necesidades." *Papeles de Población* 5(19):7–22. Centro de Investigación y Estudios Avanzados de la Población de la Universidad Autónoma del Estado de México.

INEGI. 1998. "Encuesta Nacional de Empleo 1996." Compact Disc.

Leñero Otero, Luis. 1999. "Implicaciones intrafamiliares de la población en la tercera edad." *Papeles de Población* 5(19):199–218. Centro de Investigación y Estudios Avanzados de la Población de la Universidad Autónoma del Estado de México.

Lustig, N., and M. Szekely. 1997. "Economic Trends, Poverty and Inequality in Mexico." Processed.

Montes de Oca Zavala, Verónica. 1999. "Diferencias de género en el sistema de apoyo a la población envejecida en México." *Papeles de Población* 5(19):149–72. Centro de Investigación y Estudios Avanzados de la Población de la Universidad Autónoma del Estado de México.

National Employment Survey (ENE) Module on Social Security. 1996. INEGI, Mexico.

National Income and Expenditures Survey (ENIGH). 1996. Mexico.

Parker, Susan. 1999. "Elderly Health and Salaries in the Mexican Labor Market." Inter-American Development Bank Working Paper R–353. Washington, D.C.

Partida Bush, Virgilio. 1999. "Perspectiva demográfica del envejecimiento en México." In *Envejecimiento demográfico de México: Retos y perspectivas*. CONAPO, México.

Pedrero Nieto, Mercedes. 1999. "Situación económica en la tercera edad." *Papeles de Población* 5(19):77–102. Centro de Investigación y Estudios Avanzados de la Población de la Universidad Autónoma del Estado de México.

Salas Páez, Carlos. 1999. "Empleo y tercera edad: Dinamismo y tendencias." In *Envejecimiento demográfico de México: Retos y perspectivas*. CONAPO, México.

Tuirán, Rodolfo. 1998. "Situación y perspectivas demográficas." *Papeles de Población* 4(16):17–38. Centro de Investigación y Estudios Avanzados de la Población de la Universidad Autónoma del Estado de México.

Tuirán, Rodolfo. 1999. "Desafíos del envejecimiento demográfico en México." in *Envejecimiento demográfico de México: Retos y perspectivas.* CONAPO, México.

U.S. Census Bureau. 1992. *An Aging World II.* Washington, D.C.: U.S. Department of Commerce.

Wagstaff A., and E. van Doorslaer. 1998. "Equity in the Finance and Delivery of Health Care: A Review of the Equity Project Findings." Paper prepared for the World Bank, Human Development Department, Washington, D.C.

Wong, Rebeca. 1999. "Tranferencias intrafamiliares e intergeneracionales en México." in *Envejecimiento demográfico de México: Retos y perspectivas.* CONAPO, México.

_____. 2000. "Health, Utilization of Health Care and Aging in Mexico." Mimeo.

Wong, Rebeca, and Maria Elena Figueroa. 1999. "Morbilidad y utilización de servicios de salud entre población de edad avanzada: Un análisis comparativo." *Papeles de Población* 5(19):103–24. Centro de Investigación y Estudios Avanzados de la Población de la Universidad Autónoma del Estado de México.

9
Conclusions and Policy Implications

Elizabeth Katz and Maria Correia

The chapters in this volume tell a compelling story about how the economics of gender in Mexico plays out over the course of people's lives. There is abundant evidence that different opportunities and obstacles exist for Mexican women and men in their pursuit of education, livelihood, and old age security. There is also wide scope for creative policy approaches to increasing gender equity. In this brief concluding chapter, we summarize some of the book's main arguments, discuss current gender policy in Mexico and the gender work of the World Bank's Latin America and the Caribbean Region office, and propose broad guidelines for future Mexican gender policy.

The Economics of Gender in Mexico: Work, Family, State, and Market

One of the most consistent findings throughout the book concerns the relationship between work and family. Especially for women, the trade-offs between marriage, children, and unpaid domestic labor on one hand, and formal education, paid labor force participation, and independent financial security on the other, are central features of their survival strategies. We have seen that even as children, girls' domestic responsibilities—whether paid or unpaid—detract from their educational attainment and future earnings potential. Girls who "specialize" in housework, forsaking human capital acquisition either in the form of schooling or skilled labor market experience, are more likely to become dependent on the marriage market for economic resources. Wives in both urban and rural areas have much weaker labor force attachment than single women—even when the latter are responsible for the care of young children. As women age, those who have dedicated their lives to their families become even more dependent on them for income and shelter, while those who take a more labor market–oriented path may be better able to provide for themselves. While it is unclear at what point in their lives many Mexican women are segregated into being either "workers" or "wives," men do not appear to face this same dichotomy—in exchange for providing the principal source of economic support for their families, they are allowed to be both workers *and* husbands.

A second strong theme is that institutions matter for gender outcomes. Whether these institutions are based in the market or the state, it is clear that demographic and household-level phenomena alone do not determine how women and men fare in terms of human capital formation, labor market participation, and old age security. With regard to education, girls in rural areas are more likely to go to high school where the supply of such schools is greater, implying that parents are responsive to government efforts to improve accessibility. In the case of child labor, official statistics which render girls' work relatively invisible may bias the response of governmental and nongovernmental institutions away from addressing the detrimental effects of home-based domestic work for children. At a macroeconomic level, we have seen the gender-differentiated responses to growth, recession, industrialization, and trade, such as the entry of urban wives into the labor market during times of economic downturn and the effect of changing industrial structure on the gender composition of the *maquiladora* workforce. There is also some evidence— always difficult to pin down empirically, and always controversial—that employers in both the rural labor market and in the *maquiladora* sector do not treat men and women equally with respect to employment opportunities. Also affecting the rural sector is the male bias inherent in the PRO-CAMPO income support program, which is targeted toward male heads of household. As a final example of the role of institutions, an important source of income and healthcare for elderly women is the benefits obtained in their status as widows or dependents, which suggests that many Mexican social security institutions are oriented toward providing for family members, regardless of their labor force histories.

Gender Policy in Mexico

Over the last few decades, the Mexican government has established several programs and actions related to women. The first major initiative, which dates back to 1974, was to create the National Program for Women in Development. In 1985, the government established the National Commission for Women to represent the country at the Third World Conference on Women, which was held in Nairobi in 1985. Subsequently, a National Coordination Committee was charged with preparing Mexico's participation in the Fourth World Conference on Women.

For its part, the Zedillo administration established the National Programs for Women 1995–2000 (PRONAM), with the objective of expanding women's participation in development processes and providing women and men equal opportunities. The program's broad goals include creating equal access to education; combating poverty among women; increasing women's employment opportunities and protecting the rights of women workers; enhancing women's productive capabilities; and fostering women's and men's equal rights, responsibilities, and opportunities within the family.

In 1998, to ensure institutional continuity, the government created the *Coordinación General de la Comisión Nacional de la Mujer* (CONMUJER) as a decentralized organization under the Ministry of the Interior. CONMUJER advocates for specific legislation and regulation to benefit women, and initiates sectoral programs to achieve PRONAM goals. Examples of CONMUJER's programs include textbook and curriculum reform for public schools, distance education programs and military training facilities to reduce gender stereotyping, women's adult literacy programs, employment generation, microcredit, land access, and health services and violence prevention programs.

While CONMUJER and PRONAM were created for women, CONMUJER has made important efforts to incorporate a gender focus into its work. Given its mandate to help women, however, the thrust of CONMUJER's work continues to be on compensatory programs for women. CONMUJER has devoted little attention to male issues, such as the school repetition of boys, dropout, and premature entry into the labor market.

Gender Work in the World Bank's Latin America and the Caribbean Region

With the restructuring of the World Bank in 1997, the Bank's Latin America and the Caribbean (LAC) Region office established a permanent gender unit to provide technical assistance and conduct analytical work on gender issues in economic and social development policies and programs. This volume is an example of such research.

Drawing on more than two decades of experience in women in development and gender and development, the LAC gender unit incorporates equity and efficiency perspectives into its work and attempts to address both female and male gender issues. Equity goals include recognizing the ways in which socially constructed roles and relationships influence the ability of men and women to participate in and benefit from development interventions, promoting legal and institutional reforms aimed at creating an even playing field for women and men, and addressing negative gender socialization processes. From an efficiency perspective, the Bank's gender work seeks to enhance the productive capabilities of both men and women while recognizing the potential for differential returns to income earned by women and men, particularly in terms of household well-being. With regard to male gender issues, the LAC gender unit has been working with partners across the region to learn more about the negative consequences of gender roles and stereotypes for men, such as depression, alcoholism, and violence.

Policy Recommendations

The analysis and findings of this volume suggest three broad guidelines for gender policy in Mexico.

- First, *interventions targeted at children and young adults—when critical human capital investment decisions are being made—are likely to have positive lifelong consequences for enhancing gender equity.* While Mexico has made great strides in achieving gender parity in primary education, too many girls—especially girls from poor, rural families—are dropping out of school to perform paid or unpaid domestic labor. Public support for school- and community-based childcare, together with family income support programs tied to school attendance, such as PROGRESA, have the potential to provide young women with a broader range of labor market options than are currently available. In the case of boys, who are more likely to drop out or fall behind in school due to early (nondomestic) labor force entry, programs to improve the income-generating capacity of other adult household members could help alleviate the pressure on school-age boys to work.

- Second, *gender policy must recognize the interaction between the marriage and labor markets that fundamentally shapes the economic activities of Mexican women.* While it is the case in all countries that married women have lower formal labor market participation rates than their single counterparts, the combination of Mexican family gender roles that assign girls and women primary responsibility for unpaid domestic labor, and structural features of the Mexican labor market that make it difficult for married women to find and keep jobs, creates additional barriers for women who may want to be active in both family life and the paid labor market. There is broad scope for public policy to address these barriers, including socialization of the most time-consuming domestic tasks (such as childcare), communications campaigns to encourage greater male participation in home-based work, labor market regulation to prevent employer discrimination against married women, and incentives to private employers to offer "family-friendly" work environments (such as flexible work schedules and workplace-based childcare).

- Third, the evidence presented in this volume suggests that *public sector institutions can play a leading role in recognizing the gender-specific needs of the beneficiaries of government programs.* Public high schools and universities could develop innovative programs to keep girls and young women in school, child welfare agencies could target the "invisible" home-based domestic work of girls, publicly financed job training and employment generation schemes could tailor their programs to enhance the skills of working women and accommodate the needs of working wives and mothers, rural income support programs like PROCAMPO could broaden their definition of beneficiaries to include family members of male *ejidatarios*, and social security and healthcare coverage for the elderly could continue the policy of caring for dependent elderly women.

Taken together, measures such as these would represent a coordinated effort to address gender issues throughout the life cycle, with the potential to substantially enrich the participation of women and men in Mexico's economic development.

Author Biographies

Maria Correia is Gender Lead Specialist at the World Bank. Her academic background is in natural resources management and business administration. Her publications have focused on cross sectoral analysis of gender issues and include work on Mexico, Argentina, Ecuador, Brazil, and Central America. Ms. Correia currently manages the gender unit in the Latin American and Caribbean Region of the World bank, which carries out work on gender as it relates to labor markets, education, household economics, health, social security, violence, and rural development. Her research interests include male gender issues such as alcoholism and violence, gender and vulnerability to exogenous shocks, and household economics and family dynamics.

Wendy Cunningham received her Ph.D. in economics from the University of Illinois at Urbana–Champaign in 1999. She is a labor economist with the gender unit in the Latin America and Caribbean Region office of the World Bank. Ms. Cunningham's research focuses on the role of economic crises, the family, and gender in shaping labor supply decisions in Latin America.

Susan Fleck is an international economist at the Bureau of Labor Statistics, U.S. Department of Labor. She received her Ph.D. in economics from American University and her M.Phil. in development studies from the Institute of Development Studies, University of Sussex. She has 15 years of experience in labor, gender, and development issues, particularly in Latin America.

Elizabeth Katz is Assistant Professor of Economics at St. Mary's College of California. Her research, which has been published in *World Development*, *Feminist Economics*, and *Land Economics*, focuses on gender and rural development in Latin America. She is currently doing work on gender and rural–urban migration in Ecuador, and on the relationship between household headship, labor force participation, and childcare strategies in urban Guatemala.

Felicia Marie Knaul works for the Mexican Health Foundation as Director for research. Previously she was with the World Health Organization, and prior to that she served with the Centre for Research and Teaching in Economics in Mexico City as Director of the Program on Health Economics. She holds a Ph.D. degree in economics from Harvard University. Her areas of research include child labor, female labor participation, street children, child abuse, and health systems. She has written several articles and two books on child labor.

José A. Pagán is Associate Professor of Economics in the Department of Economics and Finance, College of Business Administration, the University of Texas–Pan American in Edinburg, Texas. His research areas are labor and international economics. His academic work has appeared in many journals, including *Economic Development and Culture Change, Industrial and Labor Relations Review, Industrial Relations, Review of Development Economics,* and *Economic Inquiry.*

Susan W. Parker is currently a professor in the Center for Research and Teaching in Economics (CIDE) in Mexico City. She received her Ph.D. in economics from Yale University in 1993. Previous positions include post-doctoral fellow at El Colegio de México, financed by the Rockefeller Foundation, adviser to the Mexican Social Security Institute and the Education, Health and Nutrition Program in (PROGRESA) Mexico, and research associate at the International Food Policy Research Institute. Her research interests include poverty, labor markets, gender, and evaluation of public programs.

Carla Pederzini currently teaches at the Ibero Americano University. She holds a B.A. in economics and an M.A. in demography, and is a Ph.D. candidate in population studies at El Colegio de México in Mexico City. Her dissertation topic is gender and education in Mexico. Her research interests include migration, gender and population, education, and women's labor force participation.

Susana M. Sánchez has been a financial economist in the Latin America and Caribbean Region office of the World Bank since 1996. She has written various studies analyzing, among other topics, the performance of rural financial markets, credit constraints, investment behavior, microenterprise development, gender issues, institutional development of microfinance institutions, and linkages between financial markets and income shocks. Ms. Sanchez has a Ph.D. in agricultural economics from Ohio State University.

Rebeca Wong, a Ph.D. economist, is Research Associate Professor at the Center for Population Research at Georgetown University, and adjunct faculty of the Johns Hopkins School of Public Health. Her research projects include the study of the economic consequences of population aging. Dr. Wong's current work includes collaboration in the Mexican Health and Aging Study, a national longitudinal study in Mexico.

DATE DUE